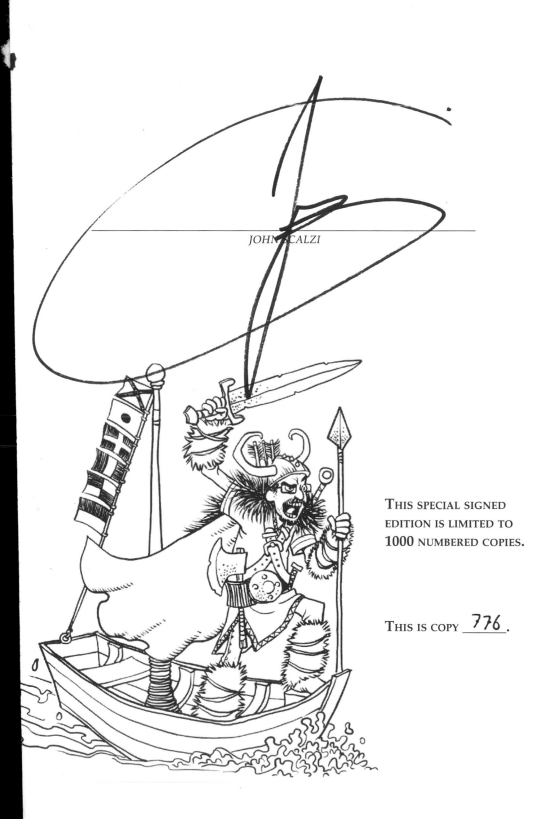

JOHN SCALZI

THIS SPECIAL SIGNED
EDITION IS LIMITED TO
1000 NUMBERED COPIES.

THIS IS COPY **776**.

VIRTUE SIGNALING AND OTHER HERESIES

VIRTUE SIGNALING AND OTHER HERESIES

SELECTED WRITINGS FROM WHATEVER 2013–2018

JOHN SCALZI

SUBTERRANEAN PRESS 2018

First Edition

ISBN
978-1-59606-894-0

Subterranean Press
PO Box 190106
Burton, MI 48519

subterraneanpress.com

Manufactured in the United States of America

DEDICATION

To Kristine and Athena, as always.

    To the staff at Subterranean Press.

    And to everyone who has read Whatever for some or even all of these last 20 years. It's been a heck of a ride.

OH, HEY, IT'S TIME FOR ANOTHER ONE OF THOSE AUTHOR INTRODUCTIONS

Don't worry, I'll be quick.

The essays in this collection run from early 2013 through May of 2018, which, alas, marks a particularly turbulent time in the life of our nation, most notably because in 2015 Donald Trump decided to run for president and in 2016, to the surprise of everyone, most definitely including Trump himself, he won. The man is a terrible human and an even worse president, probably the worst in living memory, and you may believe I write extensively about that very subject in the course of the essays you'll read in this book.

But Trump and his awfulness did not spring up out of nowhere—he was planted in the soil that had been tilled and toiled upon for decades—not just in politics but in the social life of the nation. The US has always had a mean streak in it, and in the last few years people have been working hard to get it to rise up. Well, great job, guys! You managed it.

I'm an optimist and I believe things will get better. But we have to get through *this* first; we have to work and write and fight and be better than the example that others from Trump on down have been setting for us. And we have to be loud about it.

Which, by the way, explains the title of this particular collection. "Virtue signaling" is a phrase the dim and bigoted use when they want to discount other people expressing the idea that it would be nice if we could all be essentially and fundamentally decent to each other. I guess when you are morally stunted you have a hard time believing other people might not be; you believe that people would be decent to each other only to be seen *appearing* to be a decent person, or to get something out of it. Being this sort of person is no way to live, I would argue. Yet some folks do it anyway.

I don't believe I am notably more virtuous than your average person. My list of personal flaws is extensive to the point of being comedic, and I regrettably show my ass on a regular basis. Nevertheless I also think we can and should be better, to each other and as a nation (and as a world). Occasionally I write about it. I am *delighted* to signal in the direction of virtue. It is actually the direction I want the world to go. And if this annoys particular, mostly morally stunted people, well. That's not the *intent*, but I might see it as a bonus.

The saying goes "work as if you were in the early days of a better nation." The thing is, I think we can be that better nation. And it is indeed the earliest of days. So here's some of that work.

Also a bunch of other stuff too—it's not all politics and lecturing, *I swear*. There are laughs and snarky bits in here too, honest.

This collection also marks the 20th anniversary of Whatever, the blog from which these essays are taken. This is the fifth book of essays taken from Whatever, which is kind of an amazing fact if you think about it. I've written more on Whatever at this point than anywhere else, including in books and novels. Much of this writing is silly and inconsequential day-to-day journaling, but some of it—some of what's in this book—represents the best and most meaningful writing I do. I've noted before that in many ways Whatever can be seen as my life's work. That still holds true.

A note on the organization of this book: The essays here are arranged mostly alphabetically, with a few exceptions (I interspersed the pieces about Trump rather than lumping them all in one place, as I figured that would be a hard slog). This means that they will jump around in terms of time and size and subject matter—a replication, I think, of the daily variety of the site. It also makes it easy just to pick it up at any page and start reading.

Happy reading, and here's to virtue, and signaling, and to early days of better nations.

STANDARD RESPONSES TO ONLINE STUPIDITY

Mar

2

2015

Dear Citizens of the Internet:

From time to time, in your ordinary exercise of the delights of the online world, you may find yourself accosted by clods. These oafish louts crave your time and attention, but in point of fact, life is short and you have better things to do.

For you, I have created this helpful numbered list of standard responses to online stupidity. When accosted, use the specific numbered response(s) relevant to them. Saves you time; alerts them they're a jerk, and this is all the response they rate.

Use and enjoy.

1. I don't care what you think.
2. I didn't ask you.
3. No doubt you thought that was terribly clever.
4. You've attempted logic. Not all attempts succeed.
5. One should not have that many errors in that few characters.
6. Either your educators have failed you, or you have failed them.
7. I see you've invited me to an argument. I decline.
8. It appears an asshole has hacked your account and is posting in your name.

9. Funny, most people go out of their way *not* to be a public bigot.
10. Cosplaying as a tantrum-throwing child is no way to go through life.
11. I'm sorry that you are so obviously scared of the world.
12. My attention is a privilege, not a right. This is all you get.

ABOUT THAT MARCH

Mar

25

2018

(The March For Our Lives was a nationwide protest in the wake of the Parkland, Florida school shootings, spearheaded by the surviving students themselves.)

 few thoughts on the March For Our Lives, in no particular order:

1. I personally didn't expect it to be as large as it turned out to be, with 800,000 protesters in Washington DC and hundreds of thousands more (at least) across the country. There were even several hundred marchers in Dayton, the largest city near me.

I had honestly thought the school walkout earlier this month was going to be the crescendo of the protests. Clearly, this shows what I know. If there were indeed 800k marchers in DC, it's one of the largest one-day protests in history, and that's not chicken feed.

2. And it's also clearly terrifying the NRA and its selected quislings, who have been reduced in the last couple of days to mocking the teenagers at the center of the protests, because nothing makes grown adults look more in control than making fun of children half to a third their age, who have lost friends and schoolmates due to gun violence. What makes them angrier is that the kids are having none of it; I suppose when you've seen your friends murdered, being mocked by an NRAtv apparatchik or a Twitter "personality" is not nearly as devastating as those latter folks would hope it is.

The NRA was clearly hoping to do what it's always done, which is to ride out the immediate outrage until it was over, with the tried-and-true one-two punch of "thoughts and prayers" and "it's too soon." But again, the kids weren't having it, and unfortunately for the NRA, a bunch of well-spoken, laser-focused teenagers with a legitimate grievance regarding gun violence plays better than a bunch of screaming, angry guntoters who want to sell the idea that the way to solve the problem of people shooting up schools with assault rifles is to force teachers to arm themselves.

3. Does this mean that we're finally at the bend in the curve where gun manufacturers and/or fetishists don't in fact hold the legislative process in thrall? Nope! The NRA still has a huge amount of money, and GOP primary voters are still reactionary, and it's still several months until November and even further to January. We will see whether people, particularly young people, decide that it's easier to march than vote, and whether the young marchers and protesters end up being representative of the young vote (this is where I trot out the curious statistic that in the first presidential election after 18-year-olds were given the vote, the kids, the *hippie generation*, voted for Nixon. 2018 is not 1972 in all sorts of ways, but the question is who actually gets out to the ballot box in November).

The march was a sign and perhaps a portent of November, but signs and portents can be wrong. In practical terms, what matters is the vote. The NRA is reduced to spitting on teenagers at the moment, but it's patient and it has a long-term plan and it knows March (and marches) ain't voting time. So, the moral here is: Kids, make sure you're registered to vote and then vote.

4. With that said, another leavening perspective, which is that the teens aren't going anywhere, and **they're not getting more conservative with age.** Trump didn't win the popular vote and the GOP can't win in Congress without gerrymandering, and the last two years has energized entire swathes of the voting public never to vote for the GOP again, at least on the national level. I mean, it's worked that way for *me*—I wasn't a regular GOP voter ever, but I've voted for a few here and there. Now there's literally no chance I'll vote for another GOP candidate for state or national office because there's nothing in the party's current political ethos that isn't nihilism and bigotry. And I'm a 48-year-old straight white dude with money, i.e., the GOP's natural constituency. The kids and the women and the minorities and the queer (and many of the people who love any or all of the above) are even further into the "oh hell *no*" column than I am, when it comes to the GOP and what passes for conservatism these days.

It doesn't mean that the 2018 vote is lost for the GOP (or the NRA, which has most of the GOP in its pocket, among other interest groups). As I noted above, there's a difference between marching and voting. And as an example I don't ever see where I live nudging into the Democratic column, either now or for the foreseeable future. But in the long run, these kids aren't ever going to forget who only offered "thoughts and prayers" when they were getting murdered as teenagers, and who mocked them for protesting because their friends and schoolmates were murdered. These things tend to stick with you. And that's only one legitimate grievance they have.

Mind you, this is why the GOP's revanchists are making hay while the sun shines; they know it's not going to last. *Just one more Supreme Court justice!* they cry. For my part, I'm looking forward to this iteration of the GOP and "conservatism" getting the punt. Yesterday's march may or may not be a harbinger of the 2018 elections, but it is a reminder that time will not stand still, and that one may still hope for better days ahead. The kids who marched deserve that. As do the rest of us.

Activism, and Whether I Do It

Jul

11

2016

My pal Monica Byrne (who is, incidentally, a fabulous writer), asked me the other day if I would consider myself an activist, and if so, would I call myself one publicly. It was an interesting question, especially since I'm at least partly known for having strong political and social opinions, and sharing them via this blog and other outlets.

My answer to her was no, I don't really consider myself an activist. The reason I gave her was pretty straightforward: I'm too lazy. Which is to say that while I have my beliefs and principles and largely follow them (sometimes imperfectly), and will happily tell others what those beliefs and principles are, the sort of *committed action* that to me defines activism—and the continued proselytization for a belief that activism often requires, including the desire to inspire others to take moral action—is not something I usually undertake.

There are other reasons for this besides laziness, including work and the desire to have other interests in my life, but laziness really is a large part of it. Activism is work. I'm glad other people do it, and admire their effort. But it's not something I put much effort in.

But you write here all the time on political and social topics! Yes I do. But this is not a blog for activism, it's a blog for whatever I feel like writing— or, when I'm writing a book as I am now, what I have *time* for writing. The blog is like me; all over the place and a bit pixelated.

This is not to say people I would consider activists *only* do activism. They do other things too, of course; the people who only do one thing all the time are (I would submit) maybe a lot to have to deal with. But

I would certainly say activists commit *more* of themselves and more of their time to activism than I do. Blog posts and retweets do not an activist make.

After my chat with Monica on the topic, I came up with another reason why I don't call myself an activist, which is that many of the causes I find myself agreeing on and writing about are ones that I don't consider my primarily fight to fight. For example, for more than a decade, here and elsewhere, I was (and am!) a vocal proponent of same-sex marriage in the US, and I was thrilled and happy when it was made the law of the land. Was I an *activist* for the cause? Well, as a straight person, I'm not sure it was my place to be so. I can say I was *active* for it, surely. But declaring myself an *activist* for it (aside from the fact of the laziness mentioned above) seems sort of usurp-y. I didn't need to be seen leading or directing the course of that particular parade. It wasn't my parade to lead. I was just happy to march in it.

Likewise for women's issues, or issues involving people of color, or trans issues, as examples, all of which I'm interested *in*, and have opinions *on*, but which ultimately don't have me as their focus as a white cis male. I have an ego, to be sure. But I don't think I need to pull attention to myself in these fights. I'm happy to stand with, not in front of (and hopefully not get in the way of, which could be a thing if I'm not paying attention).

Which brings up another point, which is that very often activism seems to come out of the well of having no other choice—that in some cases if you're not an activist, you're going to get steamrolled by the dominant culture. And, well, you know. I'm pretty much aware that in the US, I'm in the dominant culture, and quite bluntly I get to pick and choose what political and social issues I get to be involved in, and how deeply. And when I get fed up, I get to say "later," and go write or play video games or just disappear. I have the luxury of engagement, or not. I suspect that for a lot of folks, to declare myself an activist when I can bail whenever I feel like it would be exasperating.

(There are activist issues not specifically related to racial/gender/sexual identity, of course—tech and politics and religion and so on and so forth, where your average white straight male isn't necessarily pulling focus. Very few of these engage me to the extent that activism on the subject calls to me.)

I'd note that this is all about whether *I* would consider myself an activist; other people might have other opinions, either in a positive sense, or in a negative one. Surely every time someone labels me a "social justice warrior," for example, they pretty much implicitly accuse me of being an activist, and one for issues they don't like. And three things here: One, I don't mind; two, fuck 'em; three, it still doesn't make me an activist in my own mind.

If someone else wants to consider me an activist, for whatever reason, I couldn't stop them if I wanted to, and I don't. I do hope whoever they are, they know I'm destined to disappoint them somewhere down the road. I'm inevitably going to fail whatever standard they have for activism, in no small part because I'm not even achieving my own standard for it.

Again, it's not to say that I'm not often engaged on many issues. I am. At the end of the day, though, to my mind, what makes an activist is commitment to a cause and the commitment to change the hearts of others, and possibly the course of history. I'm happy to speak my mind and if my words make people think, and sometimes even think *differently* than they did before, then that's great. But I don't know if that's enough to consider myself an activist for any one cause. I think I'd have to do more than I do. And who knows? Maybe one day I will. We'll see.

ADULTHOOD AND WHAT BEING A FRIEND MEANS NOW

Oct

4

2015

The *New York Times* ran an interesting article today, in which the writer of the piece talked about the difficulty of making friends if one is over the age of 30. The reasons for this vary and can include the fact that one has a family and children to worry about, time pressures, scheduling, and the fact that as one gets older one becomes pickier about the people one chooses to spend time with in any event.

I found the article interesting because while not discounting all of the above, my thirties and forties have been very good years for me in terms of the acquisition of friends, both in terms of quantity and of quality of friends. I can say without reservation that a number of the people that I've met in the last decade have become some of the most important people in my life, friends that I can't imagine living my life without now. I don't disagree with the writer's general thesis—I *do* think it is generally harder to make new friends the older one gets—but it does make me wonder what the mechanics of my situation have been that make the last decade different for me than for this particular author.

The answer, think, is relatively simple: I moved into a line of work with a deeply-established social structure. Which is to say that when I became a science fiction author, I plugged into a field where there were lots of conventions and social events, i.e., opportunities to socialize with people who have similar enthusiasms, and where both fans and pros in the genre generally buy into the idea of a community. All things being equal, people are friendly and supportive rather than not.

Additionally, the way that the science fiction community comes together for conventions and similar events works really well for the general impositions that adults have making and maintaining friendships. When fans and pros go to conventions, by and large they are taking a bit of time from their "real" lives to have two or three days of highly concentrated social experiences: Hanging out in hotel bars, staying up late with deep (and not so deep) conversations about work and life, and otherwise focusing on enjoying themselves with others—not worrying (as much) about life, and kids, and other parts of their existence that distract from making a connection with other adults.

There's also the fact that people in science fiction and fantasy (and also I think in literature generally) are pretty good with the social media thing. While there's certainly the possibility of downside in blogs/Twitter/Facebook what with complete and utter assholes trying to get your attention, which we don't need to get into at the moment, the lovely upside to social media is that it makes it easy to stay in contact with friends even when you can't physically be with them at any particular moment. Snarking with my pals (authors and otherwise) on Twitter or Facebook helps keep the friendship humming along, so you don't have that start-and-stop feeling that the NYT writer mentions.

(I don't think that any of this is unique to science fiction and fantasy, mind you. There are other communities that adults can join into and have at least some of the same dynamics in play. This is just the one I lucked into.)

Finally, I think there's a personal aspect as well. I find it relatively easy to be friendly with people, and consequently, to make friends—and also (this is somewhat important, I think), I don't fret if I don't see a friend for months or even years at a stretch. Because, you know, I realize we're all adults and have lives and kids and such, and that sometimes that's just the deal. I mean, I can usually tell pretty quickly whether I want to be friends with someone. If I do, then the qualities that make them someone I'd want to be friends with are (generally) not likely to go away. So I don't worry about seeing them again. When I do, I assume it'll still be there. And in the meantime, as noted: Twitter and blogs and such.

(And also, occasionally: Email and/or phone and/or other private communication! That's right! Not everything in the New Age has to be done in public!)

I do think friendship as an adult has to be approached with the understanding that it *is* different for adults than for people in their twenties or below. If you try to do friendship like you were sixteen years old, then it's probably going to end up like anything you'd approach as if you were sixteen, i.e., kind of a hot mess. Being sixteen is fine when you're sixteen. It's problematic when you're thirty-six or forty-six. So, be a grown-up about what friendship is and how it's done in between everything else in your life, and I think you'll be fine.

I've noted before that prior to coming into the world of science fiction, I told Krissy that I was pretty sure I had made all the friends I was ever going to make. It turns out I was entirely wrong, and it turns out that I am very happy about that. I wouldn't trade the friendships I've made in the last decade for anything in the world. They were a surprise for me and I've been grateful for them. I continue to be grateful for every new friend I make. I hope to make at least a few more before I'm done.

THE AFTERMESS

Oct
18
2013

(Context: The Republicans shut down the federal government in 2013. It did not go well for them.)

Some not-terribly well-organized thoughts on the Shutdown and its immediate aftermath, in no particular order:

1. If there was one quote that for me crystallized the whole idiocy of the shutdown debacle, the sheer inchoate, juvenile foot-stompery of it, it was this one, from Indiana Representative Marlin Stutzman:

"We're not going to be disrespected. We have to get something out of this. And I don't know what that even is."

Stutzman later tried to qualify his all-too-honest statement, for which he was deservingly pilloried, but the original works well enough. Once it became clear that the ACA wasn't going to go away, the House GOP was looking for something, anything, that they thought Obama might agree to so they could declare victory to the people who would be willing to see something, anything that they got from Obama as a win. What it was didn't matter, as long as they got *something*.

And, I don't know. Maybe that was the plan all along—say they were aiming for Obamacare, which they knew they weren't going to get, and actually settle for a whole raft of other legislative goodies they wanted but couldn't get any other way, like pipelines and drilling and killing net neutrality. Basically, whatever they could get away with. I don't think it was this because I don't credit the legislators who pulled this stunt with a surfeit of genuine political savvy, and in any event rank and file schmoes like Stutzman certainly weren't clued into any deeper political machinations. But *maybe* it was. Maybe.

Obama gave them jack. They got nothing, or something as close to nothing (income verification for ACA recipients, which Rachel Maddow noted was a thing already in the law) as to make no difference. And all it cost was an estimated $24 billion divot out of the economy, the shutdown of the government and hundreds of thousands out of work, a whole bunch of points in every poll taken during the shutdown, and one of the great legislative faceplants in modern political history.

A relevant question for Stutzman and every other House GOP legislator who thought shutting down the government and taking the country to the brink of default to try to blackmail the president and Senate into giving them things they couldn't otherwise get was a *useful* idea: Dude, what makes you think you *deserve* respect in the first place? Grinding the government to a halt as a form of legislative extortion is, in the most *polite* word I can think of which applies here, shameful. To do it with no clear idea of the purpose of your actions makes you a tool. Stutzman, et al got what they deserved out of the shutdown: Nothing, including respect.

Mind you, Stutzman is back in his district saying he doesn't regret the shutdown. I wouldn't expect him or any other of the folks who precipitated the shutdown to say anything but that , for one of two reasons. The first is that it hurts when your ass is handed to you and so you try to scrape up some pride. The second is that some people are simply too deluded to never not declare victory. I don't know which Stutzman is; I will charitably ascribe him to the first.

2. I noted a week ago that there were three options as to why John Boehner was allowing the rabble-rousing wing of his party as much latitude as he did, the second (and most likely in my opinion) option of which was that they would turn on him if he didn't give them enough rope to hang themselves with, after which he could pass a sane bill raising the debt limit and getting the government back to work. And in fact that's pretty much what happened.

With hindsight being 20/20, Boehner seems to be getting some credit for managing an unmanageable group of members as best as was possible under the circumstances. I think that's true, although I think it should be noted that when your best includes a government shutdown, that's a pretty large asterisk. Politico, which labels him a "winner" of the shutdown because his stature has increased with the hard right in the House, wonders if he'll be able to capitalize on this new stature to get those folks to pass reasonably sane legislation.

I'm gonna go ahead and answer that one now: Not a chance, in part because many of the folks who precipitated this late crisis think the problem was they they didn't go far enough. The Dunning-Kruger caucus of the House GOP is still open for business, and they'll still be causing Boehner headaches, and he'll still have to deal with them like he's dealing with angry children made of boom. He must really love being Speaker, is all I can say about that.

3. On a related note, apparently Mitch McConnell is assuring various and sundry that Obamacare won't be the cause of another government shutdown. That's nice, but McConnell is in the Senate, not the House, and as noted above, there's at least a few folks in the House who seem to think the problem with their strategy this time wasn't that it was foolish and stupid, but that they didn't execute on it perfectly, and practice makes perfect. So call me unconvinced the lesson has been entirely learned. Hell, McConnell can't even get the "no more shutdown" memo to Ted Cruz.

4. About Ted Cruz: Look, the dude's an asshole, and it shouldn't be entirely surprising that an asshole who declared at Harvard Law that he wouldn't have anyone who attended a "minor Ivy" in his study group is the same asshole who accuses his fellow Republican senators of "carpetbombing" the House GOP. It's also fairly obvious that Cruz sees his senatorial tenure as an inconvenient but necessary way station on the road to the White House, so it should additionally be not terribly surprising that he's not interested in playing nice with the other senators, including the ones in his own party, or cares what damage his actions do to them. He doesn't plan to be there that long.

(Dear GOP: please have Ted Cruz as your 2016 presidential candidate. Oh, please. Oh, *please*.)

5. Obama: Dude looks *tired* these days, and that pretty much sums it up.

I have a friend who maintains that the whole plan for the shutdown and debt limit debacle was to drive the country to default so that Obama would be obliged to try to raise the debt limit via executive authority, or authorize a trillion-dollar coin, at which point the House would vote to impeach him. I think this is basically an entertaining paranoid fantasy, and even if it weren't it would be a debacle for the GOP, first because the Senate is held by the Democrats and second because Obama would be impeached for acting to protect the full faith and credit of the US *because* the House refused to do so *because* they wanted to impeach Obama for something. Again, I don't credit the GOP for much in the strategy department these days, but I suspect even they can see how that would work out for them. So, yeah: Don't think so.

On the other hand, the GOP are still who they are, and that's not going to change until January 2015 at least. I expect to see Obama looking even more tired by then.

Always and Never

Here's a question I've been sitting on for a while before I answered, mostly because of travel and other commitments but also because I was waiting for a good time to answer it. It comes from Avdi Grimm, who writes:

I just wrote an update on our family's ever-so-slow movement towards some semblance of economic security. It got me wondering: was there ever a point in your career where you felt like "OK, I think my family is safe now"? And if so—where/when was it?

I've written before about when I felt I had "made it," which provides an answer close to this question, but not precisely on topic. That question was about my own personal feeling of security; this question is about the state of my entire family. And in thinking about it, I find the answer to it is more complicated than I would have originally assumed.

The first part of the answer is that to a great extent I always felt my family was economically "safe." My own major personal economic crisis—when I was laid off from AOL and had to decide whether to try to find another regular job or go freelance—was in February/March of 1998, and Athena was born in December of that year (do the math there). By the time December rolled around I was doing very well as a freelancer and Krissy, who had been working part-time before I was laid off, was taken on full-time and was given full benefits, giving us a stable base on top of which my freelance income could ride. So our daughter emerged with us economically happy and comfortable.

By and large that situation has continued for us. With the exception of a couple of months right after we moved to Ohio, Krissy has never not worked and never not provided a stable base of income and benefits for the family, and I have never not done reasonably well in terms of income as a freelancer and author. We always made more than we needed to live on, which also allowed us to save and create a "cushion" in case something happened.

We've also been fortunate in other ways that indirectly but materially helped with our economic security. I've always been able to work from home, which means when Athena was very young I could be a caregiver to her while Krissy worked out of the home. Later, when I began to travel more, Krissy was able to get top-notch daycare from the local community college she took classes at for the eye-poppingly low rate of $2 an hour (the daycare was part of a child education program at the college). And of course, where we live—rural Ohio—allows for a pretty good standard of living for an amount relatively low to other places in the US. It all adds up.

We were smart about things, and I also fully acknowledge we were lucky. I was and have continued to be lucky that I have been able to make a good living writing, both before I was a novelist and after that became my primary job description; not every writer I know has been fortunate as I have been. I have caught breaks in my life—which I then proceeded to exploit reasonably intelligently, to be clear, but that doesn't change the fact that some things just plain fell in my lap. There were lots of opportunities for things to go poorly through no fault or effort of my own; they didn't.

Likewise, we were fortunate not to have the world fall in on us at any point. Neither Krissy nor I ever got sick or required substantial care in a way that made it a focus of our lives; Athena's been happy and healthy since she was born. Our house never burned down. We never got hit by a bus. We were never devoured by bears. We were, and are, lucky, and we used that luck to build the economic structures that will help to keep us "safe."

So that's the first part of the answer.

The second part of the answer is that I'm not entirely sure that I will ever feel my family is economically "safe"—that is, entirely insulated from economic pressures—because I don't think that's a realistic scenario. We're by any standard pretty well off, but it's also pretty easy for things to go to hell in a moment. I could get sick. Krissy could get sick Athena could get sick. A member of our extended family could get sick. People could stop buying my books. The economy could crater so spectacularly that no one is spared, including me or my family. Things could otherwise go sideways in lots of different ways that I can think of off the top of my head which scare the crap out of me. And in nearly every case, the things that can strip me and my family of economic security are things over which we have little or no control.

In that scenario, one is never "safe." Really, almost no one is. What one has is "margin": The amount of space, and time, and money, one has to maneuver one's way out of a trainwreck of woe bearing down on you and the people you care about. Depending on the circumstance and scenario, the same amount of margin can be more than enough, or not nearly enough at all. If you're not aware of that, you may not be paying attention.

Now, I realize that those last couple of paragraphs have gotten *really dark*, and it might seem that I've gone from regular friendly ol' Scalzi to a guy who has barrels of beans and rainwater in his basement, along with a lovely assortment of ranged weapons for when the Takers come for all I hold dear, *which will be soon*. I assure you on a day-to-day basis I feel fine about my life, and I suspect things will generally turn out just fine for me and mine. We've worked hard for years to make it so. What I'm saying is that my optimism about the economic safety of my family is tempered by a worldview that recognizes that *shit happens*, whether you think you've prepared for it or not. I'm not waiting for the other shoe to fall, but if it does, I don't want to be surprised by it. I want to be able to look at it, say "huh, that's a hell of a big shoe somebody dropped," and hopefully find a way to work around it.

So the answer to Avdi's question of when I felt my family was economically safe, basically, is "always, and never." In the moment, so far, it's always been the case. Existentially, well, nothing's safe, is it. I don't think these are contradictory positions to hold. It's not a case of looking at a glass and asking if you'd describe it as half-full or half-empty; it's recognizing it's both, simultaneously. It's also saying "Cool, we have enough water today. Let's see what happens tomorrow."

An Anti-Feminist Walks Into a Bar: A Play in Five Acts

Sep
25
2014

PROLOGUE

Not long ago on Twitter, a fellow named "Trent Max" declared:

> *It's very simple, I and a growing number of men will not date feminists. Ladies, make your choices.*

Which led to the following comment from me:

> *And thus did the number of women calling themselves "feminist" rocket.*

And the following five-act play.

ACT I

GUY: I WILL NOT DATE YOU IF YOU ARE A FEMINIST
Woman: Great! Thank you.
GUY: YOU ARE NOT SUPPOSED TO REACT THAT WAY
Woman: Oh, but I AM.

ACT II

GUY: OH HEY THERE BABY YOU LOOK LIKE YOU COULD USE COMPA-
Woman: I'm a feminist.
GUY: NOOOO THE BURNING MAKE IT STOP (flees)
(Woman smiles)

ACT III

GUY: HEY THERE BAB-

Woman: Feminist.

GUY: LIKE A REAL FEMINIST OR ARE YOU JUST TRYING TO GET RID OF ME

Women: Why not both?

ACT IV

GUY: HI THER-

Women: Feminist.

GUY: THIS WHOLE BAR CAN'T BE FULL OF FEMINISTS

(Every woman in bar nods)

GUY: HAS THE WORLD GONE MAD

ACT V

GUY: I STRUCK OUT AT THE BAR BUT I HAVE THIS LOTION AND MY HAND

Guy's Hand: Feminist.

GUY: OH COME ON

Lotion: Me too.

GUY: NOOOOOOOO

fin

And Now, a Small Example of What a Generation Gap Looks Like

Apr

17

2013

It looks like this:

Me (carrying the downstairs phone into Athena's room): I need someplace to put this while the new kitchen counters are installed. Do you have a phone jack in your room?

Athena: A what?

Me: A phone jack.

Athena: I... I don't know what that is.

(Both of us stare blankly at the other for several seconds in mutual but separate disbelief)

And now you know.

APOLOGIES: WHAT, WHEN AND HOW

I've apologized a fair amount for stupid and/or ignorant and/or insensitive things that I have done or said over the course of my life. This has given me the time and experience to, if not *perfect* the form of an apology, then to at least get it to a point where I am comfortable that the apology will be understood as genuine. Perhaps at some point in the near future you'll need to apologize for some stupid and/or ignorant and/or insensitive thing you have done. Here are thoughts I have for you on the subject.

First thing: What is an apology? Leaving aside classical definitions that are not directly on point to how the word is used in everyday life:

An apology is an admission that you've wronged others and that you are actually sorry for it. This is of course why it's difficult for people to apologize. No one likes to admit they are wrong or that they screwed up. No one likes the complicated, defeated feelings that come with being wrong and screwing up. No one likes having to go to *other* people, publicly or privately, and admit to them they've been wrong and have screwed up. It is, literally, humiliating, since apologizing almost always requires humility and a willingness to put the needs of those you have wronged over your own. For ego-bound creatures, and we are all ego-bound, this is a hard thing to do.

I think it becomes *less* hard, however, if you consider the following:

One, everyone's wrong at some point. Because, hello, you're a human, and humans are imperfect beings. It's okay to recognize you are not infallible.

Two, it's better to center your ego on doing what's right rather than never being wrong. Because, per point one, you're going to be wrong at some point.

Three, it takes strength to apologize and apologize well. Any jackass can refuse to apologize when they are in the wrong; indeed, refusing to admit you're wrong, or to apologize it, is one of the hallmarks of *being* a jackass. Being willing to stand up and say "I screwed up, I've wronged you and I am sorry for it," on the other hand, means you have the strength of character to own your actions, and the consequences of them, both for others and yourself.

Okay, now we know what an apology is.

So, let's say that you've said/done something, publicly or privately, that has genuinely upset someone (or more than one someone). Should you apologize? Ask yourself the following questions:

Are you actually sorry? If the answer is "no," then you shouldn't apologize, because your apology will be totally insincere. An insincere apology is worse than no apology at all; not only is it obvious that you're not sorry for the original act, but the fake apology suggests that you think people are stupid enough to believe a fake apology. Congratulations, you've just made yourself look like an even bigger assbag.

If you are actually sorry, then ask yourself this:

Are you primarily sorry for yourself, or for others? This is the classic "are you sorry you screwed up, or that you got caught?" question. Meaning that if the nexus of your concern is *your* reputation, *your* standing, and *your* status, then your apology is likely to reflect that. In which case, I have news for you: your apology will come across as "I'm sorry the rest of you ganged up on me," and I assure you that's not going to go over very well.

If on the other hand your primary concern is that your actions have affected others negatively, then the focus of your apology will reflect that, and those you have wronged will more likely appreciate that you see the problem is not what's being done to you, but what you have done to others.

I want to be clear I think it's fine if you are concerned for your own standing; we're ego-driven creatures, and damage control is a fine thing. The point here is to understand where the balance is. Remember that an apology is about owning up to what you've done to others. Making your apology all about you, or primarily about you, is missing the point of an apology.

Another question:

Are you willing to let your apology be an apology?

Meaning, once you've apologized, are you going immediately start back-tracking from it, adding caveats, exclusions, conditions and defensive annotations? It's remarkable the number of perfectly good apologies that don't stick the dismount. People can't leave them alone, I suspect, because of defensiveness and ego—*yes I was wrong but you have to admit I'm not the only one who was wrong here*, or *yes I was wrong but in general you have to admit my point still stands*, or even *yes I was wrong but it was wrong of you to make a big deal out of it*. Which, again, is going to make things worse.

If you can't *just* apologize, perhaps you should not apologize.

A final point for this part, not in the form of a question but still important to know:

An apology is directed toward other people, but is something you do for yourself.

Which is to say, the reason to apologize is not because other people expect it from you (although they may), but because *you expect it from yourself*—it is part of your personal character to own up to the wrongs you have done to others. If you're apologizing solely because of outside expectation, the apology is going to be hollow at its core. The best apologies are the ones where the moral actor for the apology is the one who is saying "I apologize." This can be learned, fortunately.

We're done with the preliminaries now, and you've decided that you should apologize. To my mind, an apology has three steps to it, which are pretty simple and straightforward.

1. Briefly, specifically and factually recount the action you're apologizing for. You've done something wrong. Say what it is. Don't try to mitigate or defend, just get it out there.

2. Acknowledge that you wronged others. Again, don't mitigate or defend. Acknowledge it and say it.

3. Apologize unreservedly. Don't drag it out. Don't qualify it. Say it, own it. Let it be there.

That's the basic format.

Some style notes:

Apologies are active. Use the active voice. "I did this," is far stronger, and indicative of personal responsibility, than "this thing happened." A passive voice in an apology comes across as a denial of responsibility or accountability. Don't do that. As a subset:

The offense is yours. Own it. "I am sorry I offended you" acknowledges the screw-up is yours, "to those who were offended, I am sorry," sounds like you're suggesting the responsibility for the offense should be shared, and "I'm sorry if you feel offended," is palming off the responsibility entirely on the other person (and makes you sound like an unrepentant jackass).

Don't try to be funny or clever. The failure mode of "clever" is "asshole." An apology is an attempt to own up to what you've done wrong. It's the last place in the world you want your communication to fail, and it's not a piece of communication that needs *spicing up*. Save your funny and clever side for something else.

Be upfront and to the point. To use a journalism term, don't bury your lede. Brevity does not mean insincerity.

Don't dilute your apology. Don't add it into something else, don't sweep by it to go on to other topics. Let it be its own thing and make sure you make it clear what you're doing and why. You don't have to dwell on it, but you have to give it its moment.

Here is an example of an apology done as suggested above. Let's say I have made an ass of myself to my friend "Joe" by, say, making a joke about cancer when a loved one of his has just passed away from the disease. Here's how I would apologize.

Dear Joe:

Yesterday I made a cancer joke in front of you, and as a result I caused you pain. I didn't intend to hurt you but I did it anyway, and the responsibility for that is mine. I am genuinely sorry I hurt you. I will try very hard not to do it again. I'm here if you want to talk to me. Let me know—JS

Simple, direct and to the point. Joe doesn't have any doubt what I'm apologizing for or that I take responsibility for it.

Now that you've apologized, is everything done and over and hunky dory? Not necessarily. Some after-apology points to consider.

1. An apology is not self-administered absolution. You apologize to acknowledge a wrong you've done to others, but simply acknowledging that wrong doesn't mean you're now off the hook for it. It helps substantially if you're willing to do a little legwork on the matter, from something as simple as letting that other person know you're there to talk (see the last sentence in the apology to "Joe") to something as life-changing as making an effort to adjust your worldview. Don't be the guy who says "Hey! I *said* I was sorry!" and expects it to settle all dispute. If that guy is over the age of ten, he doesn't get as much credit for that statement as he wants.

2. You should accept that your apology may not be accepted. And that it may not be accepted for any number of reasons. Maybe it was poorly phrased and came out as defensive, even if you didn't mean it to be. Maybe those you've wronged feel an apology isn't enough and want to see what you do next. Maybe you're the third person today to apologize to them for something and are simply all out of forgiveness for the day. Maybe you don't get an explanation at all.

Point is, this is not something that's in your control, nor should you pretend it is. This is one reason why I strongly believe that while an apology is offered to others, it is what you do for yourself—because the only person whose response to the apology you have control over is you. If you apologize and the apology is not accepted, then you have still acknowledged your error, and that's not trivial.

It's all right to *hope* an apology is accepted and forgiveness given— and to ask for it if you would like to. It shouldn't be a primary reason to offer it. And you should keep in mind that its acceptance is a gift freely given, and not a requirement.

3. Apologizing and making the same mistake a second time is worse than not apologizing at all. Because it suggests that you've learned nothing and that your apology was really just an exercise in going through the motions. Which is to say apologies are not merely the end of a bad situation. They are the beginning of a promise to do (and be) better.

If you're visibly making the effort to do and be better, if (and likely when) you screw up again, you will still have credit from that previous apology. If you're not making that effort, if (and almost certainly when) you screw up again, you will not. Quite the opposite, in fact.

So: When you apologize, mean what you say. Back it up. Move forward with it. And do it for you, to the benefit of others. That's how you make an apology stick.

ART AND ENTERTAINMENT AND NEIL deGRASSE TYSON

Mar
6
2018

Yesterday on Twitter, noted astrophysicist and Pluto killer Neil deGrasse Tyson wrote:

> *Bears repeating: Creativity that satisfies & affirms your world view is Entertainment. Creativity that challenges & disrupts your world view is Art.*

And, well. No. I responded:

> *Sounds profound and coffee mug-worthy but is not actually true (and also, "art" and "entertainment" are not either/or in this manner, even in this questionable formulation—they can overlap significantly).*

This excited at least a few people, who were hoping that this meant that me and Tyson would now commence to fight. But sadly for those folks, there will be no fighting. One, despite his Pluto-murdering ways, I am an admirer of Tyson for his tireless championing of astronomy and astrophysics and science in general. Two, I think Tyson is simply falling prey to a common misconception about both art and entertainment, which is that the former is (mostly) exclusive of and (mostly) superior to the latter. In both cases, it's not true.

To begin, "art" is not a rarified thing, or at least I don't think it is. It is, simply, the product of the creative exercise. When you write a story or play a song or draw a picture or act on a stage, you are making "art." Whether it is good art or bad art is another thing entirely—when I write, I can say I am (generally) creating good art, but when I draw, I am mostly creating bad art. But it's still *art*, good, bad or indifferent. What makes it art is the act of creative production, not its quality.

Likewise "entertainment" is also not particularly rarified. It's that which aims to amuse and engage people (or more widely, that which amuses and engages people, whether intentional or not). In a basic sense, if you are writing or composing or drawing or whatever with the intention or hope that other people will apprehend and appreciate what you are doing, that's entertainment. And again, you can succeed or not succeed, depending on your skill *and also* the interest and taste of the audience. What makes it entertainment is the intention, not the quality.

It's worth pointing out here that in the cases of both "art" and "entertainment" there are two, mostly unrelated components: The act of the creator, and the apprehension of the audience. I may create art, or aim to entertain, or both, but it's generally up to others to decide if I've done a good job in either case. I have my own internal critic in both cases, who I think usually has a good bead on both. But ultimately the success of art depends on the individual, and their take on the created thing. We can further declare that someone has good or bad *taste*, or doesn't know enough to *appreciate* art, or whatever, and those are arguments that can take us down a long and contentious road. But at the end of the day, *apprehension* of art is subjective, and you either accept that or don't.

Tyson's formulation of "art"—that it's somehow effectively better or more challenging than mere "entertainment," is not that unusual; it's at the root of the old question "Well, I know I *like* it, but is it *art?*" For the person for whom this is a serious sort of question, the answer of "Yes, it was art the moment the creator started producing it, and your *liking* it is valid in itself" possibly seems facile and a little vapid. Likewise, the devaluation of "mere" entertainment, as if something that succeeds in amusing and diverting you, and making you *happy*, cannot have the value of (or inherently has less value than) something that confronts you and aims to make you think.

Well, that seems a bit silly to me. Alt-right trolls aim to "challenge and disrupt my world view" with what passes for their cogitation; it doesn't mean what they're doing has an inherently higher artistic value than, say, an essay by Roxane Gay, whose worldview is rather more in alignment with mine. Fascist-aligned punk bands are not inherently more artistic than the Dead Kennedys, who have rather pointed things to say about Nazi punks.

("But those are extreme examples!" Yes, they are. And? There was no qualification on Tyson's initial statement; it's not "Except in cases involving fascists and thugs..." And even if it were, we could still find more than enough examples to dismiss the hypothesis.)

Likewise, the one thing "art" has over "entertainment" is *not* quality, it's intentionality. Art results from the creative drive of humans, and a purposeful act of creation. Entertainment can be, but does not have to be, intentionally created. I can be entertained by cats playing or by clouds rolling along in the sky, but neither the cats nor the clouds do what they do in the hopes of entertaining me. On YouTube, you can watch hours of logs burning in a fireplace or trains rolling through Scandinavia. It's entertainment but I think not really art (unless you count pointing a camera at a fireplace to be art, which, *meh*).

"Entertainment" is not a lesser state of "art"; they are separate conditions with substantial but not perfect overlap. Much if not most of what we think as entertainment starts off as art; most art we eventually see is intended to have an audience (i.e., is "entertainment"). The subjective entertainment value of something may not be the same as the subjective "artistic" value of the thing. I can recognize art has been finely crafted and speaks well to an audience, and also recognize that audience is not one with me in it (which is to say, not be well entertained by it). I can likewise recognize that something which amuses me vastly can be something I also find sloppy and junky and not something I'd recommend to other people—or alternately, speaks so particularly to *me* that I don't expect others to have the same reaction to it.

Also, and importantly, we don't have to excuse or rationalize or dismiss art that exists within our "world view" (and let me note that I could spend a whole other essay deconstructing *that* phrase) as "mere" entertainment. One, "entertainment" is not *mere*—the ability of anything to transport you out of your own worry cycle for even a few minutes is a pretty great thing. Two, that entertainment *is* (usually) art. And it's art that is working for you, however it works. Enjoy it and celebrate it. This is why there should be no such thing as a "guilty pleasure." You shouldn't feel guilt about enjoying art, whatever it is.

Now, what I think Tyson may have been trying to say, and if so is a thing I would agree with him on, is that one's entertainment and/or artistic diet shouldn't be only what you *already* know that you like—it's worthwhile to make a stretch here and there and try things that you don't know if you like, and on occasion to learn more about art (of whatever sort) so that when you approach new and unfamiliar art, you have tools to better understand and apprehend what you've got in front of you. Always be reaching for the new and always be learning—and as a result, what art speaks to you, and entertains you, will be a larger set than what's come before. And sometimes you won't like the art, and won't be entertained, but that's all right, too. You'll know more about yourself through the process.

This is why, fundamentally, I don't need to fight Tyson—I'm pretty sure he and I agree on the important things regarding art and entertainment. We're just using different words (and definitions of words) to say it. Mind you, I think I've said it better here. But then, I've just used 1,250 words, and he used a tweet.

BATMAN V SUPERMAN,
AND ITS REVIEWS

Mar

29

2016

First, I had a good time at *Batman v Superman*, a fact which is probably seated in the fact that a) I don't appear to care much about whether either Batman or Superman occasionally kill the people who are actively trying to kill them, b) I've already built into my worldview that Zack Snyder films are pretty but empty, and undernourished in the script department. That *BvS* is all of these things is, well, unsurprising to me. There's something about Snyder's visual aesthetic that I enjoy enough that I'm willing to deal with his films' generally hypoxic storytelling and other flaws; I mean, Jesus, I enjoy *Sucker Punch*, and that film's pretty much a shitshow from top to bottom. But it also gives me images like a tiny woman leaping 15 feet off the ground to throatpunch a giant samauri with a handheld gatling gun, and my brain goes *cooooooooooool*.

It's not (just) because Emily Browning is in a creepy babydoll get-up, although that does point directly to the key to Snyder's aesthetic: He's tuned into what a 13-year-old, newly-pubescent, white male comic book and video game geek wants to see—or *thinks* he wants to see, anyway. He wants to see Spartans kick ass, shot-for-shot recreations of graphic novels and sexy-child killbots in a boss fight. He also wants to see Batman and Superman punch the shit out of each other, and *then* team up for a boss fight, too. That's who Zack Snyder is as a filmmaker; that's the baseline you work with. Everything else is incidental; anything else you get is kind of a bonus.

Apparently I'm okay with that. And yes, we can argue about whether we should be entitled to expect *more* from Zack Snyder when he's put in charge of a beloved franchise of cultural icons (or what the fact that I'm apparently perfectly okay with the Zack Snyder aesthetic as described above says about *me*). But at the end of the day, I think Snyder is who he is as a filmmaker. The dude's 50 years old and has been massively rewarded for this particular aesthetic and workflow of his. The idea that he would change it at this point is a little much. He would, correctly, ask you why, when it's all working out so well for him. I get what Zack Snyder is about; he is an utterly known quantity to me. I found *BvS* to be standard-issue Snyder, and it turns out I like standard-issue Snyder just fine.

Which is not to say much of the criticism of *BvS* is wrong. The story telling is a mess and the motivations for everyone in this film are thin as the pages of a comic book. The *characterizations* are all pretty good, I'll note, which is what happens when you get good actors and you let them act (say what you will about Zack Snyder, he's *hugely* better with actors than, say, George Lucas ever was). But you know that thing people say? About how they could watch their favorite actor read a phone book? Well, they come very close to getting their chance here.

For all that, I didn't find it *difficult* to follow why people were doing what they were doing; the storytelling is messy but it has a through-line. Bruce Wayne feels protective about his Wayne Industries workers and then they die when Superman fights Zod, triggering Wayne's PTSD about his parents' death, so he decides to protect the Earth from Superman. Superman can't help himself from protecting Lois Lane at any cost and begins to see that this makes him vulnerable to manipulation. Lex Luthor wants to take over the world, realizes Superman is a hindrance and creates a scheme to get rid of him, with plans B and C if things don't work the way he wants. Wonder Woman is here to set up her film.

Which is the other thing: *BvS* is clearly Act II of a multi-act epic, of which *Man of Steel* was the first act. *BvS* assumes you saw *MoS*—if you didn't none of this makes sense (or, if you like, makes even *less* sense)—and it clearly assumes you know, because you're a citizen of the real world and read many entertainment web sites and magazines, that several more films in the DC universe are coming. That being the case, the film doesn't even attempt to tie up several loose ends, or explain things which (probably) Snyder and the rest of the Warner/DC brain trust know will be addressed in other films. This film sets up films for Wonder Woman, Aquaman, Cyborg and the Flash (these aren't really spoilers, these films have already been announced and are on a schedule), as well as an overall Justice League film (two, actually).

Does this work? Maybe a little. Other people have noted that thanks to this film, *Man of Steel* makes a hell of a lot more sense, which is to say, Superman and Zod wrecking Metropolis in that film has concrete consequences in this one, not the least of which is whether Superman can actually be trusted. So perhaps the things that don't make a whole lot of sense in this one will be explained later. The question here is whether a person paying their money *now* should have to wait for another film, years down the road, for things in *this* film to make sense. There is the idea that films should generally be self-contained.

But then again, Snyder and company are also aware that you're *already* in it for the long haul, no matter how much you whine and moan. For all the griping about the film, it made $420 million worldwide in its opening weekend. While people, including me, are having fun playing the backend calculus about whether the film was really *all that* successful, given its production and marketing costs, and whether it make it into the black in theatrical release (my prediction: Yup, it sure will, or come close enough not to matter in the grand scheme of things), you're already ensnared. You already want to see the Wonder Woman film (justly, as she was pretty cool in this film, and Gal Gadot does a fine job with her), and you're already hoping Snyder will just goddamn *lighten up*, already, for the Justice League film (he won't. You'll see it anyway). Warner Bros will make the same amount of money whether you hate-watch or not, so long as you *watch*, one way or another, and you will. Nerds always watch.

Or if you don't, that's fine too, because, again, this is a multi-stage, multi-year project, and theatrical release grosses are just one factor. Just as Disney/Pixar keeps making Cars sequels and spinoffs not because they make a lot of money theatrically (they don't) but because the merchandising of the Cars universe is *ridiculously* large, so too does this iteration of the DC universe offer Warner Bros all sorts of other ways to make money. Hollywood accounting doesn't just run in one direction, you know. It doesn't just try to amortize the costs of its failures on the backs of its hits. It also spreads the economic benefit of its hits across all its divisions. *BvS* will make $800 million to $1 billion worldwide—or won't—but it will help bring billions into WB through merchandising and licensing and ancillary markets for the films (as well as helping to prop up and drive interest to WB/DC's junior league of properties on television).

But they could have made so much more money if the film was good! I hear you say, and you know what, in theory, I'm with you. If *BvS* were a better film, which is to say, one where the story was tighter and hung together better, there's a chance it might make more money in the long haul than the "merely" $800 million to $1 billion I expect it to settle in with when all is said and done. But then again it might not. There's not a huge correlation between great story and massive grosses. *Avatar* is a punching bag for its story and it's the highest grossing film of all time with $2.7 billion worldwide. Other billion-grossing movies include two Transformers films, two of the terrible *Pirates of the Caribbean* sequels, and the grossly underwhelming first Hobbit film. Oh, and *The Phantom Menace*. *BvS* might have made more money with a better story, or less—no one knows, and it's hard to say. And in any event, as noted one paragraph above, the money from the box office is not the only money under consideration here.

Much of the *tsuris* about *BvS* comes from the fact that a certain segment of fans just don't *like* the Zack Snyder interpretation of the DC universe, which is fine, but the specifics of their complaints I sometimes find a little odd. For example, there's the complaint about the fact that in *Man of Steel* Superman kills Zod, who is actively trying to murder some people with his laser eyes, by breaking his neck:

Superman doesn't kill people! is the refrain here. Well, but he *does*. In fact, he's killed Zod before, in Superman II, back in 1981. And if you ask me, *that* time Superman didn't look particularly *anguished* about it. Sure, Superman didn't snap his neck, he just shoved him into an icy chasm and let him fall to a splattery death tastefully obscured by fog. But dead is dead. And Zod wasn't even trying to murder people at that moment!

Likewise, the complaint that Batman doesn't kill people, especially with guns and bullets—

Except in Frank Miller's comics, where he explicitly guns down some bad guys—

Oh. Uh, well.

But later on in the same story he breaks a gun and says guns are not the Bat Way! So, what you're saying is that Batman and his writers are kinda inconsistent on their whole stance about guns, and killing people, depending on the situation at hand? *Tell me more.*

Both Superman and Batman have been around for coming up on 80 years, and in that time have been rebooted so many different times and in so many different incarnations it's difficult to count them all. The current Snyderverse iterations of these characters aren't extreme in their portrayal, they're just *desaturated* and fairly humorless. Because that's kind of where Zach Snyder is at, basically. I'm not sure I *want* to see Zach Snyder attempt comedy or sustained humor. In fact, I'm vaguely terrified at the idea.

All of which is to say that I think it's perfectly legit to dislike the Snyder take on Batman and Superman and the DC universe in general, but I don't find the arguments that Snyder is somehow subverting the characters in his underlit-yet-still-somehow-very-teal-and-orange version particularly compelling. The good news for such complaints is that as far as comic book properties are concerned, nothing lasts forever. Hell, next year there's gonna be a LEGO Batman movie, which, by the trailer at least, looks pretty damn amusing. Not to mention that DC itself is rebooting its entire universe, *again*, like, this very week or something. Who can keep track?

Personally, and again, I think the Snyderverse iteration is just fine— not *amazing*, but perfectly serviceable with some great visual moments and an underlying (if not especially well-developed) ethos about the responsibilities that those with great power have to those who look to them for salvation, or fear their wrath. It's good enough, in other words, to keep me interested in what comes next. I'm not hatewatching these films. I'm just watching them, happily enough.

A Book Sale
at the Cost of
Your Conscience

First, some context: This tweet from author Racheline Maltese about an article in a Romance Writers of America magazine, in which the writer of an article counsels against taking a stand in social media on "controversial" topics:

> *As a gay person and romance writer an RWA article advising writers to avoid controversial topics like gay marriage on social media stings.*

As it should. No one is obliged to speak on political or social issues if they don't want, and no one is obliged to chip in their two cents on a topic that's gathering pennies on any particular day. It's perfectly fine to say, publicly or privately, "I don't know enough on this and am reading up," or "I'm on deadline and have to focus," or "I have a lot of thoughts on this topic and 140 characters can't express them" or even "addressing this topic right now feels like it would be sticking my head into a hive of angry hornets and why would I want to do that." One's participation is not required on every single topic, every single day.

But note well there is a difference between it being said that one is not required to offer up opinions, and that one should not offer them up at all—or, in this particular instance, that one should "take a more neutral approach." The first of these is about the recognition that any individual writer has only so much time, energy and knowledge to commit to commenting on social issues, and the other is, frankly, about fear: *you won't sell books if you have an opinion a reader doesn't like.*

And that's just terrible advice. It's terrible advice in part because it's simply not true—there are best-selling writers in every genre who express opinions that outrage and annoy whole packs of people, and have since before they were best sellers, and yet they sell books nonetheless—and in part because it's reductive. It's an argument that posits that once a writer enters the stream of commerce, the most important thing about that writer's life is their ability to sell books. Everything else about that writer's life suddenly takes a back seat to that single commercial goal.

Speaking as an explicitly commercial writer—I write books that I plan to sell! To a lot of people!—I'm of the opinion that one of the *worst* ways to be a writer is to shear off or trim down all parts of your life that are not obviously designed to further the goal of selling tons of books. Why? Because then you're cutting off the parts of your life that inform your writing, and which allow you to create the work that *speaks* to people, which is to say, to write the stories that people want to read and buy, and make you an author they wish to support. Being in "the business of selling books" doesn't mean simply moving units of collections of words, any words at all. Those words have to *mean* something, to you and to potential readers, otherwise it won't matter how hyperfocused you are on *selling*.

The author of this article notes "there are a million polarizing topics." That's correct, but it's too limited. *Any topic can be polarizing.* I've been on the Internet for a quarter of a century now and have seen knock-down, drag-out, friendship-ending fights on topics I personally consider absolutely trivial. Turns out these topics aren't trivial to many people—and it also turns out that "trivial" topics have social and political aspects to them that make them far less trivial than those outside those interest groups may initially expect (see: Gamergate). If one were to "take a more neutral stance" on any potentially polarizing topic, one would have to say nothing on anything, ever.

And you know what? *It wouldn't matter.* Because whosoever writes a book—any book, in any genre—has written a polarizing thing. Entire genres are polarizing simply for existing; certainly romance writers, who have to deal with condescension and sexism because their field is predominantly woman-centered, know this, even though the genre is *the single largest-selling genre of them all*. Whatever the subject matter of a book is, someone can and probably will single it out for criticism, and that criticism can and often will be about the author's presumed politics and social positions—which is why when *Old Man's War* first came out, I got criticism (and praise!) for being, among other things, a conservative gun fetishist, which is amusing to anyone who knows me.

To write publicly is to be judged and to be criticized and to be polarizing. If one avoids speaking on public issues in social media only out fear of alienating readers, all one does is possibly delay such judgment. Judgment will happen for what you say and also what you *don't* say. Judgment will happen for what you write in your books and what people assume you meant when you wrote those words, regardless of your authorial intent. Judgment will happen based on who people think you are based on the fantasy version of you they have in their head, which is almost always more about their own fears and desires than anything that has to do with the actual person you are.

So you might as well say whatever the hell you like, if you like. If nothing else, then the fantasy versions of who you are might be closer to the person you actually are.

Here's the final thing I want you to think about: Advising writers to be publicly "neutral" on "controversial" topics is *dangerous*, because it gives those who want to silence any author who has opinions they don't like a tool for that silencing. *See? Even the RWA is telling you to shut up on this. Now shut the fuck up, or you will fail, and it will be your fault.* RWA's membership is as I understand it primarily women. I'm not entirely sure that it's helpful for these writers to be given advice to be silent or "neutral". For some of them, their just *being* a woman is enough excuse for some people to actively try to silence them, and threaten them, and to try to exert control over them. I don't think that sort needs additional encouragement, intentional or otherwise, from a writer speaking to a largely women-centered audience.

Ever since I've been a published author, I've had people declaring that they will not buy my books because I wrote or said something they dislike. The intent was clear: *You exist only to amuse me. I hold the key to your success. Do as I say or suffer the consequences.* Whatever demanding or threatening I get is nothing compared to what others—different genders and ethnicities and sexualities—get. What these threateners, and apparently the author of this article, don't understand is that the world is positively *filled* with people who *will* read my work in spite of, because of, or independent of, my social and political thoughts. Those people will find my work and read it and enjoy it. They will find and read and enjoy the work of any author. Beyond that, I am not only the sum of my book sales. I write to sell and I write to amuse, but I don't exist only for those things. I exist to be a writer, and a husband, and a father, and a friend, and a citizen of my nation and my world, and as an individual who is his own person, aside from the desires of others.

Which is why when people object to my positions on social and political issues, I say: *Oh, well.* And when they try to silence or threaten me, I say: *Kiss my ass.* I neither want nor need the sort of reader who thinks a book sale gives them the right to dictate how I live my life, or what I choose to speak about in the public sphere. As a writer, I believe that neither I nor any other writer, including ones giving advice in writing magazines, should be encouraging these sorts of people to believe that they can or should tell writers what they can and cannot speak about publicly.

This is the long way of saying this: That advice? It's bad. Don't be "neutral" in public on the things that are important to you. Speak if you choose to speak. A book sale at the cost of your conscience is a very bad deal indeed.

BORN THAT WAY,
OR NOT

Jul

30

2015

Was pointed today to an interview with developmental psychologist Lisa Diamond, on the subject of sexuality, and additionally, whether it matters whether people who identify as gay or bisexual are "born that way" or not. She takes the position that ultimately it really doesn't matter:

It is time to just take the whole idea of sexuality as immutable, the born this way notion, and just come to a consensus as scientists and as legal scholars that we need to put it to rest. It's unscientific, it's unnecessary and it's unjust. It doesn't matter how we got to be this way. As a scientist, I think it's one of the most fascinating questions out there and one that I will continue to investigate. As a lesbian and a progressive, I think it's totally irrelevant and just politics.

I don't know if in fact Diamond is correct, but I'll note that for a very long time now I've personally held the position that I don't care *why* or *if* someone decides to love someone of the same sex (physically and/or emotionally and all the stuff in between), simply that if they *do*, that love should be respected, legally and socially. I think it's entirely possible that some people are "born that way," that some people become that way through environment (Diamond notes that "environment" should be considered a term rather more expansive than "how you grew up and with whom"), and that others might have become so by a combination of both, or some other factor entirely. Ultimately it doesn't matter, outside of a dry and somewhat abstract set of academic questions. However you got there, you got there.

Diamond also talks about sexual fluidity, which "means that people are born with a sexual orientation and also with a degree of sexual flexibility," which is to say (at least as I understand it), you know your general sexuality, and you also know how much leeway you give yourself inside of that understanding. So for example you might identify as straight but be willing to acknowledge that every once in a while you find someone of the same sex attractive, or gay but with occasional hetero crushes, or bisexual but with a lean one way more than another on average. Or, you know, you might identify as something rather more expansive than that.

This also makes a great deal of sense to me. People have been talking about the Kinsey scale for years, but I find that sort of linear sexuality tracking a little limiting. I picture it as multidimensional with a number of axes: Gay-straight might be one; sexual-asexual might be another; conservative-opportunistic might be a third. A guy who is largely straight but highly sexual and somewhat opportunistic might not turn down a same-sex encounter because, hey, *sex*; another man who is gay but closer to asexual and conservative might turn down the same opportunity.

These three axes are not necessarily the complete set, I would note; likewise I would note that not every dimension of sexuality has the same range on every person. And finally, of course, one's understanding of one's sexuality may change over time—again for various reasons.

All of which is to say, sexuality: There's some complex shit going down there.

And all the more reason, from the point of view of social and legal acceptance, not to actually *care* how someone arrived at their sexuality. The law should care if sexual encounters are consensual; society should discourage (to use a word *mildly*) non-consensual encounters. Other than that, you know, fair play.

Note that I think that people should know, as much as they are interested in the subject, the hows and whys of their own sexuality. I think knowing who you are and what led you to that understanding is useful to help you avoid behaviors that aren't good for you, and to help you find which ones are. But your personal knowledge of yourself is different than society or the law demanding you are who you are, sexually, is because of one factor exclusively, or more than another, in a precise recipe. You should care about your sexuality. I'm not convinced the law or society needs to care anywhere as much.

BOYCOTTS, CREATORS AND ME

Jul

17

2013

'm getting pinged by folks who want to know what my position is regarding the boycott of the *Ender's Game* movie by people repelled by author Orson Scott Card's social and political stances and actions regarding gays and lesbians and in particular his stance on same-sex marriage. With the notation that I am not in the least a disinterested party here (one, I've met Card and had a pleasant time in his company; two, I have a book being adapted to film, for which I strongly suspect the performance of *Ender's Game* at the box office will be relevant to any eventual green light), here's my position:

If your conscience tells you to boycott or avoid the film because of Card's positions on the rights of gays and lesbians, then, you know, do it. Card is entitled to speak his mind on gays and lesbians and same-sex marriage. You are equally entitled, on the basis of that speech and his political efforts, to decide not to support him or a film based on his work. That's entirely fair.

On a related topic, if in the future *Old Man's War* is made into a film, and your conscience tells you to boycott or avoid the film because of my (largely opposing to Card's) positions on the rights of gays and lesbians, then do *that*. I am entitled to speak my mind on gays and lesbians and same-sex marriage. You are equally entitled, on the basis of that speech and my political efforts, to decide not to support me or a film based on my work. That is also entirely fair.

(Mind you, I don't suspect on this particular topic, any boycotts of Card or me would *overlap*.)

In a larger sense, look: Art originates from people. People have opinions and thoughts and actions, many of which are largely unrelated to their art. In learning about those largely unrelated opinions, thoughts and actions, you may find some of them, and some the people they are coming out of, offensive, obnoxious, insulting or even dangerous. They may eventually keep you from being able to enjoy the art these people produce.

When and if that happens, that's fine. If it *doesn't* happen—if you can totally divorce the art from the human who created it—that's fine, too. Everyone has their own dividing line for this, contingent on factors that are unique to them, and unique to the creator in question. Mind you, I personally think it's good to give some serious reflection as to why some particular creator has crossed that line for you, on the grounds that it's always good to know why you think or do anything. But at the end of the day, when you get to the point where you think, *I'm done with this jerk*, then that's it, you're done.

Personally speaking, I have a pretty high tolerance for artists and creators being obnoxious/offensive/flawed/assholes/otherwise seriously imperfect. This is partly because I believe art is a highly composed, refined, edited and *intentional* end result of a process that takes place in a mind which can be *almost anything*. The only thing creators fundamentally have in common is the ability to create, and to shape their creations to speak to others.

This is why, for example, bigots and cretins through the ages could create works of art that exhibit gorgeous empathy for the other, despite their personal issues: They have time to perfect their creations, and have an understanding of what an audience will respond to emotionally. You could argue that art is the better self of every creator, but I don't know if that's accurate. Art isn't what the creator could be, any more than a 100 mile an hour fastball is what an athlete could be. Art is what we can *do*. That fact shapes the life of the creator, to be sure, just like that fastball shapes the life of that athlete. But there's a whole lot of other influences that shape the creator's life, too. Not all of those get into the art, because they're not directly relevant to what the art *is*. They do show up in the person who makes the art.

So, yeah, I can put up with a lot when it comes to creators. It's not usually the art's fault the brain it came out of is directly connected to an asshole.

However, I am also aware this is a luxury I can afford, for my own reasons. Other people can put up with less, for reasons of their own. I may think these are valid reasons, or not, but these people don't need my approval to think what they want and act on what they think, and anyway I could be wrong, so there.

There are lots of creators I don't support because I just don't like their work. This should not be a surprise. There are a (very) few creators I choose not to support for personal reasons that are unrelated to the quality of their output. No, I won't tell you who they are. The reasons are personal and therefore not relevant to anyone else. I don't tend to think of these choices as anything formal as a boycott. I just don't do business with these people anymore. I don't generally do it for any larger goal, like social change or to hurt the creator economically. I do it because my own personal sense of morality tells me not to have anything to do with them. Other people in other circumstances feel the need to be more public about their actions, and have a goal beyond their own personal disengagement. Again: It's their right to do it, and there's no reason they shouldn't.

I should note that questions of boycotts are not an entirely theoretical exercise for me. I am on at least one boycott list that I know of, albeit one that I think has been spectacularly ineffective; every once in a while I'll see my name pop up on a list of authors that someone thinks should be boycotted or otherwise economically punished for opining in public in a manner unrelated to science fiction books. Recently these people are dudes who think I am a traitor to straight white males everywhere.

My opinion about these boycotts, proposed or otherwise, tends to be, one, fuck you, I'm going to say what I want, and two, if the end result of speaking my mind is that someone decides to boycott me, then fine, they should boycott me and tell whomever they like to boycott me, too. I think a lot of other creators in a similar position are perfectly fine with the "fuck you, I'll say what I want" part, but get confused or truculent about the "if that means you're going to boycott me, that's fine" part, and this is where the problem lies.

But if you want the first, you should be a grown-up and accept that the second part is also part of the package deal. As I've noted before, freedom of speech does not mean freedom from consequence. Suggesting or demanding that you should have freedom from consequence from what you say, or (related to this) that tolerance of your freedom to speak equates to bland murmuring politeness from those who oppose your speech, indicates that ultimately you don't understand how freedom of speech works.

So, to recap: Boycotts are a perfectly valid exercise of political speech, participate in one if you think it's necessary. I don't tend to boycott creators but don't mind if you do, even if that creator happens to be me. Freedom of speech does not mean freedom from consequence and everyone should remember that, especially folks who've spent a while pissing off a bunch of folks.

I think that covers it.

A Brief Phone Text Conversation Between Me and My Daughter

Jan

30

2014

Athena (from school): I found out today I'm ranked eleventh in my class.

Me: You have ten people to push in front of a train.

Athena: This is why you're the best dad.

But Doctor,
I am Pagliacci

Following Robin Williams' death and my brief comments about depression in my entry about it, I've had some people ask me for some more detailed thoughts on the subject, and whether I myself have ever experienced depression. I wrote about the subject in 2010, and the short version is that while I have had events in my life where I was almost certainly depressed (as most of us have, I suspect), I'm not someone who suffers from depression as a disease.

But again, I know a lot of people who do. I suspect that some of this is because I know a lot of creative people and the correlation between depression and creativity is well known and well documented. But I also suspect this is also because I know *people*, and I suspect that depression, as a chronic and persistent ailment, happens to a lot of people regardless of their creativity. One of the silver lining positive things about knowing many people with depression is that it's gone a very long way to hammer against that bias against mental illnesses that I have as part of the background radiation of life—the bias that tells you that someone with a mental illness isn't merely sick but is *wrong* in some ineffable way. I know that's incorrect and actively unhelpful now; I hope it makes me a better human and a better friend for my friends who have depression.

On the tangentially-related topic of humor and depression, the world seems to be largely divided into two camps—the camp that is apparently oblivious to the idea that funny people, especially professionally funny people, might have a darker side to their life ("He was funny and seemed so happy! Who knew that other side was there?") and the one that is all too familiar with that aspect of the life of a "funny" person—the ones who, after hearing of Williams' passing, tweeted something along the lines of the quote I'm using as the headline.

With the former camp, it's easy to be exasperated, especially if you write humor yourself. Where do these folks think the capacity for humor comes *out* of? If you don't have an understanding of the whole wide range of the human condition, your attempts at humor are going to come across as insipid at best and cruel at worst; there's a reason I note that the failure state of "clever" is "asshole." People who are really funny—the sort of funny more complex than a banana peel on a slippery floor—are funny because they know *people*. They're smart. They're observant. And, very often, their own life experience, with all its ups *and* downs, is the reason *why* they know which keys turn the lock on the funny.

It's easy to become exasperated with people who don't seem to know this, but it's also at least slightly unfair, because it's *process*—it's back-stage matter. Most people don't live with a professional comedian or humorist, they're merely entertained by them, and they're entertained by the output, not by the process. We laugh at the joke, not at the work that goes into it. Likewise, humor feels easy and light; we laugh at it, and laughing seems like the simplest thing in the world to do. If people don't know about the darker parts of the minds that create humor, it's at least in part because it often ruins the humor to dwell on it.

On the flip side of this I personally get exasperated by the "but doctor, I am Pagliacci" response as well, because I think in many ways it trivializes depression. Humor needs knowledge of humans and empathy; it doesn't need depression. From everything that I know about it from friends who have it, depression doesn't heighten your access to the human condition, it deadens it—takes you out of the place where you can create and where you can say anything about life, funny or otherwise.

I get that tossing about the Pagliacci quote can be an attempt to be understanding—or at least be an attempt to explain—but I think it just ends up being the equivalent of a mental shrug. *Of course that funny person was doomed. That's just what happens to funny people.* That's no more correct or helpful than being surprised a funny person wasn't happy all the time.

I'm not saying a comedian or humorist can't take their depression and make it funny. Of course they can—it's in the heart of humor to make you understand something by making you laugh about it. But the depression isn't *why* they're funny. Depression isn't helping them be funny. Depression is a thing they have to route around. Sometimes they can't. That fact deserves an acknowledgment more than a shrug and a quote about a sad clown.

I don't have any answers about depression, in no small part because my own direct experience of it in my own head is (thankfully) limited. What I do know is that for my own part I want to be done with people being hesitant or ashamed about a disease that happens to them, despite the fact it takes place in the part of the body where who they are lives. Treating it differently than other ailments of the body doesn't do anyone any good and does active harm if it keeps people from getting help.

I also want to be done with thinking that depression is anyone's *fault*. Countless pieces out there by people who deal with depression speak to it. They know what they're talking about, because they live it.

For my part, I'm listening. I think we should all be doing that.

THE CINEMAX
THEORY OF RACISM

Nov

10

2016

Yesterday, in the immediate wake of the 2016 election, I wrote here:

If Trump's administration indulges in the racism, sexism and religious and other bigotries that Trump and his people have already promised to engage in, we can assume it's because his voters are just fine with that racism, sexism and religious and other bigotries—even if they claim to have voted for him for other reasons entirely. After all, Trump didn't hide these things about himself, or try to sneak these plans in by a side door. They were in full view this entire time. If you vote for a bigot who has bigoted plans, you need to be aware of what that says about you, and your complicity in those plans.

I also last night tweeted this:

> *This just in: supporters of a racist presidential candidate upset and offended to be called out on their racism. Get used to it, folks.*

And wouldn't you know, because of both, I've gotten comments and emails and tweets from people upset that I pointed out that voting for a public racist with clear racist policies means that one is abetting racism. I assume that they know for sure that *they're* not racist, and wouldn't *be* racist, so being accused of racism stings. They didn't vote *for* racism! They voted to make America great again!

Well, so, okay. Let me give you an analogy here.

Let's say you want HBO. So you go to your local cable provider to get HBO and the only way they'll let you get HBO is to sign up for a premium channel package, which includes HBO but also includes Cinemax.

Now, maybe you don't *want* Cinemax, and you don't *care* about Cinemax, and maybe never personally plan to ever *watch* Cinemax, but the deal is: If you want HBO, you have to sign on to Cinemax too. You *have* to be a Cinemax subscriber to get HBO. And you go ahead and sign up for the premium channel package.

Pop quiz: In this scenario, did you just subscribe to Cinemax?

And you may say, no, I subscribed to *HBO*, but I couldn't get it without Cinemax. I'm an HBO subscriber, not a Cinemax subscriber.

And then someone points out to you, well, in point of fact, you *are* a Cinemax subscriber, look, there it is on your TV channel guide. Some of the money you pay in for your premium channel package goes to Cinemax and funds its plans and strategies.

And you say, but I never watch Cinemax or ever plan to.

And they say, okay, but you still *subscribe* to it, and you *knew* that in order to get HBO you had to get Cinemax, and you signed on anyway. You're a Cinemax subscriber whether you ever watch it or not.

And you say, well, look, I *really* wanted HBO.

And they say, sure, enough that you were fine with accepting Cinemax to get it. Just don't *pretend* you're not currently subscribing to Cinemax, too. You clearly *are*. Look, it's right there on your cable bill. You're a Cinemax subscriber.

Now, to bring that analogy back to the point at hand. This election, you had two major Presidential providers. One offered you the Stronger Together plan, and the other offered you the Make America Great Again plan. You chose the Make America Great Again plan. The thing is, the Make America Great Again has in its package active, institutionalized racism (also active, institutionalized sexism. And as it happens, active, institutionalized homophobia). And you know it does, because the people who bundled up the Make America Great Again package not only *told* you it was there, they made it one of the plan's *big selling points*.

And you voted for it anyway.

So did you vote for racism?

You sure did.

And you say, but *I'm* not racist, and I would never treat people in a racist fashion, and I don't like being called out as having done a racist thing.

And others say to you, okay, but you knew that when you signed up for the Make America Great Again plan that active, institutionalized racism was part of the package. Your vote supports racism. By voting, you endorsed a racist plan.

And you say, but I didn't want *that* part. I wanted the *other* parts.

And others say to you, that's fine, but you knew that to get the other parts, you had to sign on for the racism, too. And evidently you were okay with that.

And you say, no I'm not, I hate racism.

And others say to you, but apparently you like these other things *more* than you hate racism, because you agreed to the racism in order to get these other things.

And you say, well, the Stronger Together plan had horrible things in it too.

And others say to you, yes, and you didn't vote for that, you voted for this. Which has racism in it. You voted *for* racism.

And you say, stop saying that.

And the others ask, why.

I've written before on how people can benefit from racism and other forms of discrimination without actively and intentionally discriminating against others, and if you have the time I recommend reading the piece. Lots of people benefit from an institutionalized system of bigotry, etc (including me) without being *a* bigot themselves, i.e., going out of their way to keep other people down. That's the nature of a bigoted system so endemic that you don't even notice it's there for the same reason the proverbial fish doesn't notice the water.

I think you can *very easily* make the argument that a lot people who voted for Trump are not and would not actively be racist to another person in their day-to-day lives. I live among Trump voters, and the ones I live among are lovely and kind and perfect neighbors. They are what nearly anyone would describe as good people, me included. As are, I think, the majority of the people who voted for Trump.

But the fact remains that in voting for Trump, they voted *for* racism: It was right there in the package deal, front and center, and hard to miss. They voted for it anyway. And you may argue that voting for racism as part of a larger package deal does not *a* racist make, and I wouldn't necessarily disagree, as far as what people do to others in their personal and day-to-day lives. But voting *for* racism will make personal, day-to-day life harder for the targets of that racism. Two days after the election, we're already seeing that.

It's perfectly fine to point out to people who voted for racism, that indeed, this is what they voted for. And also that if owning up to the fact that they voted for racism is uncomfortable for them, they should take a moment to think about how bad it is for the targets of that racism, and how bad it has yet to get.

For the Trump voters, Trump's racism may have been just part of the package deal, the Cinemax they had accept to get the HBO. For those who are the target of that racism (and sexism, and homophobia), however, it's not Cinemax. It's their lives. Day to day, and every day. And they're all too aware of what Trump voters signed up for, to get what they wanted.

Dear GOP: We Can't Save You If You Won't Save Yourself

And now is the part of the election cycle where the pundit class comes forward and begs the rest of the US electorate to help save the GOP from itself. In the *Atlantic*, Peter Beinart argues that liberals should support Marco Rubio over Trump, and over in the *Washington Post*, Michael R. Strain of the American Enterprise Institute is flat-out begging for people to vote for someone, *anyone*, but Trump. "We all have to stop him," reads the headline to the article.

We? *We?* I don't know if Michael R. Strain is up on the news, but Trump is polling at 49% nationally among Republican voters. He's outpolling Rubio, Ted Cruz, John Kasich and Ben Carson *combined* among the people who are actually going to go to the polls to vote Republican. Likewise, Beinart's suggestion that liberals throw in with Rubio, who aside from his pandering antediluvian positions appears to dissolve into a stammering puddle of flop sweat when people are *mean* to him, which is a quality I know *I* always look for in a potential leader of the free world, is actively insulting. *Hey, liberals! Save the GOP from Trump by supporting the establishment's hand-picked empty suit, which it will use to shore up shaky senatorial races and then push and pass a political agenda massively antithetical to everything you believe in!* Yeeeeah, thanks for the hot take, there, Pete. Let me know who you buy your weed from, because that's clearly some primo shit you're smoking.

News flash, pundit guys: No one can save the GOP from Trump *but* the GOP, and its voters clearly have no intention of doing that. To repeat: Trump currently outpolls every other GOP candidate in the race, *combined*. What, pray tell, do you want any of the rest of us to do about that? The answer may be "vote against Trump in the primaries," but this is where I point out that the rest of us are not GOP primary voters for a reason. Some of us may want to vote in the Democratic primaries. Some of us may be independents and have to wait to see what dumbasses the parties elect. Some of us may belong to third parties because we're political idealists/masochists. The point is, we have other plans for the day. They are legit plans. They don't involve keeping the GOP from setting itself on fire.

Also, you know. If I were the paranoid type, I'd look at the pundit class begging the rational portion of the electorate to save the GOP from itself as a suspicious bit of political theater orchestrated by the shadowy cabal that really runs the nation. *We can't let the GOP implode yet, we still have to pay taxes! I know! Convince the liberals to vote against their interests to save a political party whose goals oppose theirs in every relevant way! And as a bonus, that way they don't vote for that commie Sanders! Quick! To the pundits!* I'm not saying that's what's happening. But I'm also not *not* saying it, nod, wink, nod, hand signal, wink.

Even if liberals (to Beinart's point) and everyone else (to Strain's) decided to vote against Trump in the states that allow open primaries—or changed their registration to Republican to vote in closed primaries, because, yeah, *that* will happen—*again*, Trump has the support of half the GOP voters right now. Folks, it's Super friggin' Tuesday. Half the GOP delegates needed for a nomination are getting sorted out tonight (595 of the 1,237 needed, of which Trump already has 82), and it's a fair bet that Trump is taking every state except Texas, which will go to Ted Cruz, an odious fistula that walks the earth in a human skin.

Now, most of these states as I understand it will allocate delegates proportionally, so Cruz and Rubio are likely to take some. But most are going to Trump. He's likely going to end the night so far ahead that even the active intervention of *everyone else* won't keep Trump from chugging along to Cleveland with a plush stack of pledged delegates. Neither Cruz nor Rubio is going to drop out of the race—Rubio because the establishment's assassins will murder his future if he does, Cruz because his monomaniacal sense of manifest destiny doesn't allow for quittin'—and neither of them is likely to poll substantially better than the other. They're Tweedle-Dee and Tweedle-Dum all the way down the line. You want to choose between these two embarrassments to the name of Generation X? After *you*.

But that's why Beinart tells liberals to vote for Rubio! To get him ahead! Oh, you dear, sweet, precious jewel in the firmament of heaven. Yes, I'm sure that if liberals *do* cross the line, hold their noses and vote for Rubio in primaries, that absolutely positively *won't* be used against him by either Trump or Cruz, two gentlemen who are celebrated worldwide for their probity and graciousness in all things political. Indeed, I see no way this fantastic plan of Beinart's could ever possibly go wrong, or work to Trump's advantage with his core constituency of angry white people who may or may not be flaming bigots, but who certainly hate *friggin' libruls*.

Folks, I'm the first to admit that my political crystal ball is not exactly piercingly clear, but here's what I believe: It's too late to stop Trump. Probably from getting the GOP nomination, but at the very least from being a significant and possibly controlling force at the Republican convention. Is anyone under the impression that, in the case of a contested convention, Trump's pledged delegates—or his actual supporters—are suddenly going to *abandon* him after the first ballot? Bless their hearts, but no one's in love with Rubio, and no one actually *likes* Cruz. Trump's people, on the other hand, are in love with him in the way that only the simple can pine for a demagogue. If you want to see what a middle-aged riot looks like, wait until the GOP tries to torpedo Trump at the convention.

But somebody needs to do something! Well, yes. Those "somebodies" should have been the GOP, but it didn't want to, and then when it wanted to it *couldn't*, because it realized too late that its entire governing strategy for the last couple of decades, but especially since Obama came to office, has been designed to foster the emergence of a populist lectern-thumper like Trump. The GOP has made its electoral bones on low-information, high-anxiety white folks for years now, but has only ever looked at the next election, and not ever further down the road, or where that road would lead to. Well, it led to Trump.

And now the GOP wants a bailout, and people like Beinart and Strain are arguing we should give it to them, because the GOP is apparently too big to fail (and yes, this means that Trump is a festering ball of subprime loans in this scenario). And, well. We bailed out the banks in '08, but no one was punished and no one on Wall Street apparently learned anything from the experience, because why would they? No matter how hard they fucked up, someone would come along to save them, and after a couple of years of grumping about smaller bonuses, they'd be back on top, sucking up even more of the wealth of the nation while everyone else muddled along on a glide path that slowly slides them into financial insecurity.

If the rest of us somehow *could* bail out the GOP by saving it from Trump, what would *we* get out of it? The GOP establishment certainly isn't in the mood to learn—shit, it's shoving all its chips onto Rubio, whose arms are probably already fitted with the titanium eye screws through which they'll loop the strings once he's elected. There's no percentage in saving the GOP from itself; its policies are already inimical to good governance and have been for the last several election cycles. Saving the GOP from Trump doesn't change the fact that the GOP *is by conscious and intentional design* primed to create *more* Trumps—more populist demagogues who will leverage the anxious discontent of scared and aging white people into electoral victories. That won't be fixed. The GOP doesn't *want* it fixed. It just wants the demagogue to be someone it can control.

The good news is that there is a way for everyone else to stop Trump: It's called voting in the general election for the candidates who are not him. At this point as a practical matter that probably means voting for Hillary Clinton. This won't solve the GOP's problems, but again, maybe from the point of view of everyone else, the GOP's problems aren't solvable. Maybe it really *does* need to blow up and start over. Otherwise we'll be back here four years out. And eight years out. And twelve years out. And so on.

DISORGANIZED THOUGHTS ON FREE SPEECH, CHARLIE HEBDO, RELIGION AND DEATH

Jan

11

2015

(In the wake of the offices of French satirical magazine Charlie Hebdo being shot up by terrorists who were Muslim, killing several stuffers.)

Disorganized because every time I try to organize my thoughts on these topics recently they kind of squirm away. So, fine, disorganized it is, then.

1. As a former newspaper journalist, as well as, you know, writing *here*, I've done my share of enraging people with words, by mocking ideas that they hold dear, because I thought they deserved mocking. I have had my share of angry responses and even the occasional threat, and my response to those typically has been to poke harder. When I took up the #JeSuisCharlie hashtag, that's what it meant to me. I've been that guy.

2. I also recognize that I know almost nothing about *Charlie Hebdo*, the newspaper, or the tradition of satire and comment that it exemplifies in French culture. From where I sit, a lot of what I've seen of it looks kind of racist and terrible. And I understand that *Charlie Hebdo* didn't just go after Islamic extremists, and that it went after other groups and people just as hard (and just as obnoxiously). But it reminds me that "we go after everyone equally" doesn't mean that I feel equally comfortable with all of it, or that it has equal effect. When I say #JeSuisCharlie, it doesn't mean I want to create or post what I think are racist caricatures and justify them as satire, applied on a presumed equal opportunity basis.

3. But then again my comfort level is about me, not about *Charlie Hebdo* or anyone else. Free speech, taken as a principle rather than a specific constitutional practice, means everyone has a right to share their ideas, in their own space, no matter how terrible or obnoxious or racist or stupid or inconsequential I or anyone else think they and their ideas are. I also recognize that satire in particular isn't about being nice, or kind, or fair. Satire is inherently exaggerated, offensive and unfair, in order to bring the underlying injustice it's calling attention to into sharper relief. Trust me, I know this. (Satire also has a high failure rate, and the failure mode of satire, like the failure mode of clever, is "asshole.") A lot of what I've seen from *Charlie Hebdo* isn't for me and seems questionable, and that's neither here nor there in terms of whether it should have a right to be published.

4. At the moment there's an argument about whether news organizations are being cowardly about showing the *Charlie Hebdo* covers that allegedly were part of the reason it was attacked—the ones with visual depictions of the prophet Muhammad, who many Muslims feel is not supposed to be depicted visually (let us leave aside for the moment the discussion of whether all Muslims feel this way (they don't) or whether Muhammad has been visually represented in the past even in Muslim art (he has) and focus on the here and now, in which many Muslims believe he should not be represented visually). The argument seems to be that by not showing the covers (or Muhammad generally), newspapers and other media are giving in to the extremists.

I'm not going to argue that very large media companies don't have multiple reasons for what they do, including making the *realpolitik* assessment that displaying a *Charlie Hebdo* cover puts their employees (and their real estate, and their profits) at risk for an attack. But a relevant point to make here is that aside from the asshole terrorists who murdered a dozen people at *Charlie Hebdo*, there really are millions of Muslims who are just trying to get through their day like anyone else, who also strongly prefer that Muhammad is not visually represented. It's not a defeat for either the concept or right of free speech for people or organizations to say they're factoring these millions or people who neither did nor would do anything wrong into their consideration of the issue.

5. Which is a point that I think tends to get elided at moments like this—free speech, and the robust defense of it, does not oblige everyone *to offend*, just to show that one can. I can simultaneously say that I absolutely and without reservation have the *right* to visually depict Muhammad any way I choose (including in some ways devout Muslims, not to mention others, would consider horribly blasphemous), and also that, with regard to depicting Muhammad, as a default I'm going to try to respect the desire of millions of perfectly decent Muslims, and *not* do it. Because it's *polite*, and while I'm perfectly happy *not* to be polite when it suits me, I usually like to have a reason for it.

6. But isn't Muslim extremists shooting up a newspaper a *perfect* reason? For some it may be, and that's fine for them. But I tend to agree with Kareem Abdul-Jabbar here: shit like this isn't about religion, it's about money and recruiting for terrorist groups who use religion, at best, as a very thin binding material for their more prosaic concerns. I'm also persuaded by Malek Merabet, brother of Ahmed Merabet, the policeman and Muslim who was killed by the terrorists. He said: "My brother was Muslim and he was killed by two terrorists, by two false Muslims." In which case, why offend the good and decent Muslims to get back at two very bad and false Muslims. I'm a reasonably clever writer; I have the capability to make my point regarding these asshole terrorists without a gratuitous display of Muhammad.

7. Hey, did you know that according to the UN, Christian militia in Central African Republic have carried out ethnic cleansing of the Muslim population during the country's ongoing civil war? And yet I hear nothing from the so-called "good" and "moderate" Christians around me on the matter! Why have the "moderate" Christians *not* denounced these horrible people and rooted them out from their religion? Is it because maybe the so-called "moderate" Christians are actually all *for* the brutal slaughter? Christians say their religion is one of peace! And yet! Jesus *himself* says (Matthew 10:36) that he does not come to bring peace, but the sword! *Clearly* Christianity is a horrible, brutal murdering religion. And unless every single Christian in the United States denounces these murders in the Central African Republic and apologizes for them, not just to *me* but to *every single Muslim they might ever meet*, I see no reason to believe that every Christian I meet *isn't* in fact secretly planning to cut the throat of every single non-Christian out there. That's what goes on in those "churches" of theirs, you know. Secret murder planning sessions, every Sunday! *Where they "symbolically" eat human flesh!*

Please feel free to cut and paste the above paragraph the next time someone goes on about how all Muslims *must* do something about their co-religionists (of which there are more than a billion, all of whom apparently they are supposed to have on speed dial), and how Islam is in fact a warrior religion, and look, here are context-free snippets from the Koran, and so on and so forth until you just want to vomit from the stupidity of it all. And don't worry, there are similar cut-and-pastes for any major religion you might want to name, as well for those who have no religion at all, although I'm not going to bore you with those at the moment.

The point is that, no, in fact, I don't see why I or anyone else should demand that every Muslim is obliged to denounce and apologize for any bad thing that happens in the world done by someone who claims to be doing it in the name of Allah. As it happens, many prominent Muslims and Muslim organizations did condemn the Charlie Hebdo attacks, just like pretty much everyone else. But silence isn't complicity or endorsement, and if you demand that it is, you may be an asshole.

8. If there is one silver lining to the horribleness of the *Charlie Hebdo* massacre, it is that people have been confronted with the fact that something they take for granted—the right to say what they want to say, how they want to say it—is something that others will literally kill to punish. That *Charlie Hebdo* is a problematic example—that *is* offensive, and intentionally so, and it does make people uncomfortable and angry—is, well, *good* isn't the right word. *Instructive.* Sometimes we have to be reminded that free speech isn't just for the speech we like, or the speech that's easy to be reasonable about.

At the same time it's okay to ask if this welcome outpouring of solidarity is because free speech was attacked, and it was decided that it was worth fighting for, or because a newspaper that mocked Islam was attacked by gunmen purporting to be Muslims, and that this may be less about free speech than another front in a religious/ethnic clash of culture.

My thoughts are that it's probably some amount of both, and that neither is cleanly delineated. The two men who shot up *Charlie Hebdo* say they were Muslim; so were some of the people they shot. Those people—the Muslims who died—have been mourned, at least it seems from here, equally with all the other dead. They haven't been pushed out of frame for a convenient narrative.

And maybe that's part of the silver lining to this very dark cloud, too—that this isn't just "us vs. them," or at least that "us" now contain people in it who might have previously been considered "them." And that all the people who are saying #JeSuisCharlie, and #JeSuisAhmed, or who are standing for free speech, or any combination of the three, are standing in memory of them as well.

Dylann Roof
and the Denial
of Racism

Jun

21

2015

I t's been interesting watching Dylann Roof be, in himself, the very best rebuttal against all the (almost entirely white) people who were desperate for his massacre to be about anything other than what it so very obviously was: racism and racial hatred. All the scrambling and denial, from presidential candidates to news networks to Twitter commenters, all undone by Roof's insistent, persistent desire to hurt black people. There was no rationalization that stood up to that simple hatred.

Not that there probably still aren't people who are willing to try to pretzel themselves into arguing it's something other than racism or racial hatred. So, you know, again, and to be clear: If you are arguing that a white man who clearly held racist beliefs, going into a place where he knew he would find black people, waiting an hour in pretend fellow-ship with them, announcing he was there to shoot black people, shooting them while spouting racist comments at them while they begged him to stop killing them, reloading several times, and then when arrested declaring that the reason he was killed all those innocent people was to start a race war, *wasn't* motivated by racism and racial hatred,

a) you are so very laughably wrong;

b) you are being as racist as you can possibly be.

Dylann Roof is a racist. His attack was a racist attack. The denial of his racist attack being racist *is* racist. There were an appalling number of people being racist in the aftermath of this fundamentally racist act. And despite everything, there are people continuing to be racist about it now. I am continually amazed at how difficult it was, and is, for people to recognize that this was a racist attack, by a racist. I'm continually amazed by everyone who still has a hard time admitting that this country is still racist as hell, and especially toward black people.

All of the above is *stupidly* obvious. And yet some people choose to be stupid about this. This willful ignorance embarrasses me as an American. I was in the UK when all of this happened. No one over there had any doubt what it was about, as far as I could see. And when it was made clear to them that I wasn't intentionally stupid about it either, the attitude I received the most was: Sympathy. The UK has its own social crosses to bear, to be sure. They easily enough recognized the one my country bears.

I'm very sure most of us knew immediately why Dylann Roof did what he did. It's just that so many of the people who argued so very hard against the obvious are those who want to control the levers of our politics and discourse. It's embarrassing to me that so many very clearly intelligent people worked so mightily to pretend this killing was something it was not. It's ironic how difficult Roof made it for them, and gratifying that this very fact exposed their mendacity for what it is: Ridiculous, risible, and racist.

EIGHT THINGS ABOUT DONALD TRUMP

Dec

8

2015

Do I have thoughts on Donald Trump today? Why, yes. Yes I do.

1. Without offering this up as an excuse—it's rather the opposite—I don't think Trump *planned* to become the face of 21st century American fascism. I suspect rather strongly that he entered the presidential race for the usual reasons that Trump does anything publicly, i.e., for the publicity and the long-term brand benefits that accrue. He said outrageous things and when they gave him a boost, he kept on going in that direction, because why wouldn't he, and here we are. Of *course* Trump is going to escalate his rhetoric, because that's what he needs to do to keep the focus on him, and to starve the other competitors for the GOP nomination of the spotlight, forcing them off the stage.

Which is to say that Trump is running his campaign like he's on a reality show, which has no other context than itself, and of which the goal is to *win the presidency*, not actually to *be president*. He's not wrong about the reality show aspect of the campaign, and that's on all of us. He's wrong about everything else, and that's on him.

2. I don't believe that Trump actually thinks about Muslims or Mexicans in any particularly deep fashion; I think he likes and respects the members of either group exactly as much as they have money and a willingness to do business with him. So if you're a Carlos Slim or a Saudi prince, he'll like you just fine and be happy to cut you all the breaks you want (Carlos Slim, it should be noted, recently dumped Trump). Otherwise, you're an abstraction that he can use to motivate another abstract group, that is, likely GOP primary voters, who, to be clear, I suspect he thinks about and respects as much and in the same fashion as Mexicans and Muslims—for what they can do for Trump, and only exactly that much.

3. Fundamentally Donald Trump doesn't give a shit about anyone other than Donald Trump, and while this is obvious to anyone who knows anything about Trump for the last thirty years, it's still apparently confusing to a number of people, who like to offer up various conspiracy theories for his continued existence in the race. *He's a plant by the Democrats to make the Republicans look bad! He's a plant by the GOP to make the rest of the field look more moderate by comparison!*

Well, no, and no. In the former case, the modern GOP doesn't need any help; in the latter case, one need only look at the current other two front runners—Cruz and Carson—to see what nonsense that is. It's extraordinarily telling that less than a year out of the election, the top three GOP candidates can all be described by the same two words: "Career narcissists." That's something for the Republicans to ponder. But to get back to Trump, there's no reason to spin up increasingly bogus and complex conspiracy theories about who is tugging on his strings when Occam's Razor—and common sense—dictates that this is Trump doing what Trump has always done: Making things about Trump, and his need to have the spotlight on him in order to build the brand.

4. This may lead you to ponder the philosophical question of "If you espouse fascist, bigoted points of views but don't really *believe* them, are you *really* a fascist and a bigot?" In these troubled times it's useful to turn to the words of a man wiser than I, so let me quote: "By their fruits ye shall know them." (Indeed much of the surrounding context for that particular quote is useful in the case of Trump.) Trump is espousing bigoted, fascist ideas and is campaigning to become president on the strength of those ideas and the fervor they generate. Whether he's saying them because he believes them or merely because they give him a short-term benefit for a longer-term business strategy, the end result is a mainstreaming and affirmation of those ideals.

But he's an outlier! Well, no. You can't say the man who has for months led the polls to be the candidate for president of one of the two major political parties in the United States is not in the mainstream. Trust me, the bigots and the fascists are *delighted* by the amount of cover that someone like Trump gives them to say that their views are, in fact, at the heart of the American experience. There are others equally delighted that their inchoate bigotry, which before they knew enough to keep to themselves, now has a focus and cover for expression. You don't get to walk away from the responsibility for doing that.

5. Which is the thing that genuinely confuses me about this whole thing. Bluntly speaking, Trump is never going to be president*; mainstreaming fascism or not, at the end of the day the numbers won't break his way. He'll be swamped in the electoral vote certainly and probably in the popular vote as well. And then what? As noted, you don't just walk away from being a bigoted fascist; that shit follows you *around*. As a business move it's puzzling; it tarnishes the brand value of the Trump name—and burnishing that value is why I think he was in it in the first place.

It's possible Trump doesn't see that there will be long-term damage (or doesn't believe it), or believes that he'll be able to work within the universe of people who don't mind he yanked his brand toward bigotry and fascism. *Hey, it didn't stop Hugo Boss or Volkswagen,* he might say, afterwards. And, you know, maybe that *will* work out for him just fine. Maybe it'll get him new casinos in the Carolinas and speaking gigs to "values" organizations. On the other hand, speaking anecdotally, before this election I saw the Trump brand as merely vulgar. Now I find it repulsive, and I strongly suspect for the rest of my days I'm going to go out of my way to avoid anything to do with it. The question is whether the people like me do more damage to the brand than the value added by the people who don't mind bigotry and fascism.

6. Lindsey Graham today has been calling out Donald Trump, calling him "a race-baiting, xenophobic religious bigot," which is correct, and I absolutely applaud him for saying so. He's also saying that Trump "doesn't represent my party," which is, unfortunately, not correct at all. Again, Trump has been leading the GOP polls almost without interruption for months. He's not an outlier. He's there for a reason. The reason is that the GOP has made space in their party for race-baiting xenophobic religious bigots, and has done so for years by conscious and intentional strategy. Trump did not bring his supporters into the GOP. They were already there. I strongly suspect Graham knows it. The GOP wasn't always the party of race-baiting xenophobic religious bigots—there's a reason the term was "Dixiecrat" and not "Republidixies"—but they took possession of them 50 years ago and have been banking on them ever since.

The GOP's problem is that Trump is the distillation of every political strategy they've honed over the last several decades, and particularly ramped up over the last two. Lionizing the "political outsider"? Check! Fawning over billionaires? Check! Ratcheting up political rhetoric so that everyone who opposes you is the enemy and sick and awful? Check! Scaring the crap out of not-young white conservative Christians with the image of lawless racial and religious minorities? Check! Valorizing the tribalism of white conservative Christianity over the rule of law and the Constitution of the United States? Check!

There's a reason why the National Republican Senatorial Committee's executive director wants GOP candidates to "be like Trump" even as Graham bleats that Trump doesn't represent the party. Lindsey Graham, are you shitting me? Trump doesn't just represent your party. He's the *goddamn Platonic ideal* of it. You can't spend decades preparing the way for someone like Donald Trump and then pretend to be shocked, shocked when he roars down the field, flawlessly executing your playbook.

7. Also, getting rid of Trump, which the GOP now fervently wants to do, doesn't solve the party's fundamental problem, which *isn't* Trump, but rather the fact that the race-baiting, xenophobic religious bigots he's currently energizing will still be there if and when he goes. Dear GOP: Do you think that when Trump goes, the remaining candidates are planning to turn their backs on that particular constituency? Hell, Ted Cruz is *positively drooling* at the prospect of snapping up Trump's leavings. And Cruz may not even have to wait that long; he's gaining in Iowa, primarily on the strength of the same crowd Trump is riling up.

I think that the GOP wants to get back to where it was before, when it could pretend with a wink and a nod that race-baiting, xenophobic religious bigots weren't in fact one of the two twin engines of the party, the other engine being rich autocrats, who don't care for silly things like regulations or workers' rights. Guys: It's a little late for that (we figured out the rich autocrat thing, too). There's only one way to fix your race-baiting, xenophobic religious bigot problem, and it's not (just) by getting rid of Trump. He's the symptom, not the disease.

Actually, he *is* a disease. But he's an opportunistic infection allowed by a previous illness. You have to have had the one to have the other. The GOP didn't vaccinate for the first. It actually smeared the infection vector all over its body.

8. In case it wasn't clear: No one—*no one*—should be supporting Trump at this point. No one should have been supporting him at *any* point, mind you. But now more than ever is the point when anyone who *isn't* comfortable with outright fascism and bigotry should make it clear, to themselves if no one else, that they are out. It doesn't matter that Trump won't win the presidency; it doesn't matter that he might not even win the GOP nomination. Right now, in the United States, the leading candidate for president of one of the two major political parties—the leader by a *substantial* margin—is openly talking about denying an entire class of people their fundamental Constitutional and human rights, and being cheered for it. It's not right, it's bigoted and hateful, and yes, it absolutely *is* dangerous.

Trump has a right to say bigoted and fascist things. Other bigots and fascists have a right to support him. The rest of us should also exercise our rights and call Trump and the others out for what they are. And right now, the fact is: If you're supporting Trump, you're supporting a bigot and a fascist. That may or may not make *you* a bigot or a fascist, but it doesn't say good things about you in any event.

If you love the principles that make the foundation of our laws—and of the United States in a general sense—then you should take your leave of Trump, and for that matter, of any candidate who would cheerfully ride into power the same constituency Trump is mining. What you stand for and who you stand with matters. It's time to stand away from Trump. As far away as you can get.

* *I was wrong about that, alas—JS*

18

Here is a true thing: In the grand scheme of things, I've only had three things I wanted to do with my life. The first was to be a writer. The second was to be a good husband. The third was to make sure that any kid I had made it through their childhood without want or fear, and knowing that they were loved. When I was younger, I figured if I could manage those three things, then at the end of my days I could leave this planet with a content heart.

The first of these you know about, presumably, and in general I think I nailed that one. The second of these is a work in progress, but, twenty-one and a half years in, I seem to be doing all right (I just checked with Krissy on this one. She said yes, and was patiently bemused that I asked).

The third thing happened today. Athena, my daughter, is eighteen years old. Legally an adult! And while that number is arbitrary and arguable, as every human is different—there are people I know who I would have considered fully capable adults at fifteen, and people who at fifty I think are not actually grown up—nevertheless it's a significant milestone. My kid is an adult now. I am literally not the boss of her anymore. And I and Krissy have gotten her there, without want or fear, and with her knowing, with certainty, that she was and is loved.

In one sense it's obvious why this is important to me. What parent does not want these things for their child? These things are also, to be blunt, not particularly laudable; if you have the means and circumstances (I'll get back to this in just a bit), you should be doing these things as a matter of course, and even in difficult circumstances you should be striving for them. There are no medals for being a decent parent. It's a baseline.

But the thing is, I didn't have a childhood free of want or fear, and while I never doubted I was loved, at certain times and in certain circumstances, everything else was up in the air. Here at the age of 47, I don't feel the need to put my own parents up against a wall and read them a litany of their failures raising a child, in part because I know more about their lives than I did when I was younger, and in part because after a certain point I think you just have to let it go and realize that somewhere along the way who you are becomes your own responsibility (and fault), not your parents'. Parents are human, they are who they are, and you, in whatever fashion works for you, celebrate, accept, forgive or try to understand them. Or you don't. It's up to you.

So my childhood was not always an easy one, and also to the point, my parental role models were uncertain at best. What sort of parent would I be? What would I be able to do for my child? Who would I be to and for my child? How would I parent along with my wife? I'm not going to lie, and again, I'll be blunt: I was terrified I would just plain fuck it up, in all sorts of ways.

But here we are, on Athena's eighteenth birthday. She's a terrific person, and one of my favorite people, not just because she's my kid, but because of who she is, and who she's always been. All her life, there are very few people I have wanted to hang around with more, to spend time with, to have conversations with, both inane and sublime. She's not perfect, which is fine because I'm not perfect and neither are you, but as I have said so many times and am saying again now, there's no doubt she's perfect for *me*. She is, simply, the child I always dreamed I would have, of whom I live in wonder of her existence, amazed that Krissy and I made such a person, helped her grow and placed her on the path she's making for herself. I love her with such an immensity that I—whose job is to put things into words—stand mute before it. Try as I may, I can't make you feel all the love and pride and honor I have just to know her, to be part of her life, and to see her be who she is, and become who she will be.

I think you probably get it anyway.

We are fortunate, and Athena is fortunate. She always had two parents, and the same two parents, parents who both worked hard and got lucky in many ways, who during the course of her childhood always managed an upward trajectory, and who were always in love with each other and unafraid to show it to each other, and to her. Not every kid gets all of those things. It's not to suggest parents are inherently to blame if they don't. Sometimes not only do divorces happen, but they're necessary. Sometimes a parent can work hard their whole life and never catch a break. Sometimes a bus goes up on a curb, or cancer happens, or a job goes away forever, or there's a war, or any one of a million things that makes it hard for parents to give their kids the childhood they wanted to give, and that every child should have. I know it, better than most.

I look back on the last eighteen years and am thankful that during them during the part of my life where a small growing person was reliant on me and my wife—all the breaks went our way. And while I'm aware that my hard work and the hard work of my wife matters for this, and that luck truly does favor the prepared and those willing to make an effort, I'm also well aware of how much was out of our hands as well. Thank you, universe.

I'm also immensely thankful for Krissy, every step of the way through Athena's childhood. Krissy and I made a good parenting team because we make a good team, period: We have complementary skill sets and parenting styles, and a willingness to work together. This was something we talked about even before Athena was born—everything from what we'd do when Athena, as all children innocently do, tried to set us against each other to get what she wanted, to what we'd do when she and I fundamentally disagreed on something as parents (the answer, in case you're curious: I ceded final decision authority to Krissy, on the grounds that she is both the more sensible and cautious of the two of us. Nothing ever got to that point, as it happens; turns out we agree on most things, and the things we don't have been relatively trivial. Still, good to have a plan).

But more than that, the fact is my wife is just an amazing mother and human. From the earliest days I saw how she was as a parent, and

I was inspired to keep pace, for her and for Athena. Did I manage it? Not always, because I'm *me*, and between the ideal version of John Scalzi, Parent and the actual parent who is John Scalzi, there is a gap. I screwed up, did stupid things and occasionally threw up my hands and retreated into my office to play video games. But with Krissy, and because of Krissy, I kept at it.

Ultimately, neither I nor Krissy will be the best arbiter of how we were as parents. Athena is and will be. But I can say that I look at my daughter and I think: We did it. We got this human through childhood and to the door of her adult life, whole and healthy and filled with the possibilities that the world can have for her.

Athena will never not be my daughter. She will never not be my child. I and Krissy will be here for her and with her, for as long as we can and for as far as the world will allow. That's never in doubt. But here on her eighteenth birthday, it's her life now. And one part of my life—one of the best parts—is over. The part where I got to have her as my little girl.

It was a gift, and a privilege, and I wouldn't have missed it for anything in this world. It was a thing I wanted to do with my life. It has made me complete.

Happy birthday, Athena. I love you.

ENJOYING PROBLEMATIC THINGS

Mar

19

2014

H. Savinean asks:

I would like to hear your thoughts on liking problematic things, e.g. media with historically accurate but objectionable portrayals of gender/race/etc., media with no historical excuse for the above, media that simply ignore women and people of color, comedians/actors/writers who plant their feet firmly in their mouths way too often… It's something I spend a fair amount of time on.

Oh, boy! A can of worms! Let me just come over and open it!

Let me skip lightly over what "problematic" means in a larger sense and suggest that for the purposes of this piece, the word means "work/people I have issues with for some substantial and to me relevant social/moral/ethical reason." With that understood:

I think it's fine to like or recognize the value of problematic people/things. I think it helps to additionally recognize two things: One, that the person/thing *is* problematic, regardless of the fact that you like it; two, that the fact you like it doesn't mitigate the fact that it *is* problematic. You can hold the two thoughts in your head simultaneously.

So, an example from my own personal problematic files: *Chinatown.* Fantastic movie, *and* the guy who directed it drugged and raped an underage girl. The film is a classic and Roman Polanski should have gone to prison. That the film is one of the best films of the 1970s doesn't change the fact that Polanski is also a rapist. Should you feel uncomfortable about Polanski and his actions? Yes you should. Can you acknowledge *Chinatown* is still a substantial piece of work? Yes you can.

Another example: *Triumph of the Will*, by Leni Riefenstahl. For reasons relating to cinematic technique, one of the major films in cinematic history—echoes of the film pop up everywhere from *Star Wars* to *The Lion King*. For subject matter, an unapologetic celebration of the 1934 Nazi Party Congress in Nuremberg and of Adolf Hitler, it is literally horrifying. Riefenstahl herself: A brilliant filmmaker and forever (and rightly) tainted by her association with a genocidal regime; one of the first great women directors, who unquestionably lent her considerable talents to the furtherance of evil. Can we appreciate the craft she brought to the film? Absolutely. Should we argue that this craft mitigates the purpose for which it was used? Absolutely not. Should Riefenstahl's embrace of the Nazi party be excused because of her cinematic talent? Not in a thousand years.

And so on. I used two examples from film, but examples can be found in every field of creative endeavor, including—obviously—writing. Likewise, Polanski and Riefenstahl are easy examples because of the unambiguous nature of their actions, but for every clear-cut case like theirs, there are a thousand less clear cut—or at least, less clear cut to *you*. Someone else might disagree, occasionally emphatically.

If you accept that you can both appreciate a problematic work/creator and recognize its problematic issues, there are a host of other issues for you to consider. Some of them:

- Should you support the work with money? Example: Would you pay to own a copy of *Chinatown*, or merely watch it when it came on television?
- Do you differentiate works from different eras in the creator's life? For example, if you have a favorite book and over time the creator turned progressively homophobic, can you cherish the work written before that transformation, or do you judge it by the author's "final form," as it were?
- How much weight should you give to historical context?
- How much do you care about a creator's personal life?
- Does it matter whether the creator is living or dead?

(The latter, incidentally, is one I think about a lot. I anecdotally noted a resurgence of Michael Jackson's music in the common culture after his death, and I hypothesize that his passing removed a lot of the "squick" factor related to his possibly entirely inappropriate relationships with kids. It's easier to get into a "Thriller" zombie line if you're not worrying about what Jackson might be doing at one of those Neverland slumber parties, etc.)

Cards on the table: I like a lot of work I think is problematic, and I like more stuff that other people would find more problematic than I do, because they have different standards and life experiences. There's other stuff I don't like because I find it too problematic, but I also acknowledge there's room for hypocrisy in my choices there, too. For example, I find some of Chris Brown's work catchy but I'm not going to give him my money because he beat a woman and by all the evidence I can see he doesn't especially regret having done so. On the other hand, in the early 70s Jimmy Page knowingly had a sexual relationship with a 14-year-old girl—that's statutory rape despite the girl's then-consent—and I own a whole lotta Zeppelin (on the other hand, I haven't bought any since I found that bit out. Even so).

Does this dichotomy reflect my judgment regarding their respective actions, some latent baked-in racism, my preference for rock over R&B, or the fact one was just a few years ago and the other over before I even knew about it? You got me. Mix and match. And while you're doing that, I'm gonna have to think about it some more myself.

Which I think is a thing worth doing as well: When you like a problematic thing, rather than reflexively defending it with the "I like it and therefore it can't be bad and *why are you making me feel bad about it*," response, go ahead and ask yourself why you like it even though you acknowledge it's got problems. You might find after questioning it, you like it less—or more, because you've thought it through.

As a final thought here, I think it's probably likely that some readers of mine find *my* work problematic for various reasons—either for what's in the text of the work, who I am as a person (as far as they know from my public presence and/or their private interaction with me) or some combination of both. It's part of the territory of being a creative person. Are they *wrong* for doing so? No; you have to accept that everyone comes to your work with their own perspective and will have their own criticisms of it (and you), some of which you will disagree with, or find to be a feature rather than a bug, as it were.

If the reader can simultaneously hold in their mind that they enjoy the work *and* find it problematic, I appreciate it. If they decide they can't and drop me from their cultural diet, then that's fine, too. We all have to make choices. I'd hope that choice comes after some thought on the matter. Ultimately that's all you can ask for, as a creator of possibly problematic things.

FACEBOOK
AND
YOUR FRIENDS

Over on Facebook I see a fair number of people linking to the story that although the average Facebook user has 155 "friends" on Facebook, there are also on average only four of those "friends" that a Facebook user would call in a genuine crisis, suggesting that just because you are "friends" with someone on Facebook, it doesn't mean you are actual friends with them in the real world.

My thoughts on this:

One, hey, having four people you can reach out to in an actual crisis is a *pretty good* number;

Two, I'm not sure why this is at all surprising to anyone at all. Just because Facebook calls its connection mechanism "friending" doesn't mean that everyone you connect with there are actual *friends*; they're merely people who, for one reason or another, you've decided to connect with on a social media network. It's not in the least relevatory to me that the number of "friends" one has on social media doesn't make much difference to the number of people you consider actual friends, or the number of people who would help you bury the proverbial body.

Here's a thing about social media, in my experience of it. The people (or entities) one follows on it tends to be part of three groups which overlap but are not exactly the same: The people one cares about, the people one knows of, and the people who one is entertained by. Only one group of these is properly friends; the other groups may or may not be acquaintances, and their presence in one's feed comes down to the fact that most of us like to have a varied mix of things to look at when we sign on and scroll down. Someone does not need to be your friend to entertain you, either by telling you tidbits of their own life or by putting up links to material they've found online that they find interesting.

Can people you otherwise do not know become your friend through online interaction? Sure, although (also in my experience) eventually it helps to make an offline connection as well, to confirm that the comfort level you have with them isn't just an artifact of online presentation and the fact that it's mediated in a way that face-to-face encounters aren't. I have a number of friends I've met online. I'm not going to rely on any of them to bury a body with me until we have that *click* in the offline world.

But then again, how many people *do* you need to be willing to help you in a crisis? Four really does seem sufficient in most cases. Likewise, if you have two or three dozen people you would call your true friends, well. That seems a *lucky* amount to me. That's a person a day for a month you'd be delighted to hang out and spend time with and involve in your various shenanigans. That's a full life right there, folks.

My personal Facebook feed has (currently) 641 people in it, most of them people who I've known personally (meaning, actual physical face-to-face time) at some point in my life, starting from elementary school and moving through my life now as a writer and author. Are they *all* my friends? Well, some were friends back in the day, and might be friends again if I got to spend face time with them in the physical world. Some are people I've more recently met who I would like to think could become friends with me if circumstances allowed.

Not every one of my Facebook Friends is a current friend, but the way I curate that list, the *potential* for friendship is there, at least. One of the reasons to connect on Facebook is to keep that potential humming along, through the exhibition of pictures and news about our lives. This qualifies as mutual entertainment as well; I like knowing about them and I hope they like knowing about me.

But I don't expect the vast majority of my Facebook cohort to feel obliged to help me in a crisis. It seems a little much for me to pick up the phone and expect the guy I knew best when we were in elementary school to drop everything and tend to me. And maybe he would! But it seems a lot to ask. I save that for the few people that I already know are there for me in that capacity (and for whom I'm willing to serve in that capacity as well). It's more than four, I'm happy to say, but not so much more than four that it invalidates the general concept.

The article I referred to above says "The results suggest that people with hundreds of Facebook friends are kidding themselves if they think they can maintain a network so large." Well, no. They're not kidding themselves if, one, and again, they realize that just because Facebook calls their connection "friending" it does not oblige them to actually be friends, and two, if they recognize that some people they've "friended" are there to be entertainment (and for whom they are likewise entertainment).

And there's not a thing wrong with that! Thank you, Facebook friends, for entertaining me with your lives and links. I hope I do likewise. And don't worry that I'll send a message asking for money, or a kidney, or for you to show up somewhere in the middle of a rainstorm with a shovel and several gallons of lye. Most of you will never get that call. I think you're happy about that, or should be, anyway.

FREE SPEECH
OR NOT

May

11

2015

van H asks:

There seems to be increasing polarization between those who view freedom of speech as an absolute, unfettered necessity for free society, and those who argue that since speech can cause harm, and the job of government is to protect its citizens from harm, the government should be allowed to limit speech in some (perhaps restricted) way.

Philosophically, where do you fall on this issue? Do you think speech is fundamentally different from other potentially harm-causing actions? Should the government ever be able to limit speech in pursuit of the greater good?

Tangentially: large free services like Twitter and Facebook are severely blurring the line between privately-owned spaces (where they have complete control over what speech is permitted) and public forums (where they do not). Twitter is legally a private space, but most of the time it *feels* a lot more like a public forum. Do you think the law needs to "catch up" in how it handles these quasi-public forums?

Let's begin by noting that "free speech" here is by no means an absolute on the level of individual governments. People, and on the Internet particularly, often seem to take their concept and definition of "free speech" from United States constitutional norms, but, strangely enough, no country in the world is actually bound to the United States constitution but the United States. This is a state of affairs that often appears to confuse people.

In point of fact, however, the First Amendment of the Constitution of the United States and the assorted Supreme Court rulings associated with it apply only to the United States. Everyone else works under whatever rules regarding free speech their countries have. By and large, particularly in Western countries, this means quite a lot of leeway in what one is legally able to express, but there are limits (generally) which are more strenuous than those in the United States, and obviously there are other countries where these limits are even more strenuous than that.

Let's also put onto the table that even in the United States, which is generally acknowledged to have the fewest legal impediments to unfettered free speech, there are still limits, which the government has acknowledged. The old chestnut that free speech does not include the right to (falsely) yell "fire!" in a crowded theater is still applicable (even if the reasoning in the Supreme Court case in which the comment appeared has been largely overturned by more recent jurisprudence). These limits are few, but they are there, and over the course of US history, they have been continually reinterpreted by the courts. I imagine this goes on in other countries as well. So anyone who argues (other than philosophically) for a state in which "free speech" was indeed ever unfettered by government expectation is either referring to a point before actual human governments larger than a family unit, or doesn't much know what they're talking about.

Let's also do acknowledge that as a practical matter, "free speech" laws and obligations apply to governments and public institutions, to private institutions rather substantially less (although the government, in the US at least, may try to oblige private institutions to these laws in some manner and through various mechanisms) and to individuals and their private spaces almost not at all. This is also deeply, deeply confusing to many people, apparently.

Finally, let's make the point that your right to "free speech" does not mean I (or anyone else) is obliged to listen. I can, and often will, walk away if I think you're spouting nonsense. This is another fact which seems to deeply confuse certain people; the idea that being dismissed or ignored equates to censorship appears to be hardwired in their heads.

But it's wrong, and they're wrong for believing it, which makes them wrong twice.

With all that as the landscape in which we will walk during this discussion:

Personally speaking, I tend to be, both philosophically and as a political actor, a believer in the value of a robust definition of "free speech" as it applies to governments and public institutions, not just in the United States but worldwide. This belief in a robust definition of free speech means that I acknowledge that hateful, hurtful, triggering and generally awful speech must be given a place by the government in the public sphere. Racists, sexists, homophobes and other assorted bigots cannot have their soapboxes in the square removed—not just for the defensive measure of "and then the government will come for *me*" but because, simply, I believe in the end you acknowledge a human right to express yourself, even if that other human is *wrong*, or you don't. The limits I would place on speech are pretty high and of the "imminent harm" level—exhorting a mob to violence against someone and giving them directions to their house is an example I would give as speech that crosses that line. Short of that: It's got to be allowed by the government.

But I also place a pretty hard line between the government and everything else. The government has to tolerate your bullshit and give space for it; *I* don't. Neither, for that matter, does Twitter, or Facebook or any online social media network or construct not run by the government. I *don't* accept the argument that services like Twitter or Facebook blur the line between private entity and public service, regardless of whether they are "free" (i.e., no cost to use); that's a little like saying my local Kroger's or Safeway is a public gathering place because anyone can walk through the sliding doors (shopping malls? The same, unless you are in California or New Jersey).

If you want to argue that Twitter/Facebook/etc are in fact "quasi-public" spaces, my first response would be "show me the law." I doubt there is one there that makes it so. My second response would be "have you asked Twitter/Facebook/etc what *they* think?" Because I'm reasonably certain that their corporate lawyers would mount a pretty robust argument that they are, in fact, private entities rather than a public good or utility. Their lives become immensely more complicated if they are judged the latter.

Not to mention everyone else's lives: If the Supreme Court of the United States ruled, for example, that Twitter/Facebook/etc are public services, with regard to the First Amendment, I don't suspect the ruling would be confined to those specific services; it would probably apply to online sites generally—including my blog, as it is housed on WordPress—and what a mess *that* would be. My own response to such a ruling would likely be to close comments forever, since if I am not allowed to moderate that space I'm responsible for, then I'm just not going to bother having comments. I have standards.

So, no: Twitter/Facebook/etc are not "quasi-public"; they are in fact private entities, and they have a right to dictate to the people on them— as I have a right to dictate to people who comment here—the rules of the virtual road. The First Amendment (and, I suspect, whatever free speech protections that exist in other countries) simply do not exist on these services. Facebook is not obliged to house your bigotry, nor Twitter your harassment of people you don't like, nor I your bad arguments that offend me in their stupidity. Whether any of us do allow them is up to our own particular levels of tolerance for such things. I myself make it pretty clear what I'm willing to put up with. I don't think the law needs to "catch up" to this in any way; I'm not a proponent of the government nationalizing Twitter, or Facebook, or, well, my blog.

As for whether the government should protect people from the harm of free speech, well, per above, I don't believe that speech needs to be curtailed by the government, but let's also recognize that speech doesn't occur in a vacuum. Context matters, and government should recognize that speech—even and perhaps especially protected speech—has consequences, and that an appropriate role of government may be to protect speech *and* to handle the effects *of* it. What form and shape might that "handling" take? Well, that's indeed an *interesting* question, and one that is neither simple nor likely to be resolved in the scope of this entry. But it is a question worth asking and trying to answer. If a government wants to promote free speech—as it should—it should also be ready for what comes *from* free speech.

On a personal note, it does seem to me that a lot of the kvetching about "free speech" and censorship comes down to people wanting the right to be just plain assholes in every possible situation. Well, fine: You can be an asshole in every possible situation, if that's a thing you want, and bless your heart. But I do believe that a great deal of free speech is not about what you have the right to say, but what you choose to do. I made a joke recently that (without specific intent on my part) referenced child sexual abuse, and some folks called me on it. I had the right to say "it stays because I think it's funny," but what I did was to say "whoops, you're right, let me fix that," and to change it to something else funny that didn't have the same set of problems. I have the right to display visual images of Mohammad; I haven't because I know that many Muslims dislike that, and I can work with that as part of my world view. I have the right to call trans folks by the gender they are transitioning from, but I would prefer to acknowledge them for who they are rather than who they were. And so on.

The point is that it's not really difficult to pay attention to the concerns and interests of others and still be able to say what you need to say; I have not found it difficult to do so, in any event (unless you are a complete bigot, I suppose, but, well. I guess you just have to live with that). My point is that I haven't found my own ability to speak freely— and pointedly—on any subject at all constrained in any real sense by being aware of other people's concerns. It *is* slightly more work. But, you know what, one, I'm a writer, this is kind of in my wheelhouse, and two, if a little more work means more people are receptive to what I say because I don't *unnecessarily* antagonize them, it's worth the investment (I *do* occasionally antagonize people on purpose).

And you may say: But what about the people who *demand* trigger warnings and that the world revolve around *their* sensitivities? Well, personally, trigger warnings don't really bother me, in part because, look, if you've had trauma and reading what I wrote (or what I'm pointing you to) will cause that trauma to revisit you, I think it's reasonable for you to know that ahead of time. I don't think trigger warnings are a demand that the world revolve around you; they might be a simple recognition that you exist in the world, which is a different thing. Likewise,

I don't think everything has to be tailored to the people who have triggers or other concerns, but letting them know they might want to route around things is fine. This is, I don't know, courtesy? Courtesy seems okay to give.

I'll close by noting that obviously this piece speaks only in broad strokes—as noted, speech is not a free-floating concept; it's heavily embedded in the real world and all its complexities. Anyone who tries to separate the two of them is showing they don't really understand the issue. With that said, I think it's possible to be a free speech maximalist and someone who understands that with the right to free speech comes a responsibility to consider one's speech. Rights are what one *can* do; but it's what one *should* do that is equally important.

THE FOUR LEVELS OF DISCRIMINATION (AND YOU) (AND ME, TOO)

Apr

17

2014

I've been talking about sexism recently—my own and others—and I have to say I've found it increasingly exasperating to see the massively defensive response of "not all men are sexist" that inevitably follows. One, because it's wrong (more on that in a bit), and two, because the more I see it, the more it's obvious that it's a derail, as in, "Holy shit any discussion of sexism makes *me* uncomfortable so I want to make it clear *I* am not sexist so I'll just demand recognition that not all men are sexist so I can be lumped in with those men who are not sexist and *I can be okay with myself.*"

(I also note a fair correlation between the men who demand acknowledgment that men are not all sexist and the men who show some general hostility either to women or to the idea that they are being actively sexist through their own words or actions. But then, I don't really find this correlation all *that* surprising.)

The silver lining to this exasperation is that it's been making me think about sexism, and the more general concept of discrimination, more carefully. At the crux of the "Not all..." formulation, it appears, is the (honest or otherwise) assertion that in order to participate in discrimination, one has to actively and with malice aforethought choose to discriminate—in order to be sexist, one has to be *a* sexist, in other words (or to be racist, one has to be *a* racist; in order to be homophobic, one has to be *a* homophobe, etc).

And, well. No. In fact, you don't actively have to go out of your way *to* discriminate in order to participate *in* discrimination—that's kind of the point. Some of that is already built into the system that everyone is part of. You get it, positively and/or negatively, no matter what; everyone does. You may then also *decide* to support discrimination in one way or another, and that's the thing that changes you from being (for example) sexist to being *a* sexist. But to deny that baseline discrimination we all deal with because you're not by your own lights actively trying to promote that discrimination is silly. It's there, it's real and it's measurable, and you take part in it, one way or another.

But where does the line get drawn between being [x]ist and being *an* [x]ist, as it were? Let me posit what I think are four (very) general states of discrimination, as a way to suss out my own thoughts on the matter.

(And here is where I add the following disclaimers: **One,** these are my own thoughts, not rigorous research. **Two,** people who routinely and rigorously study discrimination may find this delightfully naive. **Three,** I acknowledge that the following framework is both very general, simplified and "chunky," as in, reality is a great deal more subtle than four easy-to-conceptualize levels. **Four,** this is a work in progress. Got it? Okay, then:)

So, here are four basic levels of discrimination as I see them, each building on from the other, each with generally increasing negative effect on those discriminated against:

Level One: Ambient—This is the discrimination that is given to you, by society in general, by the particular groups you participate with in our general society, and by immediate influences (i.e., family, friends, teachers and authority figures). Your own ambient mix of discriminatory things will vary due to all of the above, as you drill down from the general to the specifics of your own life. But that doesn't mean you *avoid* discrimination (or its effects); it merely dials in what *particular* discriminatory things you are more strongly influenced by. Everyone is influenced by the ambient discrimination, which is why, in fact, *everyone* is sexist, racist, classist, etc—we all got given this stuff early, often and before we could think about it critically. This is the baggage we deal with.

Level Two: Advantageous—This is the level where you realize that sometimes discrimination works for you, and you take advantage of it…or at least, are willing uncritically to accept the benefits of it. You may or may not wish to acknowledge that you have these certain advantages, and when you do acknowledge it, you may or may not try to assert that those advantages don't apply to you specifically, i.e., that you didn't get an automatic benefit due to discrimination and instead what benefit you've accrued is due to something *intentional* about you ("No one ever gave me anything! I worked for it all!"). But your recognition and acceptance of this advantageous discrimination is neither here nor there about **a)** whether it works for you, **b)** whether by participating in it, you're helping to reinforce that discrimination.

Level Three: Argumentative—This is the level where you take on board the idea that discrimination is desirable in some way (usually in a way that benefits you directly, or benefits a group you belong to, so you accrue general and indirect benefits), and as a result you argue for and/or defend discrimination. This can take on a number of forms, from the relatively benign (the "not all…" argument) to the not at *all* benign (arguing that being a slave in the US was not so bad, or that women aren't mentally composed to do math or physics or computer programming, or that Muslims are naturally inclined toward violence, as examples), and the use of rhetorical process to drive a discussion of discrimination either away from recognition of discrimination, or toward a different topic in order to control and contain the discussion.

Level Four: Antagonistic—The level where you choose to actively set yourself against others due to their differences from you, by (as examples and not limited to) acting to obtain or calling for limits to their freedoms (or to maintain current, actively discriminatory practices), actively minimizing their participation in society, either in general or in a specific subset, threatening them by word or by action and/or encouraging others to do the same.

So: I am sexist in that I have a raft of general assumptions and expectations about women and men that I got just from living in the world that I do; some things seem "girly" and "womanly" to me while some other things seem "boyish" and "manly." But I am willing to argue that I am probably not *a* sexist, because I don't, for example, believe that men have inherent rights and privileges that women should not, nor do I believe women's roles are lesser or subservient to men's, nor do I, say, threaten them with rape or violence when they say or do something I dislike.

But of course that's an easy formulation, isn't it. We don't really do or say anything *useful* if we only acknowledge the most extreme examples of discrimination as evidence that someone is a bigot in one way or another. This is part and parcel of the "not all..." assertion—one, that the ambient discrimination in the world *doesn't count* when considering someone's discriminatory assumptions and behavior, and two, that somewhere along the way, there's a big, bright line at which one can say "hey, *now* you're being a sexist/racist/homophobe/whatever."

And, you know, I don't think it works that way. Ambient discrimination makes us discriminatory. We all do it; we're all that way because that's what we get all around us. What makes us not *a* sexist, or *a* racist, or *a* homophobe, or whatever, is what we choose to do when we recognize our discriminatory behaviors or attitudes (or have them pointed out by others). If you work to minimize them going forward, in yourself and in your larger world, then you're probably not *a* sexist/racist/homophobe/whatever. If you sort of shrug, and go, *yeah, well, that's life,* then, yes. You're totally *a* sexist/racist/homophobe/whatever. You don't have to wait to claim that title, or have it justifiably applied to you.

(And yes, before the angry straight white male brigade descends, this applies to everyone, not just straight white men. If you're not aware of it already, please bone up on the concept of intersectionality. But let's also not *pretend* that straight white dudes aren't first among equals when it comes to these issues, please. You all know my thoughts on my own social group by now.)

So. Am I, John Scalzi, sexist, and racist, and other forms of discriminatory? Yup. That stuff got built in, mostly when I was young and/or wasn't paying attention. It happened to you, too. Sorry. But I also try to work against being *a* sexist, and *a* racist and other such things, by seeing those things in myself and working to correct them, and to correct them outside of myself as well. Am I work in progress? Yes. I'm not perfect at it, either. I show my ass from time to time. But I'm happy to keep on progressing. It's a lifetime effort.

What I hope is that because of that effort, the ambient discrimination that people will get born into and participate in will suck less in the future than it does now. That's what I can do, and what you can do, too.

FRIGHTENED, IGNORANT AND COWARDLY IS NO WAY TO GO THROUGH LIFE, SON

(Written in the aftermath of quite a few people were losing their shit over Syrian refugees.)

So, this week.

The last few days are a reminder that a large number of Americans are in fact shrieking, bigoted cowards, and that's a sad thing, indeed.

Seriously, I don't think the bedwetting about Muslims has been this bad in a very long time, which is saying something, and the panic on Syrian refugees is particularly ridiculous. Here's a nice, juicy quote from a just-released essay on the subject:

Of the 859,629 refugees admitted from 2001 onwards, only three have been convicted of planning terrorist attacks on targets outside of the United States and none was successfully carried out. That is one terrorism-planning conviction for a refugee for every 286,543 of them who have been admitted. To put that in perspective, about 1 in every 22,541 Americans committed murder in 2014. The terrorist threat from Syrian refugees in the United States is hyperbolically over-exaggerated and we have very little to fear from them because the refugee vetting system is so thorough...

The security threat posed by refugees in the United States is insignificant. Halting America's processing of refugees due to a terrorist attack in another country that may have had one asylum-seeker as a co-plotter would be an extremely expensive overreaction to very minor threat.

What horrifyingly liberal commie soviet came up with this load of codswallop? The Cato Institute, the libertarian think tank co-founded by Charles Koch, i.e., the fellow who with his brother is currently trying to buy the entire right side of the political spectrum for his own personal ends. When *the Cato Institute* is telling you to maybe take down the pearl-clutching over the Syrian refugees a notch or two, it's an indication that you've lost all perspective.

It's been particularly embarrassing how the mostly-but-not-exclusively (and thankfully not all-encompassing) GOP/conservative politician freakout about the Syrian refugees points out that, why, hello, bigotry really *is* a thing, still. From small-town mayors declaring that FDR had it right when he put all those US citizens of Japanese descent into camps to presidential candidates alluding that it might *not* actually be a bad idea to make special IDs exclusively for Muslims here in the US, to the House of Representatives passing a bill to piss on the Syrian refugees, it's been a banner week for bigotry here in the US, enough so that the United States Holocaust Memorial Museum took the extraordinary step of issuing a statement of concern with reference to the Syrian refugees. And as many have noted, there is irony in the freakout about Syrian refugees coming into a season which celebrates a notable middle eastern family who famously were refugees at one point in their history, according to some tales.

But as a certain asshole politician named Brian Babin said this week, "Mary and Jesus didn't have suicide bomb vests strapped on them, and these folks do." Well, no, they don't. Leaving aside that the perpetrators on the attacks in Paris all appeared to live in Europe to begin with, the actual process for placing refugees in new countries is so long and arduous and so selective, with just 1% of applicants being placed, that (as the Cato Institute astutely notes) there's a vanishingly small chance that someone with ill intent will make it through the process at all—and an even *smaller* chance that they would be assigned to the US when all the vetting is done. To worry about terrorists in the refugee pool is, flatly, stupid—no terrorist organization is going to pour resources into an avenue with such a small chance of success, especially when it's easier to apply for a friggin' visa and get on a plane (they can buy their guns when they get here, don't you know). The reasons why so many people are voiding their bowels about it are simple: Ignorance, racism, xenophobia and bigotry.

"But people are scared!" Okay, and? Being *scared* may be the excuse for abandoning all sense and reason in the moment one is actively under attack; it's not even close to a reasonable excuse for, thousands of miles away from an attack and with no immediate threat on the horizon, vilifying innocent co-religionists of the attackers and plotting to slam the door on refugees running from the very people who claimed responsibility for the Paris attacks. Taking the Paris attacks out on Syrian refugees is security theater—it doesn't make us safer, it'll just make the most ignorant among us feel safer. It's the TSA of solutions to the Daesh/ISIS problem.

This has been a bad week for the United States, folks. France was directly attacked by terrorists and its response was to promise to house 30,000 Syrian refugees; we weren't and one branch of our government fell over itself to put the brakes on accepting a third of that number. France is defying the very organization that attacked it while we, on the other hand, are doing exactly what that organization hoped we would do. We're being the cowardly bigots they hoped we would be, and as loudly as possible.

So congratulations, America. We've successfully wrested the title of "cheese-eating surrender monkeys" from France. Enjoy it.

Genius
and Master

Aug

23

2017

Just posted a thought on a friend's Facebook post that I think I'd like to expand on here. The friend was talking (basically) about how he was annoyed that the fans of a certain person insisted that person was a genius when my friend saw that person's output as largely just okay. I wrote:

Calling someone you're a fan of a "genius" is mostly just second-order complimenting of one's self (because you have the good taste to be a fan of a genius, you see). Most of the people I'm fans of are not geniuses, they're just really really good at what they do, and because they are, they sometimes make great and/or enduring art.

And I think that's true. "Genius," in the context of creativity, is bandied around a lot and is typically used as shorthand for "that person/ group I like who does stuff I really like and which for some reason I have incorporated into my self-identity." There's also often but not always a whiff of "and they do something I don't know how to do myself" in there. In short, "genius" means "people who are highly skilled and super-talented in their creative field, who produce high quality material that speaks to me ineffably."

I think being one of those people is nice work if you can get it, but I don't think it equates to being a "genius." I think to be a creative genius (very incompletely, here) is to bring something new(ish)* to a culture, and to have it affect enough people that it is incorporated *into* the culture, and (this is the really unfair part) to have enough people notice that you have done it to be remembered for it. If you're doing genius-level stuff and it's all stuffed in a drawer and it never gets out, you're going to miss out on being a creative genius, sorry.

So genius is both rare—it's difficult to bring something new to the creative table—and a lot of it is down to luck and the fortunes of history, i.e., whether someone finds your work and celebrates it. Emily Dickinson and Vincent Van Gogh count as two geniuses whose stock rose well after their death; in my own field Philip K. Dick was celebrated in the small circle of science fiction while he was alive but only ascended in the culture after death. Not everyone gets to be the Beatles, and see in their lifetimes how their creative genius changed the world.

Most creative people aren't in my opinion *geniuses*, since it seems to me that genius has a lot to do with being in the right place at the right time, and failing that, at least having the right people find out about you when you're dead. Which is to say, things that are completely out of one's control and with a large element of luck involved. So much of genius has nothing to do with native ability and/or acquired skill. And in being recognized as a genius, it helps to get in early, before all the ground has been broken (or alternately, there when a field is in crisis, and everything is up for grabs).

But—and this is an important conjunction—this doesn't mean that creative folks who aren't geniuses *aren't* making good art, or great art. They very often are, because the one element of genius they have some control over—craft—is something they work on, and they keep working on, hopefully through their careers. In point of fact I think there's an argument to make that much of the work of non-geniuses is as good as or even exceeds the quality of the work of "geniuses," who, while their reputation benefited from being the first to explore a field or technique, also (and necessarily) didn't have the same fluidity or experience with the subject as others who came later and worked with it longer and incorporated it at a much earlier stage into their creativity.

So again: Not very many creative people should be called a genius, which is to my mind a highly contingent title, and one's ascendance to the title might not even be settled in one's lifetime. But certainly quite a lot of creative people should be acknowledged as *masters* of their field, and of their craft. "Master" is about the things you can control—your skill and the work you put into it—and it's something that others can concretely argue for by pointing to the quality of one's work in itself.

Examples! you say. Okay, let's take, oh, I don't know, film director Ron Howard. Is Ron Howard a genius? I think history is going to come down on the "probably not" side of that one—there's very little in his canon of work that's groundbreaking or startlingly innovative or so influential that you can see its mark in other filmed works. Is Ron Howard a master? Yup—leaving aside the Oscars he picked up for *A Beautiful Mind,* one can easily pick out the very good and near-great work he's done (my trio: *Parenthood, Apollo 13, Frost/Nixon*) and point to his reputation for no-nonsense competence—there's a reason LucasFilm had him parachute into the Han Solo film. Howard may not be a genius, but when *Apollo 13* or *Parenthood* shows up on cable, I stop skipping and start watching. He's really good at what he does, and some of his work is legitimately classic. He deserves the honors and accolades that have come his way. He's a master.

As I note above, I think people who are fans of a creative person want to label that person a genius, not just because it's complimentary to the artist (no one dislikes being called a genius) but because it speaks well to their own taste. I'm not going to stop anyone from using the word, or tsk-tsk that hard when they do. But for myself I think it's worth it to say that not everyone's a genius, and it's not an insult in itself to say someone's not one. And also for myself, I'm more likely to call someone whose creative work I admire a "master." In many ways, I consider that to be the higher compliment. You can become a genius by circumstance. Becoming a master takes work.

Let me suggest "new" here can mean either something wholly new, and often springing from an advance in creative technology of some sort, or something that is an unexpected synthesis of existing forms.

GETTING LUCKY
WITH
COLLEGE COSTS

The bill for Athena's fall semester at Miami University arrived a couple of days ago, and we paid it, and I have some various thoughts about that I want to share.

When I went to college, 30 years ago now, I couldn't pay for it. I did what the majority of people did then and do now—I cobbled together various sorts of funding from multiple sources. A scholarship here, a Pell grant there, a work study job and loans—and still it wasn't quite enough when one of my funding sources fumbled the ball pretty badly and I had to ask my grandfather for help (which to be clear, he was happy to provide, with the only provision being that I would write him a letter a month, a request very much in my wheelhouse). I graduated with a fair amount of student debt, rather more than the average amount back in 1991, which was around $8,200. I think I was around 30 when we paid it off.

I don't regret my college debt—I'm of the opinion that my education was worth what I paid for it and then some—but at the time I didn't really like having the anxiety of wondering how it was all going to be paid for, and my education being contingent on outside financial forces, over which I had no control. I was lucky I was able to find ways to cover it all. I was also lucky that I got a good job right out of college (in 1991, during a recession), and was always financially solvent afterward. That college debt never became a drag or a worry, as it easily could have been, and which it did become for a number of my friends.

I don't think scrambling for money or paying down college debt added anything *beneficial* to my life, however. As much as certain people might make a fetish of having to struggle in one way or another for one's education, and that struggle having a value in itself, I'm not especially convinced that the current American manner of "struggle"—pricing college education at excessive rates and then requiring students and family to take on significant amounts of debt, effectively transferring decades of capital from the poor, working and middle classes to banks and their (generally wealthy) shareholders—is really such a great way to do that, especially since wages in general have stagnated over the last 40 years, the same period of time in which college tuition costs have skyrocketed, consistently above the rate of inflation. Worrying about college funding and paying off college debt isn't character-building in any real sense. It's opportunity cost, time wasted that might be productively spent doing something else educationally or financially beneficial.

So: I don't regret my college debt, but I don't think it was something that added *value*, either, to my education or my life. All things being equal, I suspect I would have been better off not having to worry whether I had enough funding for college any particular quarter, or being able to take the monthly post-collegiate debt payment and use it for something *else*, including investment. Not just *me*, of course; I don't think anyone, students or parents (or colleges, for that matter), benefits from the current patchwork method of college funding, or the decade-long (or longer) hangover of college debt service.

We always assumed Athena would go to college; very early on we began saving and investing with the specific goal of funding her education. Along the way we caught the break of my writing career taking off, which meant the account intended for her education plumped out substantially. By the time it was the moment for Athena to decide where to go to college, we were in the fortunate position of being able to pay for it—all of it—wherever it was she decided to go. So, to go back to the initial paragraph, when that first Miami University bill came up, we were able to cut that check and send it off. No muss, no fuss. We'll be able to do the same for the other college bills over the next four years.

Which is great for us! And not bad for Athena, who will end her college experience debt-free in a world where the average US student with college debt in 2016 was in the hole for $37,000, with that number only likely to go up from here. But let's also look at everything that had to happen in order for us to get to that point: We saved early, which was smart of us, but we also had the *wherewithal* to save, which meant we got lucky that Krissy and I both had work, that in her case her gig included health insurance for all of us and that in my case I was in constant demand as a freelance writer, which, I assure you, is not always the case. We got lucky that the books took off as they did; the odds on that were not great. We were lucky that no one of us got seriously or chronically ill, or that other family crises depleted savings. Athena is an only child; that's not necessarily lucky, but it definitely was a factor when it came to paying for college. We only have to do this once.

All of which is to say that Athena will be getting out of college debt-free partly because we planned early but *mostly* because of factors that we had only some control over, and over which she had almost none. She didn't choose her parents or her circumstances; she got what she got. And in this case, she got lucky.

That's fine for her. But it's not a very useful strategy for paying for college. "Get lucky picking your parents" should not be the determining factor for whether you leave college debt-free, leave with tens of thousands of dollars of debt, or can't afford to go to college at all. Every single one of those circumstances can have a substantial effect on how the rest of one's economic life will go—and how the economic life of one's children will go. There's a reason why in the United States, home of the "American Dream," it's actually pretty difficult to move up the social ladder. Yes, I did it, but I also don't pretend I didn't get lucky—a lot—or that my path is easily repeatable. Take it from someone who is living the American Dream: It stays only a dream for most of those dreaming of it.

I'm proud that we can pay for our daughter's college education. I'm also well aware how many things had to break our way to be at this point, which just as easily could have gone another way. It would be better to live in a world where luck, one way or another, is not a salient, determinative factor for whether one can afford college, or whether one can graduate from college without debt. In fact, that world does exist; just not here in the US. College tuition in most developed countries is substantially less than it is here, including being basically free in places like Germany and France. We could do that here, for state schools at least, if we decided we wanted to.

But we don't. I know we have our reasons. I just don't think those reasons are very good.

GHLAGHGHEE, 2003—2015

(A memorial for my cat.)

Ghlaghghee came to us in May of 2003 when my then next-door neighbor Jerry knocked on my door, said, "here's the kitten your wife said she wanted," thrust a small, furry thing into my hands, and then walked off. I looked at the small puff of fur, literally no larger than my hand, said "okay" to myself and then took it upstairs with me.

Then I called my wife, who was at work, and the conversation went like this:

Me: You didn't tell me you ordered a cat.

Krissy: I ordered a what?

Me: A cat.

Krissy: I didn't order a cat.

Me: Jerry just came over with a kitten that he said you wanted. He mentioned you specifically.

Krissy: Oh, lord. I was talking to him the other day and he said that his cat had had kittens and that he thought that one of them was an albino. I said, "Oh, I'd like to see that." I didn't say I *wanted* it!

Me: In that case, surprise, we have a new kitten.

Also, as an albino cat Ghlaghghee was a bust, because she had markings that made her look like a Himalayan; for all of her life when people saw photos of her they complimented me on what a lovely example of the breed she was. She wasn't. Her mother, who lived next door, was a mixed breed cat with tortoiseshell markings, and we strongly suspect her father was a Siamese mix feral cat who we would see wandering about the first couple of years we were here. Ghlaghghee, despite appearances, was a common moggie, genetically speaking.

But she was just about adorable, I like cats, and I sensed a real "no takebacks" vibe from Jerry. Deciding to keep her was not really a problem. We also decided that we would let Athena, age four, name the cat. More accurately, Krissy decided it, and I went along, with caveats. Specifically, that we would ask her to think of another name than something dreadfully boring, like "Fluffy," because, honestly, we were a creative people, we Scalzis, and we could do better.

And this is how *that* went down:

Me: Athena, we have a new kitten and we've decided to let you name it—

(produces kitten)

—but before you do, I want you to try to think of a creative name, not something like—

Athena: I WANT TO NAME IT FLUFFY

Me:—*crap.*

I was not really down with the name "Fluffy," but you try getting a four-year-old child to change her mind about a new kitten name and see how far you get. In this moment of domestic crisis, I turned, as I so often did, to the wisdom of George Bernard Shaw, who once commented that the English language is so nonsensical in its rules regarding pronunciation that one could spell "fish" as "ghoti" and it could still sound the same.

Well, I could live with "Fluffy" if it was spelled "Ghlaghghee," so that's what I did. And thus our cat was named, and also twelve years of people asking how "Ghlaghghee" was pronounced and/or trying to pronounce the word as if their epiglottis was spasming. Which amused *me*, at least.

Ghlaghghee quickly decided that I was her human, which was fine with me because I like cats and she was both a pretty cat and an exceedingly well-tempered one. She was one of those rare cats who enjoyed being rubbed on her belly, and never complained when she was picked up. I would frequently cradle her like a baby, and she was fine with that;

indeed, she often had an expression that I translated as "why yes, I should be carried around and spoiled. I am surprised this is even a question."

That said, her cuddliness was highly contingent on who you were; she wasn't much for strangers and even Athena she would sometimes treat as a person below her station. As for the other cats, well. She was the smallest of the three cats we currently have, but there was no doubt which cat ran the household. A prime example of this was the fact that Ghlaghghee had claimed my and Krissy's bed as her space; if Zeus or Lopsided Cat tried to share it with her, she would make her displeasure with their presumptuousness clear almost instantly. For a decade, the bed was a no-go zone. She got along very well with the other cats, as long as they remembered who was boss.

Ghlaghghee was always popular with Whatever readers, because she was a handsome cat who I would frequently photograph, but she became famous to the entire world in September of 2006, when I taped bacon to her, posted a picture of it here on the site, and for two days that post with a picture of bacon taped to a cat became the most popular thing on the English-language Internet.

Looking back now, it's difficult to believe that in all the time prior to that moment, no one had thought to tape bacon to a cat, and then put that picture on the Internet, but apparently no one had. The Internet loves bacon; the Internet loves cats. Combining the two was perfect synergy.

For a brief period of time, Ghlaghghee, aka BaconCat, was one of the most famous cats on the Internet and substantially more famous than I was. I had more than one conversation that went like so:

Person I Don't Know, Who I've Just Met: So, what do you do?

Me: Well, I write books. Science fiction books. My most famous one at the moment is called *Old Man's War*.

Person: Sorry, I don't know it.

Me: I also once taped bacon to my cat.

Person (visibly excited): Oh my God! That was *you?!?* I love that cat!

Ghlaghghee was written up in the *New York Times* and *Wired* and several other places; she was unimpressed with them all because she's a cat and it's not as if she actually cared about any of that stuff ever, and it never really occurred to me to try to keep my cat's moment going. Ghlaghghee's celebrity has long since been eclipsed by the Grumpy Cat and Lil' Bub and other such creatures, which is fine. Ghlaghghee didn't seem to mind. A quiet country life, with a few fan club members frequenting Whatever and a Twitter feed, seemed to suit her.

Ghlaghghee always slept with me and Krissy on our bed, and then one morning in December we both realized that she hadn't come up to sleep with us at all. I went looking for her and she was lethargic and wheezy. I took her to the vet soon after and she told us that Ghlaghghee had suffered from congestive heart failure. Ghlaghghee was not, on balance, a particularly old cat, but congestive heart failure can happen in cats at any point, and more frequently after middle age. Our vet gave us some medicine to help her clear out her lungs, which had been experiencing fluid backup, and let us know that we should be preparing for what comes next.

Cats with congestive heart failure can sometimes live for a couple of years with the condition, but Ghlaghghee was not one of those cats. Literally overnight she went from active to feeble. It was hard to get her to eat or to do anything other than sleep. We did what we could to make her feel safe and loved.

Yesterday it was clear that prolonging her life at this point made no sense. We made an appointment with the vet for Monday. Last night I made her as comfortable as I could, wrapped a towel around her to keep her warm, kissed her on the head and told her good night. I went to sleep and in the night had a dream that she had come to bed with me and Krissy again, sleeping between us as she often did.

I woke up and she was gone.

We buried Ghlaghghee in the back yard, by our maple tree there. She had lived literally her entire life, from the moment of her birth to the moment of her death, within two hundred yards of our house. She belongs here in death, too, in the place she knew, to become part of the landscape and to still be with us.

I'm taking her death badly. I've had a month to prepare but as Krissy told me today, preparing isn't the same thing as being in the moment. Pets are part of your family; you love them and in their way they love you back. Ghlaghghee was indisputably *my* cat, and I've spent a dozen years with her, every day, as part of my life. I knew this was coming and I thought I was ready to say goodbye.

I was, but I wasn't ready for how much saying goodbye to this particular cat would hurt. I suppose it's just that I loved her a lot. And it hurts when those you love go away.

Trump,
the GOP,
and the Fall

At this point there is no doubt that Donald Trump is the single worst major party presidential candidate in living memory, almost certainly the worst since the Civil War, and arguably the worst in the history of this nation. He is boastful and ignorant and petty, disdainful of the Constitution, a racist and a sexist, the enabler of the worst elements of society, either the willing tool of, or the useful idiot for, Vladimir Putin, an admirer of despots, an insecure braggart, a sexual assaulter, a man who refuses to honor contracts, and a bore.

He is, in sum, just about the biggest asshole in all of the United States of America. He's lucky that Syrian dictator Bashar Hafez al-Assad is out there keeping him from taking the global title, not that he wouldn't try for that, too, should he become president. It's appalling that he is the standard bearer for one of the two major political parties in the United States. It's appalling that he is a candidate for the presidency at all.

But note well: Donald Trump is not a black swan, an unforeseen event erupting upon an unsuspecting Republican Party. He is the end result of conscious and deliberate choices by the GOP, going back decades, to demonize its opponents, to polarize and obstruct, to pursue policies that enfeeble the political weal and to yoke the bigot and the ignorant to their wagon and to drive them by dangling carrots that they only ever intended to feed to the rich. Trump's road to the candidacy was laid down and paved by the Southern Strategy, by Lee Atwater and Newt Gingrich and Karl Rove, by Fox News and the Tea Party, and by the smirking cynicism of three generations of GOP operatives, who have been fracking the white middle and working classes for years, crushing their fortunes with their social and economic policies, never imagining it would cause an earthquake.

Well, surprise! Here's Donald Trump. He is the actual and physical embodiment of every single thing the GOP has trained its base to want and to be over the last forty years—ignorant, bigoted and money-grubbing, disdainful of facts and frightened of everything because of it, an angry drunk buzzed off of wood-grain patriotism, threatening brown people and leering at women. He was planned. He was intended. He was expected. He was *wanted*.

But not, I think, in the exact form of Donald Trump. The GOP were busily genetically engineering the perfect host for their message, someone smooth and telegenic and possibly just ethnic enough to make people hesitant to point out the latent but real racism inherent in its social policies, while making the GOP's white base feel like they were making a progressive choice, and with that person installed, further pursuing its agenda of slouching toward oligarchy, with just enough anti-abortion and pro-gun glitter tossed into the sky to distract the religious and the paranoid. Someone the GOP made. Someone they could control.

But they *don't* control Trump, which they are currently learning to their great misery. And the reason the GOP doesn't control Trump is that they no longer control their base. The GOP trained their base election cycle after election cycle to be disdainful of government and to mistrust authority, which ultimately is an odd thing for a political party whose very rationale for existence is rooted in the concept of governmental authority to do. The GOP created a monster, *but the monster isn't Trump*. The monster is the GOP's base. Trump is the guy who stole their monster from them, for his own purposes.

And this is why the GOP deserves the chaos that's happening to it now, with its appalling and parasitic standard bearer, driving his GOP host body toward the cliff. If it accepts the parasite, it will be driven off the cliff. If it resists, the parasite Trump will rip himself from it, leaving bloody marks as it does so, and then shove the dazed and wounded GOP from the precipice. That there is a fall in the GOP's future is inevitable; all that is left is which plunge to take.

I feel sorry for many of my individual friends who are Republicans and/or conservatives, who have to deal with the damage Trump is doing to their party and to their movement, even if I belong to neither. But I don't feel sorry for the GOP at all. It deserves Trump. It fostered an environment of ignorance and fear and bigotry, assumed it could control the mob those elements created, and was utterly stunned when a huckster from outside claimed the mob as his own and forced the party along for the ride. It was hubris, plain and simple, and Trump is the GOP's vulgar, orange nemesis.

Trump will do the GOP long and lasting damage, and moreover, Trump *doesn't care* that he will do the GOP long and lasting damage. Trump was never about being a Republican; he was just looking to expand his brand. As it turns out, like apparently so many things Trump does, he's done an awful job of it—the name *Trump*, formerly merely associated with garish ostentation and bankruptcy, is now synonymous with white nationalism, sexual battery and failure—but the point is on November 9th Trump is going to move on and leave the wreckage of the GOP in his wake, off to his next thing (everyone assumes "Trump TV," in which Trump combines with Breitbart to make white pride propaganda for the kind of millennial racist who thinks a Pepe the Frog Twitter icon is the height of wit—and I hope he does, because the Trump touch will drive that enterprise into the ground, and little would warm my heart more than a bankrupt Breitbart).

Trump is the party guest who sets fire to your house, gropes your spouse and drives over your neighbor's cat when he leaves; the GOP is left to deal with the police and the angry neighbors. It's almost piteous, except when you scrub back to five hours earlier to hear the GOP say "What, Trump wants to come to the party? Well, he's an asshole who drove Fred Jones' car into the pool the other weekend, but he's always good for a laugh, isn't he? Surely it will be *fine*," and then tells him to bring his bad boy self right on over.

There is no good way for the GOP or its members to extricate itself from this mess. Trump has doomed them for this election cycle. But there is a moral way, and they should take it. When a grifter and a con man has suckered you into a shitshow, you have two options: bail out early and admit you got shit all over yourself, or stick with the con and affirmatively choose to drown in the shit. No GOP politician should ever have endorsed him; the moral hazard he presented was obvious and clear and became clearer the further he went along. But if they were foolish enough to have endorsed him, it's not too late to bail out. He's going to lose either way and drag the GOP down with him; these politicians might as well come out of it with their souls, besmirched but still their own.

And obviously to me, no one with sense should cast a vote for Trump. He's not just a candidate, he is an active repudiation of what we should expect from the United States and those who lead it. A candidate who can't open his mouth without a lie falling out—a lie that everyone including him knows is a lie—doesn't deserve to be president. A candidate who threatens millions because of their religion does not deserve to be president. A candidate who promises to extralegally throw his political opponent into jail does not deserve to be president. A candidate who fosters white nationalism, racism and anti-semitism does not deserve to be president. A candidate who brags about sexual assault and then tries to dismiss it as mere talk does not deserve to be president.

These are not merely Democratic or Republican issues. These are American issues, human issues and moral issues. You can't vote for Donald Trump and say you don't know what you're voting for. You're voting for hate, and chaos, and the deluge. Anything else that you think you get from voting for him will be washed away in the flood.

Trump is the single worst major party presidential candidate in living memory, but he's there because the GOP spent decades making him possible, and its base, trained for decades to look for someone like him, made him its standard bearer. He needs to lose and the GOP needs to be punished for him. Conservatism and classical Republican ideas won't go away, nor should they. But if the GOP can't break itself from its addiction to the bigoted and the ignorant, then it certainly deserves to die. It's brought the country to the edge. Shame is only the beginning of what it should feel for it.

THE GREATEST
OF ALL TIME

Jun

4

2016

I cried for Muhammad Ali when I was eight years old, the night he fought and lost to Leon Spinks, February 15, 1978. When I was eight years old Muhammad Ali was everywhere, the best known and most admired athlete in the world—he even had an animated television series, for heaven's sake!—and everyone knew, without qualification, that he was The Greatest of All Time. I knew that too, took it as an article of faith. The Greatest of All Time, a living legend, was a man who simply could not be defeated, certainly not by Leon Spinks, who I had never heard of before and who I, in the depth of my understanding at the advanced age of eight years old, considered something of a palooka (had I known what the word "palooka" meant at that age, which I didn't). But he did lose to Spinks, and I sobbed for hours. For Ali to lose to someone like that unmoored my understanding of the world. It was literally my first crisis of faith.

What I didn't understand then, and wouldn't fully understand for years afterwards, was that Ali was not called The Greatest of All Time because he was undefeatable in the ring. He was defeatable, five times in his career, even if the other 56 times he out-thought, out-fought, out-danced, and out-psyched the other men in the ring with him, his artistry in doing so becoming the foundation of his greatness for most people, including me. What made Ali The Greatest of All Time was the totality of who he was, outside the ring as well as in it.

The world doesn't need me to recount the details of his life—there will be enough obituaries that will do that, and I can say with utter confidence that there are vast numbers of people better equipped, for all sorts of reasons, to eulogize the man. What I can say is that from that early crisis of faith at age eight to today, almost 40 years later, my understanding of Ali changed from him being a simple god on a pedestal, someone who was The Greatest of All Time by acclamation—and who was I at eight years old to argue—to him being a complex, difficult, imperfect and inspiring human being, a product of and a shaper of his time. What was true at age eight is true at age 47: He was The Greatest of All Time. What changed was not Ali. What changed is my understanding of him, and what greatness is.

Let me talk a moment about Ali being both a black man and a Muslim. In the wake of his death, you're going to see people saying that Ali transcended his race or his religion, or both of them, to become someone who belonged to all people. I think two things about this. First, it's undeniable that people of all races and creeds admired him, his life and his accomplishments. I loved him as a child, when my understanding of him was simple, and I honored him as an adult, when my understanding of him was more complex.

But—and this is the second thing—you *cannot* love or honor Ali properly without acknowledging that blackness and Islam are *at the core* of his greatness. It seems to me, and I think the events of his life bear this out, that the greatness of Ali—who *he* was—did not come out *to* you, was not there *for* you, and in a fundamental way did not care what you *thought* of it. It was *there*, and you could come to it or not, and if you did, you had to take it on its on terms. On *Ali's* terms. And Ali's terms were: He was a black man, in America and in the world. He was a Muslim man, in America and in the world. He was who he was. *He* did not have to transcend those things about himself. *You*, however, might have to overcome your understanding of what you thought of both blackness and Islam to appreciate him. People did or did not; Ali went on regardless.

I think it's important that when I was an eight-year-old child, one of my idols, one of my pantheon, someone whose greatness I accepted uncritically, was a black man. I'd like to think in a small, early way that my love for Ali made a difference in how I grew up thinking about race. As I grew up, and I learned about his experiences being black in the US in the mid-20th century, his refusal to submit for the draft and his rea-soning for it, and his conversion and movement through Islam—and the responses to all of these by others as they happened—Ali was an unwitting but invaluable teacher.

I can't say I have a perfect understanding of race or religion or of blackness in America or of Islam. The imperfections of understanding of each of those is on me. But I can say that to the extent I engage in any of them with any measure of success, Muhammad Ali is part of the rea-son why. Because he was black. Because he was Muslim. And because he made me understand that both of those were fundamental to his greatness, not things he needed to transcend to be seen as great.

My friend and classmate Josh Marshall noted earlier today that the decline in interest in the sport of boxing over the last few decades makes it difficult for younger people—especially under the age of 30—to understand the scope of Ali's greatness in his time. I think it also means, particularly with regard to the sport of boxing, that Ali's appel-lation as The Greatest of All Time is unlikely to be seriously challenged, ever. It's not that other boxers won't have better records; it's not that other boxers won't be great. It's that for a moment in time, boxing had in its ranks a man who could and did shape his nation and his world with his athletic talent, his political courage, his devastatingly sharp mind, and his great heart.

He was Muhammad Ali and there will never be another like him. I cried for him when I was eight because I did not understand why he was The Greatest of All Time. I understand now. I cry for him again because I do.

GUILT, MINE, AND PAYING IT FORWARD, ME

Jun

19

2013

You know, every now and again some dude will read my "Straight White Male" piece or one of the similar follow-on pieces, decide to put me in my place, and barf up a blog nugget consisting of straw men, bad logic, projection and anger issues with me as its target. This is fine, of course. Everyone needs a hobby and at the end of the day I'm not generally psychically or materially injured by the venting, and indeed I'm often amused. So let the blog nuggets fly.

Be that as it may, it's worth it every once in a while to note a particular poor argument about me and point and laugh at it. The one I'd like to address today is the one which asserts that I have guilt for being white and/or straight and/or male and/or what passes for "liberal" here in the United States. The "guilt" assertion is a favorite tactic of bad rhetoricians, because, oh, I don't know, if you feel guilt then you are weak, and if you are weak then your arguments aren't good because SHUT UP YOU PATHETIC WEAKLING I LAUGH AS YOU MEWL IN THE DIRT STOMP STOMP STOMP or something along that line.

Let's put aside for now the inherent poor logic of "You feel guilt therefore your argument is invalid" and ask the relevant question of: Do I, in fact, feel guilty for being white and/or straight and/or male and/or what passes for "liberal" here in the United States?

Short answer:

BWA HAH HA HA HA HAH HA you gotta be kidding me.

Longer answer:

BWA HA HA HA HAH AH HA HA HAH HA HA HA AH HA HA HA no, seriously, you *have* to be absolutely, totally, *completely* joking. And if you're not, that's about seven different tangy flavors of stupid.

And now, the answer that offers detail and some nuance:

So, not too long ago, I was at an amusement park with a friend of mine who is notable in his field, which is not my field. And because he is notable in his field, he has fans. At least one of those fans worked at this amusement park and said to my friend, hey, if you come to the park, let me know and I'll make sure you get the VIP treatment. And who doesn't like getting the VIP treatment? Very few, that's who.

So we went and we got the VIP treatment and I have to tell you it was pretty sweet. For example, all those lines everyone else had to wait in to get a popular ride? We totally didn't. We went down an open path and got escorted right to the head of the line. We passed all those folks who had been waiting for 90 minutes or so while we did it and slipped into a car for the ride. It was a fun ride.

Do I feel *guilty* for breezing past all the folks who had to wait an hour and a half to get on the ride? Nope. I was offered a break and I took advantage of it, and was happy to do so. It meant that I had an extra ninety minutes to go on more rides, and that my overall amusement park experience was not one of complete exasperation. It worked out well for me.

But let's be clear: I got a break there, something other people don't always get. And in my particular case, it was a break that *I* did nothing to receive—I got a break because I knew a guy. I don't feel guilty about getting that break, but I also don't pretend that it was deserved or earned, or that the people we walked past wouldn't be within their rights to be irritated with me blowing right on by. And I don't pretend that, for the fact that I *just happened* to know a guy, I wouldn't have been in that line for an hour and a half. So, no guilt, but come *on*. I know what I got out of that situation, through no effort of my own.

Out here in the real world of the United States, me being white and straight and male is kind of like me going to the amusement park with my notable pal. I get some breaks and advantages, at least some of which I didn't do anything on my own to get. Do I feel guilty about them? No.

I have things I want to do in my life—and things I'm happy to *avoid* in my life—and if I get breaks that let me do/avoid them, I'll take them. I *do* take them. But again, I don't pretend I'm not getting breaks other people aren't, and avoiding aggravations that other people have to deal with. I recognize what I get that's due to me and my efforts, and what I get because of things that aren't fundamentally about *me* at all.

Now, if you're unsophisticated enough to confuse this sort of self-awareness with guilt, then yes, I suppose that indeed looks like guilt to you. If you are the sort of person who then additionally confuses guilt with weakness, because you don't think things through, or because your own set of insecurities and neuroses compels you to do so, or whatever reason causes you to make such transmutations in your head, and you fear or despise weakness for whatever reasons you might have, then I can see why you might be inclined to treat people you see as having guilt with contempt, and their thoughts and opinions unworthy of your consideration. So sure, I get that.

It makes you look like a fucking idiot, however. I really wish you would stop doing that.

(Likewise, the whole bit about "liberal guilt." Dude, please. Your 1993-era set of Newt Gingrich™ Brand "Mean Things to Say About Liberals" Cue Cards are worn from all the thumbing through they get.)

I don't feel guilty about the breaks I've gotten. I don't feel guilty about the breaks I still get. But—and I think this is relevant here—I also think it's important that today and moving forward people who aren't straight and white and male get access to the same set of breaks that I've gotten. I also think that as someone who's gotten breaks that have worked to my advantage, I should be willing to put in the effort to make that happen. With great breaks comes at least some responsibility.

Now, as it happens, this belief dovetails very nicely with a central tenet of the Science Fiction and Fantasy community: "Pay it Forward." This means, in its most basic form, that when you're helped get to where you are, the way to repay that debt is to then help others who need it— take what's been given to you and send it on. The fact of the matter is that I've been given a lot, by people and by the culture I live in. I have a large debt, so to speak, that can be repaid only by paying it forward. I am happy to do it, and I'm especially happy to do it in a way that makes sure that the largest possible field of people, of all sorts, have the chance to pay it forward from there.

So, no. I have no guilt about being a Straight White Male. Why should I? What I *would* have guilt about is if, as a Straight White Male, with all the advantages I have, earned *and* unearned, I wasn't working to make my various communities better for those in them (and for those who wished they would be welcome as part of them). If I weren't doing that I would feel very guilty indeed. It's much better to believe in "Pay it Forward" than "I Got Mine."

GUILTY
PLEASURES

Apr
9
2013

John Glaenzer asks:

What guilty pleasures do you have? Belting out CW McCall songs on Friday night? Watching reruns of "Mythbusters" in your bathrobe, because dressing on Saturday is too much of a hassle? Writing mildly amusing comments on a semi-famous science fiction writers blo...

Oh dear.

Anyway, what are your guilty pleasures?

I don't have any, because I don't feel guilty about my pleasures.

Which is not to say that I don't have a lot of silly or simple or even stupid pleasures. Among them, the joy of blowing the heads off zombies in the Left 4 Dead video games, listening to Journey after the age of twenty-one, eating an astounding array of junk food mitigated only by a daily multivitamin, or making up songs about my pets and singing them when one enters the room (Yes, my pets have theme songs? Don't yours? Hmmm). I do all of these things—and more! Really, a large percentage of my pleasures are, shall we say, *uncomplicated*.

I don't feel guilty about them, however, because, eh, why should I? My pleasures make me happier to a greater or lesser degree, they don't hurt anyone else, and in any event one of the great advantages to being a grown-up is being able to do what the hell you want and not have to apologize for it or run it past anyone else. The reason we call things "guilty pleasures" is usually because we substitute someone else's judgment for their value over our own.

I'm not inclined to do that. One, because I feel comfortable with my own judgment on what gives me pleasure and don't need validation from anyone else. Two, because even if I did need validation from everyone else, everyone else would be a hypocrite on this score, since everyone (or at least everyone I've ever met in my life) has their own set of pleasures that someone else would look askance upon—and because every pleasure in life has almost certainly been looked askance upon. Every pleasure is a guilty pleasure to someone. Eventually you just have to stop caring if your pleasure has the approval of the majority, or of a critically-minded minority, or of, you know, your *mom*.

The flip side of this is that it makes it easier for you to not care what gives other people pleasure. You like Nickelback? I'm not a fan at all and I don't mind cracking the occasional joke at their expense, but you know what? If you like them and listening to them gives you happiness, then listen to them and be happy. A huge fan of basketball? I'm not much for it outside of a highlight reel, but that shouldn't stop you. Enjoy your bouncy ball heaved about by tall persons. Enjoy you some sparkly vampires? I am painfully aware that sparkly vampires give me no pleasure whatsoever. But if they give you pleasure, then please to enjoy you some shiny bloodsuckers. I don't need to care about what you like, and more to the point, you don't need to care what I think about what you like.

(There's also the fact that, to be blunt about it, what I do professionally is likely seen as a "guilty pleasure" by some, because there are people who look down at genre fiction and/or science fiction and/or me as a writer. And, well. I don't want people to feel like they have to make an excuse or feel guilty for reading what I write to anyone; I just want them to enjoy it.)

So, yeah: No guilty pleasures. I like what I like, and I don't care what anyone else thinks about it. Wheee!

HAMILTON, AND THOUGHTS ON THE UNCANNY VALLEY OF MUSICALS

Feb

20

2017

On Saturday night Krissy and I went and saw *Hamilton* in New York. This was a moment greatly anticipated by a large number of my friends who had seen the show (or at least listened to the soundtrack), had fallen head over heels in love with it, and who wanted to induct me into their Hamiltonian cult. I had previously refused to listen to the cast album of the show, choosing to go into it fresh (although only to a point—I obviously knew who Alexander Hamilton was, and I had read the Ron Chernow book that Lin-Manuel Miranda used as a basis for his play), so Saturday was my entrance into the congregation. Having been thus baptized, I would now be available for Hamilton sing-alongs and arguments as to which Schuyler sister was the best and so on.

Having now seen *Hamilton*, here's what I have to say about it:

One, it is in fact really good. I see why all my friends went nuts for it, and also why it won all the awards it did and propelled Lin-Manuel Miranda into the stratosphere of celebrity. It's all entirely deserved. I suppose I could quibble here and there if I was feeling contrary—the play is notably episodic, particularly in the second act, and some characters and plot points are jammed in and then dropped out, which suggests the play could have been more tightly edited—but one can always quibble on details and miss out on the overall effect of a work, which in this case is significant. I hugely enjoyed myself, and was thrilled in particular with the second half of the first act. I'd see it again, surely.

Two, I don't love *Hamilton* like my friends love *Hamilton*. This is not the fault of the play, nor a matter of me being contrarian to be contrary, and choosing not to love that which my friends love, simply because it's already gotten all their love. It's because of something that I already knew about myself, which is that generally speaking I have a level of emotional remove from a lot of live action musicals, both in theater and in film. I can like them and enjoy them, and certainly admire the craft and skill that go into making them, but I don't always engage with them emotionally. A really good live action musical can easily capture my brain, but in my experience they rarely capture my heart.

Why? The short answer is a lot of live action musicals exist in the emotional equivalent of the Uncanny Valley for me—an unsweet spot where the particular artifices of musicals make me aware of their artificiality. The longer answer is I'm perfectly willing to engage in live musicals intellectually—and why wouldn't I, says the writer of science fiction, a genre with its own slate of artifices—but seem to have trouble with them emotionally. Live humans stepping outside of their lived experience to burst into a song directed to an audience pretty much always makes my suspension of disbelief go "bwuh?", and then I'm not lost in the story, I'm aware I'm a member of an audience. That sets me at a remove.

Which is, to be clear, entirely on me. This is *my* quirk, and not an indictment of live action musicals. They clearly work perfectly well for large numbers of people, who do not suffer from my own issues regarding emotional engagement with the form. Nor does it mean I don't enjoy musicals in general. I do. Not being at 100% with musicals doesn't mean that the experience is like ashes in my mouth. Getting 90% of the effect of a musical can still be pretty great, and was, in the case of *Hamilton*. It does mean, however, that the fervor so many of my friends feel about a really great musical is usually not something I feel.

Interestingly, in my experience the way for me to engage emotionally in a musical is to add *more* artifice to it. For example, I'm a sucker for animated musicals—I think *Beauty and the Beast* is one of the best musical films of all time, *The Nightmare Before Christmas* is a brilliant operetta, and *Moana*, whose songs were written or co-written by Miranda, made me cry where *Hamilton* didn't—precisely because the animated format adds another layer of willing suspension of disbelief. I mean, if you're willing to accept talking candelabras, or skeleton kings or the ocean as a comic foil, it's not *that* hard to accept characters breaking out into song, either.

Likewise, I have an easier time with funny musicals—or more accurately, musicals intended to be comedies as well (*Hamilton* has several funny moments, including the bits with King George, but is not meant to be a comedy). I enjoyed the hell out of *The Producers* and *The Book of Mormon* and *Spamalot* because they were fundamentally ridiculous *anyway*, so the breaking out into song doesn't pull me out the way it does with more serious musical work.

Going the other direction—movies with songs in them which yet are not musicals—also works for me too. *Strictly Ballroom* (the film) feels like a musical and yet *isn't*, and I love it insensibly. The concert film *Stop Making Sense* is a perfect film, from my point of view; watching it is like going to church. And I'm looking forward to *Sing Street* because everything about it suggests I'll get the thrill watching it like I got watching *The Commitments* back in the 90s.

Again, this is about *my* quirks, not an argument that, say, *Hamilton* would have been better as *Hamilton!*, a funny farce where a zany founding father gets into all sorts of hilarious hijinx with his best ol' frenemy Aaron Burr. It wouldn't have (although I have no doubt now that someone will try it). It's merely to the point that for whatever reason, a lot of live action musicals exist in a place I can't get fully emotionally engaged with it. I find that interesting, and wonder if I'm alone in this.

The real irony? Not only did I perform in musical theater as a kid (and enjoyed it! And would do it again!) I'd kind of like to *write* a musical one day. Not to say "you people have been doing musicals *all wrong*, this is how you do it" because, yeah, no, I'm not *that* asshole. But because I think *Redshirts* in particular would make a damn fine musical, of the funny sort, and because I know I appreciate and engage with science fiction better, having written science fiction, so who knows? Maybe that trick will work again in another genre and medium. Or (actually "and"), maybe I should just go and see more musicals. That would probably help too.

In the meantime: *Hamilton* is excellent, as advertised. Go see it when you can. I'm not likely to join the HamilCult, but that shouldn't dissuade you, should you be of a mind to.

(Also: Angelica Schuyler was the best Schuyler sister. I mean, come on.)

HARRY POTTER AND THE INITIALLY DISMISSIVE BUT ULTIMATELY APPRECIATIVE FAN

Jun
26
2017

The first time I personally encountered Harry Potter was not long after the third book, *Harry Potter and the Prisoner of Azkaban,* came out. I was 30 and my daughter was an infant, so in neither case were these particular Scalzis the target demographic for the books, but by that time the buzz (and sales) of the series were pretty significant. So one day in the airport, while I was browsing in a bookstore, I picked up *Harry Potter and the Chamber of Secrets* and opened it up near the end, to the part where Dobby the House Elf is given a sock.

I read it for a few pages to get the sense of Rowling's style, and then put the book back on the shelf and thought, "well, okay, that's not for me." Why not for me? In this case, it was something about the writing of that particular scene. I could see how all the pieces fit together, and I could see how it was working, and I could also see that all of it seemed pitched to someone who wasn't *me*, 30-year-old John Scalzi. This didn't mean it wasn't a good book or the right book for someone else; by the age of thirty I had gathered enough wisdom (and, dare I say it, humility) to recognize that "not for me" was not the same as "not for anyone." But I didn't feel the click that made me want to keep reading. Evidently, Harry Potter was not for me.

And that was okay! There is a lot of stuff in the common culture that is not for me, particularly when it's pitched to people who are younger or older than I am. *Dawson's Creek* and *The Vampire Diaries* are not for me, just like *My Three Sons* or *Dark Shadows* were not for me. Emerson Lake and Palmer was not for me, nor was N*Sync, nor is Ariana Grande. *Doctor*

Who's first iteration was not for me and I have to admit I'm only passably interested in the current version. I could be here for days with a list of all the things that are not for me. Again, which is fine! There are lots of things that I decided *are* for me. I was happy with them.

And so with Harry Potter and J.K. Rowling, whose niche in my mind I pretty much figured had been occupied by Will Stanton and Meg Murry, and Susan Cooper and Madeleine L'Engle. I didn't worry too much about whether Kids These Days were reading *The Dark is Rising* or the Wrinkle in Time series, for the same reason I didn't worry too much if today's kids were really into Tears for Fears or the Go-Gos, to name but two bands whose discographies were pertinent to my teenage years. Every generation finds their storytellers, in literature and music and art in general. I was okay letting J.K. Rowling and her stories belong to the generation of young people after mine. Yes, I know, very gracious of me.

But as it turns out neither Harry Potter nor J.K. Rowling were done with me. First, of course, it turned out that Harry Potter, Hermione Granger and Ron Weasley (and Rowling) weren't Tears for Fears; they were the Beatles. And like the Beatles they weren't just *popular*. They materially changed common culture—for a *start*, because they also changed the industry that they came out of, and the work of everyone in their field, who either responded to them or were influenced by them. Now, one may, like me, decide a phenomenon like that isn't *for* you, but when literally(!) the world is changing to deal with and make room for that phenomenon, you still have to acknowledge that it's there and work with it, or at least around it. Particularly when and if, like me, it comes out of the fields (in this case publishing and writing) you hope to be in, and in my case were eventually part of.

Second, I found another way in to Rowling's wizarding world: through the movies, which were for me in a way that I, from that snippet of the second book, assumed the books were not. In retrospect this is not at all surprising—I was a professional film critic for several years, and I've written two books on film, and, as anyone who has ever read my novels can tell you, the storytelling *structure* of film is a huge influence on my storytelling in prose. My professional and creative interest in film helped *that* version of Harry Potter's story speak to me.

(And in point of fact this is not the first time I had found the film/ TV version of a story working better for me. I've written in detail about how I think the Peter Jackson's take on The Lord of the Rings is better— or at least better for *me*, in terms of story presentation—than the Tolkien books; likewise I am deeper into the Game of Thrones universe through the TV series than I was through the books. In all these cases, I'm not suggesting the prose version has failed in some way and the films "fix" them. They obviously work for millions of people. More to the point, different media allow creators to do different things, and reach different people. As was the case here.)

Having gotten through the door with the series via film was a good thing, because as it turned out Harry Potter *is* for me—which is to say that I find the world that Rowling created to be deep and thoughtful and interesting in ways I didn't expect. And because it's interesting and engaging to me as someone who approached it as an adult, I understand better why it's so *very* deeply affecting for the readers who literally grew up in tandem with Harry and Hermione and Ron and all the rest of the students at Hogwarts. They aren't just characters to them, any more than Will Stanton or Meg Murry were just characters to me. They were and are contemporaries and friends. Harry Potter's Hogwarts year had several million students in it. It's a miracle they all fit in the dining hall.

One way or another, lightly or deeply, it's turned out Harry Potter is for more people than I would have expected, all those years ago. This is one reason why 20 years after the release of *Harry Potter and the Philosopher's Stone*, we're getting the sort of retrospectives on the series that *Sgt. Pepper's* got 20 years down the road from its release, and why, just like everyone knew which Beatle was their favorite, now everyone knows which Hogwarts house they'd personally be sorted into, or would want to be.

(Personal moment here: I assumed I was a Ravenclaw, because *come on*, but then went to the Pottermore site and was sorted into Gryffindor, which annoyed me but on reflection I realized was correct, damn it. Also, re: the Beatles, John is Slytherin, Paul is Gryffindor, George is Ravenclaw and Ringo is so very Hufflepuff. Fight me on this).

This is not to say the Potterverse is perfect or that J.K. Rowling is infallable as a writer or human. It's not and she's not. But then again, none of the universes I've written are perfect, and I sure as hell am not infallible, either. Fictional universes don't have to be perfect, they just have to be a space people want to explore and keep exploring, year after year. I can't say that I know Rowling to any great extent—we've exchanged pleasantries on Twitter, which I try not to let her know I've geeked out about—but I do admire her, as a writer and a worldbuilder, and as someone who has decided that she needs to be engaged in our world and time. From her public persona at least, it's no great surprise that Harry and Hermione and Ron came out of her brain, or that she created such great antagonists for them. I think she sees what the world can run downhill toward, and how quickly that can happen, and that people need to stand against that, and stand with each other as they do so.

Which is another reason I'm glad that I found Harry Potter is for me, and for millions of other people. We need that now in 2017. *I* need it now. There's very little chance J.K. Rowling knew, 20 years ago, that her books and her characters would be needed like this today. But I hope she knows it now, today and every day.

HARVEY WEINSTEIN AND OTHER ABUSERS

Oct

10

2017

(For those who need it, a warning: I'm talking rape and sexual assault here today.)

In the wake of the latest on Harvey Weinstein's history of sexual abuse of women, some thoughts, not necessarily in order of importance.

1. Harvey Weinstein is by all indications a rapist and general piece of shit. Just to put that out there up front, so there's no confusion. He deserved to be fired by his company (as he was) and should almost certainly be in jail.

2. He's also solely responsible for his own actions. Which apparently comes as a shock to the scads of people who, when the news got out, started wanting to blame prominent film people who knew him (particularly women) for their silence, and the people who worked for him for not taking a stand against him. I'll get to both of these things in a minute, but look: Harvey Weinstein intentionally and systematically sexually abused women, sexually harassed women and targeted them for sexual coercion. He promised professional advancement and threatened professional oblivion in order to compel sexual compliance, and bribed and threatened women for their silence. And he did this, it appears, over three decades. He owns it.

3. But what about the systematic problem of harassment in the film and television industry, you ask? Well: Yes, it is there, and yes, Weinstein both participated in it and furthered it for his own pleasure, and yes, it needs to be addressed and rooted out, and anyone who sexually coerces another person should be punted hard on their ass. But let's be clear that Weinstein was not *compelled* against his will to participate in it and to further it. He did that on his own. He was the author of his own moral story, and his moral story sucks. Acknowledging that Weinstein is solely responsible for his own choices neither ignores or exculpates the systematic issues of the entertainment industry. He raped and assaulted women. He owns that.

4. While we're on the topic, let's dispense of some other nonsense. Weinstein tried to imply that coming of age in the 60s and 70s meant his moral compass was pointed a few degrees off true. Well, that's bullshit; I know *lots* of people who came of age in the 60s and 70s who know perfectly well sexual coercion and rape is immoral. Pretty much *all* of them, in fact. Donna Karan (who is apparently one of the few who does not) just made news by sort of airily suggesting that the issue with Weinstein was more that he was a symbol of various sexual issues than a real live man who raped and sexually assaulted numerous women, and well. No. It's possible he is *both*, but any story framing that attempts to keep his personal actions from being front and center is crap. He wouldn't be a synecdoche for these issues if he wasn't a coercive assaulting piece of shit. Any explanation of Weinstein's behavior that does not center his own choices is a bad one. He's a grown man. He knew what he was doing, and he knew what he was doing was wrong. He did it anyway.

5. What about the staff at Miramax and The Weinstein Company who knew—or at least could guess—what their boss was up to but did nothing about it? I'm not here to excuse them, and we are all responsible for our moral choices. I am also aware it's easy to judge when your career and income aren't riding on the necessity of not looking too closely at what your boss is doing. Bear in mind that the film industry is the industry that perfected blacklisting—one day you're fine and the next no one's returning your calls. At the height of his powers there's no doubt Harvey Weinstein could make working in the industry very difficult, and the further down the food chain you were, the more difficult he could make it.

I am fortunate that when I was working for others, I never had a boss whose moral baseline (as far as I knew) substantially conflicted with mine. I was never put in a position of having to cover for, or look away from, a boss's actions. I would like to think that if I had been, I would have done the correct thing, even in the face of losing my job. I'd like to *think* that, but it's easy to think about what you would do when you've never been confronted by that actual decision point.

Again, I'm not here to excuse the moral choices Weinstein's employees made—or didn't make—and they'll have the burden of their choices for the rest of their professional lives. I do know that the burden of their choices was placed on them *because* Weinstein chose to sexually assault and coerce women. His actions had consequences beyond him.

6. As for the issue of very famous people apparently not knowing what Weinstein was up to, I'm going to tell you a story. In my line of work there was an editor named Jim Frenkel, who worked for Tor, my publisher, and who as it turned out was a harassing piece of shit. It also turned out that he was very good at hiding that fact from his bosses and fellow editors and from authors, like me, who did not fit the profile of the sort of person he liked to harass. I was male, I was already published and successful, and I suspect Frenkel knew I would talk if I found out anything. I found out because Frenkel finally harassed a person who was more than happy to talk out loud about it, and who had people who would amplify her voice. Lots of people lateral to or above his status were shocked. Lots of women below his status asked how the hell the rest of us did not know.

We didn't know because we didn't see it personally; we didn't know because the "whisper network" didn't reach us. And why didn't it reach us? Maybe because the women were scared about what Frenkel could do to their careers. Maybe because they assumed some of us already knew and were doing nothing about it. Maybe because some of us were men and the women didn't want to have to deal with the emotional burden of trying to make us believe harassment was a real thing. "Whisper networks" can be useful, but they're full of holes. And more than that: They propagate downward and attenuate upward. After a certain height, you don't hear many whispers.

No one knows a food chain better than a predator. Harvey Weinstein was not going to prey near or above his station; doing so served none of his purposes and represented risk. He wasn't going to prey on (say) Meryl Streep or Hillary Clinton, and the chances that someone he would prey on would be able to tell either of those two women—or other women of a similar stature, or men on the same level—was pretty slim, and what reaches someone at that level is often spotty and inconclusive, for all the reasons noted above.

(Please note I'm not originating these observations; I'm merely making the same point women have been making for years.)

This doesn't mean *no* people above certain level didn't know. But it does mean predators are good at hiding their tracks, or at least making their path confusing. It also means that predators know how to leverage their power—and in the case of Harvey Weinstein, he was very powerful indeed.

And for the women of power who did know and who kept quiet, or at least quietish: Surprise! This is where the systematic sexism and harassment in the film/TV industry raises its head. You knew it would show up sometime!

7. Anyone who voted for an admitted sexual predator for president who is now blaming women for not knowing or not confronting Harvey Weinstein: Sit the *fuck* down. You don't even have the veil of plausible deniability to cover the fact that you helped make Mr. "Grab 'Em By the Pussy" the President of the United States. You knew and you didn't care. To go after Clinton because she knew Weinstein after you cast your vote for Trump, well, shit. Motes and beams, son.

And, not that I've seen it, but in case it's out there (and it probably is, somewhere): Anyone defending Weinstein on the basis of his ostensible politics or because of the great art he's helped produce, you can sit the fuck down, too. The correct politics and the ability to spot good films and filmmakers isn't a pass for being sexually coercive and a rapist. I'm happy to cede this piece of shit human has very fine taste in cinema. He's still a piece of shit human.

8. I'm all for condemning both Trump *and* Weinstein, and any other man who uses his power to sexually coerce other people. Weinstein is a liberal and Trump is, well, whatever the hell he is (white supremacist authoritarian populist masquerading as a conservative), but both are men who have decided that they get to force themselves on women, and women should be happy or at least quiet about it. There's no political angle to it; or more accurately, certain men of any political stripe seem happy to be predatory pieces of shit. Nor should there be any political separation to the solution to this problem: Kick *all* that shit to the curb.

9. And of course some of the backlash from this is that some men in corporate settings are now avoiding women, which makes me want to smack my head and wonder what the fuck is wrong with my sex. The solution is not to cut women out of your professional life, you assholes. The solution is to fix your goddamned corporate culture and root out the sexual harassers and predators so *neither you nor any woman* have to worry that a closed-door meeting means a quick two-step to the HR department. Redlining women from professional advancement because you don't know how else to deal with the issues of harassment and pre-dation means *you* are the problem, not them.

10. Harvey Weinstein is a piece of shit, but he's not the only piece of shit out there. The film/TV industry has a sexism and harassment problem, but it's not the only industry with a sexism and harassment problem. Today is Weinstein's moment in the barrel, and he should be shot to the moon for it. But there's a whole line of dudes waiting after him, starting from the president and working on down.

All of which you would know already, my dudes, if you listened to women *and believed them*. I've been working on that one myself a lot recently. I'm not perfect, but I like to think I'm getting better at it. We'll see. Maybe you should make an effort at it too, if you've not done so already.

HENRY ROLLINS
SHOWS HIS ASS, GETS
TOLD, OWNS IT

So, in the wake of Robin Williams' suicide, Henry Rollins wrote a piece in *LA Weekly* called "Fuck Suicide," in which he basically engages in a bit of "tough love" victim-blaming. This caused the world to drop on Henry Rollins. Henry Rollins, to his credit, has offered up a reasonably decent apology, and plans to follow up in the same forum where the original piece ran. So that's good, so far. Apologies are hard and hard to do well, and I think he hits the basics.

A number of years ago a girl who I knew in high school committed suicide in college, in a way that at the time I thought was astoundingly dramatic. For years, when I thought of her at all, I was kind of pissed off at her. I thought of all the people she hurt with her actions, and I thought that fundamentally, what she had done was selfish and stupid and designed to get her attention that she thought she was owed and now would not be able to appreciate because she was dead—not that I thought she had thought about what would happen after she committed suicide. So that was my thinking about her, like I said, for years.

And then somewhere along the way, and I don't remember when precisely it was, I realized that someone in this scenario was indeed an asshole, it's just that I was putting the finger on the wrong person. The asshole was me. Because in fact I knew nothing about what was going on her head, or how much pain she may have been in, knew very little about depression or how it works on people—basically I knew *nothing*, period, about anything relevant. All I knew were my own opinions, based on my own life experience, in which neither suicidal thoughts, nor depression outside of a few occasional bad days, had ever featured. I wasn't qualified to judge. Life is one long process of discovery about just how little you know about pretty much everything, and that includes people and the insides of their heads.

When I think of this young woman now, I mostly, simply, feel sad. I wish there would have been a way she could have seen her way through to sticking around. And I'm sorry that I spent years generally being pissed off at her. It was wrong of me, and it didn't do either of us any good.

This is my way of saying that I get why Henry Rollins wrote what he did, and why he was the asshole in that scenario, and why I'm pleased, in that vague way that one is when thinking about people more famous than you, whose work you've enjoyed, that he's accepted that he blew it and is trying to walk it back. As I've said many times, we all show our ass from time to time. I certainly have. What you do after you show your ass matters.

HERE'S
A QUARTER

Many years ago—actually about a quarter of a century ago—I had applied for the job of Student Ombudsperson at the University of Chicago. The job of the Ombudsperson was to help students navigate the bureaucracy of the university, and to help them get their concerns heard when the usual channels weren't working. It was a job where I got to problem-solve and advocate for people, and that appealed to me.

One part of the process for being considered for the job was an interview with a selection committee, which featured members of the faculty, administration and student body, who asked me (and presumably the other candidates) questions and offered hypothetical issues to resolve. It was during one of the hypotheticals, the details of which are not especially important, that I was confronted with a hypothetical student who simply wouldn't be happy with any outcome. So, like this:

Q: A student comes with "X" problem. How would you resolve it?

A: I would do "Y", and here's why [explain why].

Q: Okay, but they're not happy with that solution. What do you do then?

A: Then I would try "Z," and here's why [explain why].

Q: Okay, but they're still not happy. Now what?

A: Well, then let's try "Q," because [explain why].

Q: They're still not happy.

A: Fine, I would try "K," because [explain why].

"Okay," my interviewer then said, "But they're still not happy with your solution or your efforts. What do you do then?"

"I give them a quarter to call someone who cares," I said. "Because at that point it's clear they're more interested in being upset than anything else, and I have other work to do."

Yes, I actually did say that (or something very close to it; it was 25 years ago and I didn't record it).

And yes, I got the job.

Here's the thing: I believe that we owe our fellow human beings a certain amount of compassion and courtesy and respect, and to listen to their complaints and grievances. We should ask ourselves whether those complaints and grievances are valid, and whether we can help—and in some cases, ask whether we are the author of those grievances, and if so what we can do to resolve them.

But I also believe that after a certain point, it may become obvious that some people just want to complain, or to be angry, or to be an asshole, or whatever, and that nothing a reasonable person can do will ever make those people happy or satisfied. So you give them a quarter, metaphorically or otherwise, and tell them to call someone who cares. Because you have other things to do. And then you go on doing those things you need to do.

They won't be happy, but then they were never going to be happy, and it's not your responsibility to fix their problem—"their problem" not being whatever specific complaint or grievance they might have, but a worldview that requires them to always *have* a complaint or grievance, and/or to believe that the root of that complaint is somehow about you. That's something for therapy, perhaps, not for you, or anyone else who isn't getting paid by the session.

You should be a kind and compassionate person to others when they have a problem or grievance. You should also know when it's a problem you can't solve, and also, when the person doesn't actually want the problem to be solved. It's neither kind nor compassionate to them *nor to you* to keep being involved after that point. And to be sure, after you've given them their quarter, they will likely complain that you are a terrible person, and/or part of a conspiracy to keep them down, and so on and so forth. That's their karma, not yours.

I was and am pretty proud of my time as Student Ombudsperson at the University of Chicago. I ended up helping a good number of people, and making sure that the students could get their voices heard. But I never forgot that part of the reason I got the job is because they knew I knew where to draw a line. It was a useful skill in that job. It continues to be useful to me today.

Hillary Clinton, Considered in Herself

<table>
<tr><td>Jul</td></tr>
<tr><td>28</td></tr>
<tr><td>2016</td></tr>
</table>

So, before Hillary Clinton puts a cap on the DNC convention with her appearance tonight, let me talk a little about what I think of her as a presidential nominee, (mostly) independent of the fact of Donald Trump as her opponent for the office. And to talk about her as a presidential nominee, I need to talk a little bit about me as a political being.

And who am I as a political being? As I've noted elsewhere, among the various political labels that have been used over the last several decades, I'm probably closest to what used to be called a "Rockefeller Republican," a person who is relatively socially liberal but relatively economically conservative. But that label doesn't precisely describe me, either. I am both of those things, generally, but it doesn't get to the root of my political ethos.

To get to that, I need to go back to high school, to a class I took called Individual Humanities. The class was the brainchild of teacher Larry McMillin, and it was a year-long class (interestingly, divided between the last half of one's junior year and the first half of one's senior year) that took a look at portrayals of the individual in Western Literature—from Oedipus Rex through Joan of Arc through Huckleberry Finn—to chart the development of the idea of the individual and what it means to be one, in the larger context of western civilization.

The specific details of the class are something I'll leave out for now, but the takeaway of the class—the summation of its goals—was to argue that one of western civilization's great achievements was the development of the independently acting and thinking individuals who saw as their *greatest life crisis* service to their community. Which is to say: In our world, we get built to think for ourselves, and when that happens, we realize we can't be in it *just* for ourselves.

And, importantly, this ethos and the benefits thereof are not the purview of one group or class. *Everyone* should be encouraged to develop into who they have the potential to become. *Everyone* in turn uses that realized potential for the overall benefit their community or communities.

Well, that sounds communist! Yes, I suppose if you wanted you could argue that "from each according to ability, to each according to needs" is an expression of this concept, but then again, so is "TANSTAAFL" as long as it's applied alongside "Pay it forward"; even the concept of *noblesse oblige* holds its echo. Like the "golden rule" which is found in most major religions, the concept is adaptable to a number of situations. The important things: Development of people as individuals; recognition of the individual's responsibilities to their communities.

This is, to my mind, a powerful, adaptable and *moral* ethos, first because it encourages each of us to find our full expression and to develop those gifts we have within us—to become *us*—and at the same time reminds us that these talents and gifts need to be used not only for ourselves but for the benefit of others. It's not (just) self-interest, or even (just) enlightened self-interest; it's realization of self and a commitment to others *as the result* of that realization. It doesn't mean one can't do well for one's self; most of us are not built to be monks. It does mean you should see "doing good" as an equal or higher goal than "doing well."

This idea of the enlightened individual in service to their community is a significant part of my own personal ethical toolbox; likewise, it's part of my political thinking as well, and a thing I want to see in politicians.

Along with this ethos, I have a very large streak of pragmatism, which is to say, I generally think it's okay to get half a loaf when the full loaf is manifestly not on offer. Should you go in saying "sure, I'll take half a loaf"? No, go ahead and see how much of the loaf you can get—if you can get the whole damn thing, good on you. But if you get 80% or 50% or 25% or whatever, depending on circumstances, well, fine—that fraction can be a basis to build on. Applying "All or nothing" thinking to *every* situation is for amateurs, nihilists and fools.

So, let's apply both of these concepts to Hillary Clinton. I think that Clinton has shown amply over the years that, whatever personal ambitions or her willingness to cash a check for speaking fees (and as an ambitious person who occasionally speaks for money, I don't see either as inherently a problem), time and again she's put herself in service. Not with 100% success and not without flaws even when successful, but there are none of us perfect, and the end result of her putting herself back into the arena again and again is that much of that service has had an impact. Her ambition and service are not just about her and what it gets her. She's done much, and at a high level, for others.

As for pragmatic—well, look. One does not work at the levels she does and has for decades without it, and if there's any ding on the Clintons as a political couple, it's their willingness to make a deal. Again, I don't see that as necessarily a bad thing, even if one's line for "acceptable deal" is elsewhere than theirs. This is definitely a "your mileage may vary" sort of thing, but I'm okay with the mileage I get out of it.

Independent of anything else, Clinton is an attractive presidential candidate for me for the reasons noted above. Service and pragmaticism go a long way for me. In the context of where the GOP is right now, and who they are fielding as their candidate this cycle, it's not even a contest. In the case of John McCain and Mitt Romney, the two previous GOP presidential candidates, even as I disliked their overall policies and plans for the country, I could not say they had not acted in service to their communities and country, or that they didn't have the ability to be pragmatic when being pragmatic was what was needed. I can't say that about Trump. There's nothing in his past actions that suggests he's in this life for anyone but himself.

But Hillary Clinton is—is *what*, exactly? A criminal? Corrupt? Dishonest? Evil? Terrible? Awful? A bitch? Satan in a pantsuit ensemble? As I've noted before, a quarter century of entirely outsized investigations into her life and actions have come up with nothing criminal or found corruption that rises to indictable levels. As for the rest of it, whatever Clinton's own personal characteristics, she also had the misfortune of stepping into the political spotlight concurrent to the GOP wholesale adopting the Gingrich playbook of demonizing the opposition. She's had an entire political party and its media apparatus spending two full decades telling the world she's a bitch, and evil, and a criminal. It's still happening; the Republican National Convention resounded with the words *lock her up, lock her up, lock her up.* And yet *she is still here.* She is still in service. Now, you can see that as ego or delusion or the inability to take a hint. I see it as an unwillingness to yield the floor to those whose political playbook is simply "demonize your opponent," with the rest to be figured out later.

(And make no mistake—should Clinton win the presidency, the fury isn't going away. The GOP is all in this year with sexism and bigotry and hate, and at this point it has no other gear; it literally cannot do otherwise without entirely losing its primary voter base. This is what the Gingrich playbook has gotten the GOP. It's made them fury addicts, and the withdrawal symptoms are as likely to kill them as not.)

Maybe ultimately the issue is that she's not likable, i.e., she's not the candidate you'll have a beer with. Well, now there's Tim Kaine for that if that's important to you; he'll have a beer with you, and if you have too many he'll take your keys when you're not looking, pretend to help you look for them when you're ready to go, and then let you sleep it off on the couch. But honestly, I've never gotten that whole construct. One, I don't need to have a beer with my President; I assume they have other things to do. Two, if that's a controlling aspect of your presidential decision making, I mean, if it actually *is* important to you, then you're the problem and you need to pull your head out and maybe have more relevant criteria, or at least put "beer buddy" as far down the goddamned list as possible.

And three, says who? I don't need Clinton to be likable in order to vote for her for president, especially as I'm not likely to ever meet her and spend time with her and have late night phone calls where we gossip and share secrets. She's not my *friend.* But I also don't find her *unlikable* today, and I don't remember that ever being the baseline of my opinion of her (she's had unlikable moments, to be sure. Welcome to being human). But then, I also don't tend to think women who express opinions, or who don't feel the need to excuse their ambition or their place near the top of the power structure, are inherently unlikable. Let's not pretend that in fact that's *not* a problem, still, for a lot of people—and that this being a problem hasn't been exploited by others.

(Also, you know. Maybe it's a personal quirk, but I just don't get that invested in politicians as inspirational figures. I'm perfectly happy with them being essentially colorless and efficient and boring. Maybe even prefer it!)

At the end of the day, without reference to any other aspect of this particular presidential race, Hillary Clinton offers more than enough for me to vote for her. With reference to other aspects of this race—namely, that Donald Trump's candidacy is as close to being an actual existential threat to US democracy as we've had, possibly ever—voting for Clinton becomes not only a preference but a moral necessity. I can't *not* vote for Hillary Clinton in this election. So it's nice to know I would have been happy to vote for her, no matter what.

How I Knew
I'd Made It

Jan

31

2014

I n conversation not too long ago, someone asked me when I felt I had "made it." It's a fair question; for a writer, there are a lot of milestones that could be the points at which one feels one has made it. Selling that first book is an obvious one (selling the *second* book, a less obvious but no less relevant one), as is the first time you are nominated for an award, or win one, or hit a bestseller list, or get a starred review in the trades. Getting a movie or TV option is a big one. Seeing someone you don't know reading a book of yours out in the world. Any of these are perfectly good moments to stop and say, hey, I guess I've made it.

My moment isn't any one of those. My moment came a couple of years ago, when I was driving out of town and noticed my gas tank was almost empty. So I stopped at the gas station, slid my credit card into the pump, filled up my gas tank, replaced the nozzle, got back into my car and drove away. And then realized a couple of miles down the road that at no point did I look to see how much the gas cost per gallon, or how much the whole tank of gas cost me. I didn't look because I didn't have to. No matter how much it cost, I knew I had it. I knew I could afford it.

That was my moment.

Some of you, I suspect, are looking a bit puzzled at this. So it's here that I need to give you a bit of context.

When I wrote "Being Poor" back in 2005, the very first thing I wrote in the piece was "Being poor is knowing exactly how much everything costs." The reason I wrote that is because when you are poor, you *have* to know how much everything costs, because you know exactly how little you have to spend, and how much you need to get through your day. You have to strategize how to apply your money.

Like so: You have $10 for the whole day. Gas costs $3.12 a gallon. You have a quarter tank of gas to go somewhere 25 miles away and then get back. Do you *need* to put in more gas? How much do you *have* to put in to do what you have to do? Is the gas going to be cheaper ten miles down the road? Will you have enough left over when you've put gas in your tank to buy the other things you have to get today? Can they wait? If they can't wait, how much will you need for *them?* Will what you have left give you enough for gas? And so on.

I've seen people here in town come into the gas station and ask for very specific amounts of gas. I don't have to ask why they're asking the cashier for exactly three dollars and twenty-five cents worth of gas, or whatever amount they ask for. I know why. It's *exactly* the amount they can afford that day, and, hopefully, exactly the amount they need. They've thought it out. They've made the numbers work as well as they can. I know it because I've seen it done in my own life, growing up; the calculus of what you can afford today, what will have to wait for tomorrow and what things can be put off until the absolute last minute.

If you grow up with that sort of resource calculus as part of your daily existence, you almost never get free of it; you're always checking tallies in your head. And to be sure, in a very real sense this is not a bad thing at all—not knowing what you're spending on things is a very fine way for anyone to quickly and suddenly go broke. You *should* be keeping track of your income and outgoes. It's a basic and laudable life skill.

But I would argue that with folks who do it (or have done it) from a place of poverty, there's a difference in both degree and kind. Like your grandmother who lived through the Great Depression and never threw out a piece of string because "you never knew when it will come in handy" and therefore had a ratty ball of string no one wanted to touch, much less use, there's something pathological about poverty accounting—a need to know the *precise* cost of things and the worry that at the end of the day, no matter what you do, there's just not going to be enough. You keep track of costs not because it's a smart thing to do. You keep track of costs because you're waiting for the other shoe to drop.

I have that sensibility in my head. And again, on one hand, it's not all bad: we save a lot of the money we have come in, and I have what I think is a realistic sense of what we can afford and what we can't—and as a full-time writer, whose income is (heh) *variable*, it's good to have more than a little ingrained awareness of one's financial circumstances.

On the other hand, sometimes I wake up in the middle of the night, and for no good reason plan out a strategy for an imminent income apocalypse. *What if everything you've ever written stops selling? What if you can't sell the next book? What if Krissy loses her job? What if you can't get back into marketing and consulting? What then what then WHAT THEN?* And then I spend three hours imagining how we downsize to survive on nothing until I finally fall back asleep from mental exhaustion. When I wake up in the morning I'm fine, because rationally I know that I'm doing all right, and my writing career is unlikely to go up in a sudden, inexplicable flash. But the *WHAT THEN?* voice stays in the background, because it remembers what it was like to *have* to think about those contingency plans in one's day-to-day life.

And this is why, a couple miles down the road from the gas station, the sudden realization that I *didn't* worry about the price of gas, that I had just gassed up and went, hit me like an electric shock. I had literally never done that before. It wasn't about the not knowing the exact cost of the gas; I could find that out just by looking at my credit card statement. It was that it finally had gotten into my brain that I could *afford* things. That I didn't have to do the mental calculation of the cost of the gas from a place of anxiety. That I had the confidence that I could afford what I just spent—not the confidence intellectually, which I had, but confidence in the part of my brain that wakes me up at 3am in a panic about everything going to hell. For that part of my brain, miraculously, everything checked out.

That's when I knew I had made it.

The irony is that since then, I can't not look at the cost of the gas I'm pumping into my car, if only because I remember driving away that one time, not looking. The difference is now, when I look at the amount, it's not because my brain is having a tiny, muted but still real bit of panic about the cost. It's because I just need to know how much I spend, like any person should.

It's a small difference, and unnoticeable from the outside. But on the inside, it means that a lot has changed. It means I made it. I am grateful I have done so.

How Not to Talk
About Your Money,
Very Rich Edition

Jun

24

2014

illary Clinton: Likely to be the next president of the United States, I suspect, but in the last several days, apparently clueless about how to talk about her money, of which there is a lot, and for which her ability to get more is pretty much assured until she shuffles off this mortal coil. Complaining that she and Bill were dead broke when they left the White House was at the least slightly overdramatic, considering all the apparatus, from book contracts to speeches, that exist to allow ex-presidents and first ladies to quickly pad out their bank accounts. It's like complaining about your Ivy League law school debt when you already have a job lined up at a white shoe law firm and a clear path to partnership. Yes, you have debt; no, you're not going to have any sort of problem getting rid of it.

Likewise, noting that you pay income tax like a common troll, unlike so many other rich people, is not a great call. One, you don't get a pat on the back for paying your taxes like you're supposed to be doing. Two, if you're noting that you pay taxes on income, while other rich people pay taxes on capital gains, and that those two rates are different, **a)** it's not quite kosher to imply that other people are skirting their taxes if they're actually paying what the law requires and **b)** you're Hillary Clinton, I'm not sure how much you want to advertise that fact considering President Clinton reduced capital gains taxes while in office. Three, even if you paid full freight on your taxes, if your household net worth is reportedly upward of $100 million, I expect the best you can hope for from a statement like that is a bit of eyerolling.

Very rich people, please note: In this world of Internets and Twitters and informations at fingertips, everyone knows that you are very rich. Trying to assure everyone that you're different from all the other very rich people—and that your vast fortune is not quite like every other very rich person's vast fortune—is probably not the winning strategy you think it is. There also comes a certain point at which "working hard" is not a reasonably complete explanation for the millions one accrues in life, at least not to the millions of people who are also working hard and paying the same full freight on taxes and somehow lack the millions of dollars in income and net worth to show for it.

It's nice to be in the rare air where one can make six figures for showing up to give a speech. Don't confuse that place in the world with one that is available merely through simple "hard work." There's a lot more that goes into it than that, much of it not directly owing to one's own planning or exertions. Context, as always, matters.

If I had a net worth of nine figures or more, any time I was asked for comment about it, the short version of it would be "I have been very fortunate, and I know it." Hell, that's my standard response *now*, and I am nowhere near worth that much.

In Which I Rank the Months, Because Why Not

Oct
1
2015

In order from best to worst:

1. October: Halloween. Cool weather. Foliage.

2. May: My birthday. Spring in full bloom. Memorial Day starts summer.

3. December: Come on, it's the holidays.

4. September: Start of the school year (traditional). Football, if you care.

5. June: Summer's nice month.

6. November: The middle child of the 4th quarter. Thanksgiving in the US.

7. April: Usually Easter. Usually somewhat green.

8. January: New year, but first half feels like December's hangover.

9. February: Screw you, Valentine's Day, don't tell me how to feel.

10. July: July 4th plus two weeks of errant fireworks.

11. August: Summer's asshole month.

12. March: Drunks and mud.

INCELS AND
OTHER MISOGYNISTS

<table>
<tr><td>May</td></tr>
<tr><td>7</td></tr>
<tr><td>2018</td></tr>
</table>

Laura has a question about a regrettably hot topic of 2018:

What are your thoughts on Incels? While I think the type of guy has been around for always, their organizing and magnifying seems different and concerning.

For those of you not up on the recent news on these folks, "incel" is a term that means "involuntary celebate" and is used as a self-identifier by a certain subset of whiny misogynist man-child who believes he is owed sex by "hot" women, pretty much because he is a man and wants sex with a hot woman. When the sex with a hot woman is *somehow* not in the offing, he gets pissy about it.

And, unfortunately, sometimes murderous about it too—the recent surfacing of the term in the public consciousness occurred when one of these self-identified incels drove a van into a bunch of pedestrians in Toronto, killing several. This action, along with this fellow's self-association with "incels," prompted several deeply regrettable hand-wringing articles from conservative commentators, more or less along the line of "well, *shouldn't* we be redistributing sex, or at least sex *robots*, to these angry, congested men?" This prompted some well-deserved dragging of said commentators on social media and elsewhere, which in turn prompted some of them to attempt to qualify their previous statements, which in turn led them to digging their own holes deeper. At this point, for example, someone should gently lead the *New York Times'* Ross Douthat away from his keyboard and the internet, set him in a dandelion patch and leave him there until just about forever.

As you might be able to surmise from the previous two paragraphs, I'm not notably sympathetic either to the "incels" or to the gormlessly dim sort of straight white male commentator who rends his garments wondering how to get them sex while their victims are still fresh in their graves. As many, many, *many* people have already noted, no one has a "right" to sex, the way these fellows think about sex reduces women to objects at best and objects of contempt at worst, and all the bloviating about the abstract concept of "redistributing sex" that these oh-so-serious commentators engage in is once more objectifying women as sex-gratifying objects, just one rhetorical step removed.

(And as for "sex robots": dudes, if "incels" already don't want to fuck women they don't consider "9s" at the minimum, the idea they're going to be satisfied with an oversized silicone sleeve for their johnson is *optimistic* at best. They might consider women to be objects, but it's important to the incels that their objects are, in fact, women).

I don't tend to think of incels as a group in isolation. Rather they lay on the general misogynist scatter plot, along with "men's rights" activists, pick up artists, "men going their own way" and the sort of person who just simply believes women are inferior to men and uses their own personal set of scripture (whether based on religion or politics or "science" or some combination thereof) to justify their sexism. Gross, unapologetic misogyny has been having a moment thanks to a president who has delighted in treating women the way incels wish they could treat women, if only they had millions of dollars to get into the room with them in the first place, and then a lawyer to make them go away when they were done. It's also been helped by a shift in the sexism Overton window that, for example, allows a man who was for women being hanged for having abortions to get a plum job in a mainstream media publication until the convenient fig leaf of him lying to his editor about how serious he was in that opinion got him fired (yes, I'm aware Kevin Williamson has attempted, wailing of the chilling unfairness of it all the while, to qualify his position after the fact. Set him in the same dandelion patch as Mr. Douthat, please). So it's not exactly surprising that in this particular environment, the incels may feel their moment has come around at last, if not to get laid, then at least to be taken seriously.

I'd take incels seriously as a threat to women in particular and to people in general (the victims in Toronto were not just women), and it's important to know their pathology in order to deal with them when they're inspired to criminality. I don't in the least take them seriously as a social movement. For one thing, it's incorrectly labeled. There's very little *involuntary* about their celibacy; they're making the affirmative choice to be so by being childish misogynist assbags. *Strange* how women don't want to have anything to do with jerks who see them solely as a warm hole to stick their dicks into! Who could have foreseen this might be the case! Surely it's a *mystery of the ages* that such a thing would come to pass. And these fellows are only making their situation worse by loitering around online with others who validate their anti-social women-hating bullshit by suggesting it's neither right nor fair that they, as men, should not be able to have sex on demand from hot women. *Are we not Nice Men?* they cry, if not in unison, then in threaded harmony.

Well, no. You're *not* nice men. *Nice* men recognize the fundamental humanity and agency of women. Nice men work on themselves to become better people. Nice men understand they're not owed sex by anyone. Nice men learn to recognize that grading people on a scale based on appearance is childish and reductive and will keep you from discovering the amazingness of people as they are. Nice men are nice not as a way to get sex, but because they recognize the value of being nice in itself, for themselves. Nice men realize that "nice" means nothing if it's not attached to an actual core of kindness and decency and principle—and that kindness and decency and principle are virtues, not weaknesses. Nice men don't tally up every action they make as if they're accruing points redeemable for sticking their penis into a moist orifice. Nice men don't go whining about it when their "orifice" scheme doesn't work out as they wanted it to, and they don't blame others who neither consented to the scheme nor go along with it when it's sprung on them. Nice guys don't think consent is an impediment. Nice guys don't have to declare themselves to be "nice guys." But nice guys don't mind noting there are always ways for them to keep improving themselves and being better to and for other people.

Mind you, I don't expect anyone who identifies as an "incel" to be swayed by anything here—it's much easier to believe the problem lies with the "Chads" and "Stacies" and "Beckys" of the world, and that *I'm* a beta cuck in any event, than it is to undertake a critical examination of self and work to improve one's self as a human being, and as a result perhaps be seen as someone who someone else might wish to spend time with and affection on, and be a better person in any event. *C'est la vie.* This is, of course, their own karma.

What should anyone else do with regard to incels? Remember they are actually "volcels"—*voluntarily* celibate, because they've chosen to be crap human beings no sensible woman (or anyone else) would want to spend time with—and then leave them to their own chosen lifestyle, because apparently they would rather do that than put in the work to be attractive, engaging people. If they really *do* want to have sex with other people, they should make the effort and then take their chances like the rest of us, and it should be noted that a lot of the rest of us, having made the effort, have seen it pay off, in ways both obvious (Yay! Sex! Possibly!) and less obvious (being content with ourselves and our lives, even if and when no sex partner is in the offing).

And if they don't want to do that, well. I guess then they can just go fuck themselves.

In Which I Select a Current GOP Presidential Candidate to Vote For, 2015 Edition

Nov

23

2015

F our years ago this month, I took a look at the field of Republican candidates for the office of President of the United States and ranked them, from the one I would be least likely to vote for to the one I would be most likely to, if it came to that, (i.e., if a series of microstrokes robbed me of all sense and sensibility, because at this stage in the GOP's evolution that's the only reason I would vote for a Republican as President).

Now it's 2015 and it's time once more to do the same sort of ranking. Note that once again this election cycle I would rather take a refreshing shower of hot lava than to vote the GOP into the presidency, and so you should be aware my selections and rankings come from that point of view. Which is to say: Brace yourselves, this is not going to be pretty.

In order of the least likely (i.e., I'd rather feed my fingers to bears than to vote for this jerk) to the most likely (i.e., I won't be happy about it but I don't think he'll entirely trash the joint in four years, please don't take that as a challenge), here are my choices:

14. Mike Huckabee: As near as I can tell, what passes for Huckabee's presidential campaign is in reality a months-long audition for Pat Robertson's gig on *The 700 Club* once Robertson finally but clearly reluctantly shuffles off this mortal coil to the Hell that awaits terrible people who think they're in with God. If so, good luck, Mr. Huckabee! You'll finally become the smug and awful bigoted fossil you've always aspired to be!

13. Rick Santorum: Sadly for Santorum, there's only room for one smug and awful bigoted fossil at the bottom of the GOP polling charts, and that's Mike Huckabee, because he's got seniority. I rank Santorum slightly higher than Huckabee in my preferences, but that's like ranking "puke on your shoe" slightly higher than "bloody puke on your shoe." It's still puke on your shoe.

12. Ted Cruz: You know, I can appreciate Cruz's painfully obvious sense of manifest destiny when it comes to him and the presidency, and the fact that that every step of his life has been a direct and calculated step to that goal. Good for him! It's nice to have ambitions. However, it also hasn't escaped my notice that at every step of the way, the thing that most people apparently have to say about Cruz is "wow, what an *asshole*." I can't help but think that's kind of a telling fact. Even his fellow GOP senators think he's a real prick and don't want anything to do with him.

Leaving aside that everything that comes out of his mouth is at best meretricious claptrap that would shame even Newt Gingrich, and the fact he has no real legislative record to speak of, I think it would be good for his growth as a human being to learn that being a complete douchenozzle at every available opportunity won't, in fact, get you the highest office in the land. Humility, Mr. Cruz! It's well past time you tried some.

11. Donald Trump: The GOP establishment would like you to believe Trump was their summer fling, who in September didn't take the hint that it was over, followed the GOP back home, and now drives by its house every hour to peer through the window, and texts at 4am asking if the GOP wants to go to the local Waffle House *just to talk*.

But in reality, it's terribly unfair to Trump to suggest this has not been an *entirely consensual* affair. Fact is, the GOP has been actively looking for a populist demagogue for years, one it could control with money. The GOP's problem is that Trump *has* money—as he's very happy to tell you, as often as you would like to hear and then again a few dozen more times after that—and he's apparently perfectly happy to go full fascist, when the GOP knows you *never* go full fascist, you just hint and wink. But Trump's looking at his supporters and seeing that *they*, at least, are ready for him to go full fascist, and Trump didn't get where he is in American culture by being *subtle*, now, did he?

And here we are: With a billionaire would be oligarch who the GOP can't use its only real lever—cash—to control. And maybe they'll wash him out in the primaries, and then maybe Trump will run as an independent and take his tribe of hopped-up jingoists with him—or maybe not! Maybe he goes *all the way* with the GOP. Some summer flings just keep on going, whether they should or not.

10. Ben Carson: Carson's problem is that running for president isn't brain surgery—which is to say it involves a whole bunch of things he appears to know absolutely nothing about. While the idea of Chauncey Gardiner, MD, is compelling as a literary character, the idea of Carson's brain grinding horribly into neutral in the middle of a legitimate crisis fills me with an unholy terror. Trust him with a scalpel? Sure, probably. Trust him with The Button? Oh, let's *not*.

9. Carly Fiorina: Well, she's only the second-worst businessperson in the race, I'll give her that. But my thought is that when someone promises to run the country like they ran a company whose stock value declined by more than half and also ditched 30,000 workers while they were in charge, I should take them at their word, and run the other way.

8. Rand Paul: Every time I think of Rand Paul, I imagine that on his bedside table is a copy of *Atlas Shrugged*, the pages of which are stiff and stuck together and smell vaguely of corn chips. Then I shudder for five whole minutes and try to think of something else.

7. Marco Rubio: Rubio is these days apparently emerging as the GOP favorite for the nomination, which undoubtedly pisses Jeb Bush off to no end. Well, okay: Rubio is generically handsome and seems pleasant and is what passes for smart in the GOP these days, and I'm sure he will be perfectly happy to jump through whatever various hoops his handlers require. So he's got that going for him, which is nice.

Thing is every time I hear him talk I get the impression of a fellow who is trying very hard not to let others know he is ever so slightly in over his head and not quite managing it. Hilary Clinton's gonna gnaw on him in a debate like he's a chew toy. Can't we put him back into a cool, humidity-controlled cellar for a couple more election cycles until he's aged up a bit? No? Well, fine, then, GOP, do what you want, I'm not the boss of you.

6. Chris Christie: Angry dude with a demeanor of a schoolyard bully who may or may not be above pulling shenanigans involving a bridge to annoy people he doesn't like, and is apparently of the opinion that five-year-old Syrian refugee orphans are a clear and present danger to our country. Bless his heart.

He should not be president; he'd stroke out within the first six months, I'm certain of it. For all that, there is worse in the current field of candidates—much worse, in fact—and this is where we are here in 2015.

5 (tie). Jim Gilmore and George Pataki: Former governors, perfectly competent and utterly colorless and have no chance because "competent and colorless" is not what anyone wants these days. I mean, *I* would be okay with it, obviously given the rest of the field, which is why these guys are as far up as they are on my list, obviously. But the GOP isn't going to ask me.

This particular spot, by the way, marks the dividing line between "Things could be worse" and "Check out the Canadian immigration Web site to see if you could get in" on this list for me. I'll also note that currently none of the remaining candidates on the list are polling above 4% nationally. I am not an *actual* GOP primary voter, is what I'm saying.

3. Jeb Bush: I feel kind of sorry for Jeb Bush, because for years we've been told that he was the "smart" one, and his campaign has just been *so* flabby and disappointing and tired, and as for Jeb, if this is what passes for smart in the Bush family then we're all just going to have to admit that our standards for smart when it comes to politicians, or at least Bushes, are too damn low (search your heart. You already knew this to be true).

So why is he so high on my list of GOP candidates? One, please see *the rest of this list*, which makes the 2012 GOP clown car look like the friggin' Athenian Agora, and two, because Jeb may be tired and listless and doesn't actually give any indication of running for any other reason but familial obligation, but he's also got *infrastructure*, i.e., two previous presidential administrations worth of resources to pick and choose from to keep the nation going despite him. I mean, shit, even *W.* couldn't sink the country, and he put *real effort* into it. Jeb literally could not be any worse. His people will see to that.

On the other hand, if Bush lets a Cheney within 700 miles of him or his proposed administration I *swear to God* I will literally shove *all my money* into a Hillary Clinton SuperPAC. Don't make me do it, Jeb.

2. Lindsey Graham: Apparently a decent human being, has a record of reasonable bipartisanship and is what passes for a moderate these days, and his current polling in the field is at, like, 1%. Which makes him almost perfect for the likes of me. I suspect he'll get some nice speaking gigs out of this run. Good for him.

1. John Kasich: He's cranky and too conservative for my tastes and he's got a hard-on for defunding Planned Parenthood here in Ohio (not to mention an attempted union-bust which required a citizen initiative to smack back) and he said a genuinely dumbass thing about opening a government office for Judeo-Christian values like he's never heard of the Establishment Clause before *and* has shamefully said he doesn't want Syrian refugees *and yet* I look around at who is running in the GOP field this year, and Kasich is one of the few I trust not to run the whole country into the ground either through incompetence or ideological rigidity, or both.

Part of it is that at least some of his crankiness is directed at his own party and its current slate of candidates, which appear to strike him as fumbling doofuses. He's not wrong. Part of it is that he hasn't been entirely horrible for Ohio, and occasionally signals that there's an actual working brain inside of that suit. Which sounds like faint praise, and it *is*, but look: This is 2015 and we're grading on a *very serious curve,* here. Kasich is the best we're getting out of the GOP in this election cycle. So of course he's polling at 3% nationally and I wouldn't give him much of a chance in the primaries, just like my 2012 first choice, Jon Huntsman. I'm sorry, John Kasich—by choosing you, I've probably doomed your candidacy.

Be that as it may: If I had to vote for one of these folks, he is the one I'd vote for. May God have mercy on him. May God have mercy on us all.

IT'S OVER, BERNIE SANDERS FANS. LET IT GO.

May

19

2016

Bernie Sanders is not going to be president, nor is he going to be the Democratic candidate for President of the United States. To date, he has won fewer electoral contests, pledged delegates and total votes than Hillary Clinton, and in each of these cases the margins aren't close. While it is *technically* possible for Sanders to close the gap with Clinton in the nine contests remaining, from a practical point of view it's impossible. In order to pull ahead in pledged delegates, Sanders would have to win something like 70% of all remaining delegates; given that he is substantially behind in polling in California and New Jersey, the two largest remaining contests, this is extremely unlikely.

Even when Sanders wins, he doesn't win by enough—his win in Oregon, for example, netted him only nine pledged delegates over Clinton, which leaves her 272 delegates ahead. To be clear, and as I've said before, Hillary Clinton doesn't *have* to win any more states to win the Democratic nomination for President of the United States; all she has to do is not lose too widely. If Sanders could win all nine remaining contests—which he won't—Clinton would still end up with an overall larger number of pledged delegates and votes, so long as the contests were close enough, *close enough* in this case being a margin less than 68%-32%.

Bernie Sanders is not going to going to be president, nor is he going to be the Democratic candidate for President of the United States. I know it. Clinton knows it. Most disinterested observers know it. Sanders himself almost certainly knows it, because he is not a stupid man. He's being beaten, fair and square, in contests, pledged delegates and vote counts, even before things like superdelegates are added into the mix. The only people who don't seem to know it are some of Sanders' supporters.

Or, to be more accurate, a number of Sanders' supporters are aware he's losing, but are under the impression that the reason he's losing is because of nefarious action and the game being "rigged," rather than, simply, he's won fewer contests, pledged delegates and overall votes than Hillary Clinton. Why? Because apparently these supporters just really really *really* want Sanders to win, and because he isn't ahead there has to be something else at play than more Democratic primary voters preferring Hillary Clinton to their man.

This is not to say Clinton hasn't been the preferred candidate of the Democratic establishment all along; she clearly has been. But then again, Jeb Bush was the preferred candidate of the Republican establishment this cycle, and look where that got him. You can be the preferred candidate and still have things go south. Heck, Clinton was the establishment candidate of 2008, too—she took her campaign into June, just like Sanders plans to, and still lost, to Barack Obama. Being the establishment candidate doesn't mean much if at the end of the day someone else wins more contests, delegates and total votes than you do.

Sanders has won fewer contests, pledged delegates and overall votes than Clinton and has done so consistently since the start of the primary season; Clinton's been ahead in all three since February 20 and the Nevada caucus, unless you think there was some skullduggery involved there, in which case she's been ahead since February 27. It is pretty much impossible that Clinton won't come into the Democratic convention in Philadelphia with more pledged delegates and total votes than Sanders. Sanders' team and his supporters are floating the idea that at the convention they will try to dislodge the superdelegates currently declared for Clinton to bring them to their side and win the candidacy that way. But this would require the superdelegates to ignore the fact that Hillary Clinton was the clearly preferred candidate of both the overall Democratic primary voters, and won more pledged delegates than Sanders. Why would they do that? Why *should* they do that?

The answer for a number of Sanders supporters seems to be, basically, *well, because we really really really want it, and we should get what we want*. And I guess it's *nice* that you really really want something, but, look: Sanders has won fewer contests, pledged delegates and overall votes than Clinton, and we don't always get what we really really want, and sometimes you just have to suck it up and be a goddamned *grown up* about that fact.

And then you start thinking, well, if I can't have this thing I really, really want, what *can* I have? At this point, truculent Sanders supporters, either you can have someone in the White House who voted with your preferred candidate 93% of the time when they were both in the Senate, and who generally wants most of the same things your candidate wants (albeit in slightly more establishment ways), or you can have Donald Trump, who isn't the buffoon you think he is (or, more accurately, isn't *just* the buffoon you think he is), who just released a list of potential Supreme Court candidates that reads like a wish list for the reactionary right, and who will soon have the entire apparatus of the GOP chugging away for him because the GOP would rather be in the White House with an ignorant, racist buffoon than not be in the White House at all. And while I suppose a number of you would rather be "principled" and say, *my guy or let it all burn*, my friends, it will indeed *all* burn, and you will be trapped in the fire with the rest of us.

(Yes, you can also go third party, and vote for either Jill Stein of the Green Party or Gary Johnson in the Libertarian Party, etc. Have fun! But if it gets to October and the polls are depressingly close, let the specter of Ralph Nader remind you that third party votes offered primarily for protest have consequences in our political system. Yes, that sucks. Doesn't change the fact.)

In 2008, right around this time in the election cycle, I wrote a piece about how Hillary Clinton, who was clearly not going to be the Democratic candidate that time around, but whose team and followers were thinking of certain parliamentary calisthenics which will sound familiar to Sanders supporters right about now, should let it go. She didn't listen, of course; she slogged on through to June. Here in 2016, Bernie Sanders is not going to be the Democratic candidate, either. He, too, should let it go. I don't expect him to listen, either. But this time the people I want to listen are his more fevered followers. Guys, you have to get ready for him not to win. He might win concessions in the platform, which would be groovy. But that's as far as it's going to go. He's not going to be president, and he's not going to be the Democratic candidate.

And when all is said and done, there will still be the general election. It's going to be Clinton versus Trump. You're going to have to decide what you really want for the next four years at least. It's going to matter what you choose. Not just for yourself but for everyone else.

Jacqueline Kahn

<table>
<tr><td>Jun</td></tr>
<tr><td>8</td></tr>
<tr><td>2015</td></tr>
</table>

My friend Jacqueline Kahn died yesterday morning. I want to tell you a little bit about her, and what she meant to me.

First, you have to know that in the 4th grade, I broke my leg. I broke it by hitting a moving Ford Pinto. Technically I was at a cross walk so I was not at fault, but there was a parked car directly in front of me and I ran out into the street, and the poor man who hit me couldn't have possibly stopped in time. Regardless, my leg was well and truly smashed up, and I was in a cast and wheelchair for a big chunk of my 4th grade year.

The folks at my school decided it was not a great idea to have me tooling around the playground in a wheelchair, so for recess and lunchtimes I was carted into the school office, where Jackie was working, I believe, as a receptionist/secretary. I was ten and very very very chatty, so naturally I spent a lot of time blathering in her direction. Jackie, to her credit, was kind to me and talked back, rather than just genially ignoring me. Later, when my leg healed, I in my ten-year-old egotism thought that she would be sad that I was no longer there, so every day after that, as I headed to the bus to take me home, I would stop in and tell her a joke before I left.

I did that every single day through the end of my sixth grade year, my last year at elementary school. Most of the jokes were terrible. Jackie, bless her, continued to be kind to me.

And more than that. My mother went through a terrible divorce early in my sixth grade year, after which my mother, sister and I were briefly homeless, and then moved several times in the course of that last year, to cities other than Covina, which is where my school was. When we moved out of Covina, I should have no longer been able to attend Ben Lomond, the elementary school I was in. But of course I didn't want that, and my mother didn't want that, and I'm pretty sure that my mother didn't go out of her way to tell anyone we had moved. But sooner or later it got out, and I think there was some question about whether or not I would be able to continue at Ben Lomond.

What happened then, as I understand it, is that Jackie said that if I was made to leave the school, she would quit her job.

And that was that. I stayed.

I didn't know any of this at the time, of course. I learned about it much later. But I can't tell you how important it was. As I said: Rough divorce, homelessness, and shuttling around to several houses, all in the space of a few months. We were terribly poor and because my mother had to find work where she could, when she could, I and my sister were left alone to our own devices a lot of the time. What stability I had— honestly, the one place I could depend on *not* suddenly changing—came from my elementary school, where I had Jackie, my teachers (particularly Keith Johnson, my 6th grade teacher) and my friends. If I were to have lost that, among everything else I lost, I couldn't tell you how I would have dealt with it. I suspect I would have dealt with it poorly. So I think I can say without exaggeration that Jackie's act saved me, in ways I wasn't aware of at the time, but am aware of now.

Jackie's kindness to me didn't stop once I left elementary school. We became friends and she was someone I depended on. She stayed in contact with me in junior high and high school. She took me to movies—a lot of movies, and good movies because she was a film buff—and let me visit her house, where she kept Corgis before Corgis were cool. In many ways she made me part of her extended family. I knew it and loved it, and thought of her in so many ways as another grandmother, equal to, and in most ways one I was closer to, than my own actual grandmothers.

In high school she read my stories and came to all the plays I was in. When I went off to college I would come back on holidays to see her and say hello. When it became clear Krissy and I were a serious item, I took her to Jackie's house so she could meet her (she approved). She was there for my wedding. When I moved away she kept in touch with me through e-mail, sharing her own writing (she was a playwright, and a pretty good one) and keeping me up to date with her family, as I kept her up to date with mine. When my very first book came out, in 2000, I co-dedicated the book to her. She liked that. I knew she was proud of me and the life I've made.

And now she's gone.

I had advance warning of this day, so I was able to prepare for it, which I think in many ways was a kindness. She was so important to me that having the news cold would have come like a hammer blow. Instead I had time to think of her and the totality of her life and everything I owe to her, in ways obvious and not so obvious, so that when this final door closed I could feel, not pain, but joy in a life that was well-lived and was generous enough to encompass me in it.

Jacqueline Kahn was a woman who was good to me as a child, a friend to me as an adult, and always, a home spirit—someone I knew cared for me, no matter what, and with whom I felt safe, and cherished, and loved. I love her, and will miss her, and will carry her and her kindness in my heart all of my days.

All my love now goes to her family, and to all of those who knew her and cared for her, and for whom she cared. May her memory be a blessing to each of them.

And thank you for letting me share a little bit of who she was with you. When you see me, you see a little bit of her in me. I'm glad of that. She was the best of people.

JIAN GHOMESHI
AND THE
WOMEN HE KNEW

Oct
31
2014

S ome thoughts on Jian Ghomeshi, about whom I feel entitled to opine because I was once a guest on his show—talking about the little fundraising thing I did last year which included RAINN, an interview which now in retrospect is sadly ironic.

(For those of you not up on this, Mr. Ghomeshi was a radio show host in Canada, who was let go by the CBC because of then-mysterious reasons. Mr. Ghomeshi took to Facebook to allege that he was fired because he participated in consensual BDSM play which was now being used against him by vengeful exes, and sued CBC for "breach of confidence and bad faith." Since then a number of women have come forward to allege totally non-consensual abuse and/or harassment at the hands of Mr. Ghomeshi.)

So, a numbered list.

1. There's nothing wrong with consensual BDSM play; if that's your thing and you can get other people to go along with it in a safe and consenting manner, then you kids have fun with that.

2. Suddenly smacking the hell out of someone and/or choking them without prior discussion or agreement is pretty much the *opposite* of consensual BDSM play, now, isn't it. (Note: this is a rhetorical question. The answer is: Yes, it is the opposite.)

3. As a matter of law (to the extent that I know anything about Canadian/Ontario provincial law, which I don't so I might be entirely wrong), Mr. Ghomeshi is innocent until proven guilty.

4. The procedurally laudable governmental presumption of innocence *does not mean*, however, that as a matter of opinion, one cannot believe the allegations against Mr. Ghomeshi. As a matter of personal opinion, I believe the women who are coming forward and saying that Mr. Ghomeshi attacked, abused and harassed them. I could be wrong, but I don't really think that I am.

5. I think it's possible that Mr. Ghomeshi deluded himself into thinking these attacks equated to consensual sexual play, which is both not an excuse at all, and a good argument for availing one's self of educators in that particular field who can teach one how to do one's play safely and to know what "consensual" actually means. However, I think it's rather more likely that Mr. Ghomeshi, who is a full-fledged adult and someone with some evident facility for words, was in fact quite aware that what he was doing was not in the least consensual and relied on his position at the top of the Canadian cultural heap to protect him from the consequences of his actions, as indeed it appears to have done for a very long time.

6. If what is alleged against Mr. Ghomeshi is true, and to reiterate I rather strongly suspect that it is, then his being fired from the CBC is, bluntly, the least worst thing that could happen to him at this point. If the allegations are true, he deserves a stint in prison, full stop, end of sentence.

7. It was canny of Mr. Ghomeshi to try to frame his assaults in the context of BDSM, but also disingenuous and false. BDSM is not my thing, but I know a lot of people for whom it is. None of them would see what Mr. Ghomeshi did as something relating to their particular kink. Attacking someone without their consent isn't about sexual gratification, it's about the assertion of power—the ability to say "I can do this to you and there's *nothing* you can do about it." And sure, maybe Mr. Ghomeshi got a *rise* out of that, too. But at the end of the day choking a woman who is not consenting to the experience and saying it's BDSM is akin to stabbing someone in a bar and claiming it was a martial arts test match. Again, BDSM isn't my thing, but it's a thing I know enough about to know that what Mr. Ghomeshi was doing wasn't that.

8. The irony of the above point is that if it really *was* about BDSM (which it was not), then there was no reason for any of that to happen. What little I know about BDSM is that those who enjoy it are happy to share and to teach and to provide a safe space for that enthusiasm. Mr. Ghomeshi, I am certain, would not have lacked for willing, consenting partners—if this *was* really about consensual sexual exploration and enjoyment. But, again, I don't really think it was ever about that.

9. I don't know Mr. Ghomeshi other than through a very brief professional encounter. I don't envy the people who *do* know him who are now learning about the allegations and who suspect that they are true. What do you do with a friend like that? Do you drop him? Do you maintain he is your friend but acknowledge what he's done is wrong? Do you fight for your friend, right or wrong? I don't have any answers for this one. I know what I think I would want to do; I don't know if it's what I *would* do because I've never had to be in this situation. What I can say is that I hope I never am in this situation.

10. To reiterate, because it's important: I believe the women who have come forward to allege assault and harassment. It's been noted by other people better able to testify on the subject that one of the most radical things you can do when a woman speaks up about abuse and harassment is to believe her. Which initially seems like an incredible statement to someone like me, who is almost always believed by default when he chooses to speak up about something. I have that luxury. Not everyone does. It's a fact I strongly suspect Mr. Ghomeshi knew, and used.

John Boehner's
Stepping Down

Sep

25

2015

And honestly, can you blame him? He's had to ride herd on an increasingly dysfunctional GOP Caucus in the House for four years now, a group that sees actually shutting down the government to get its way as just another political tactic. That's got to have taken its toll on the man, who I believe at his heart does see government needing to be useful, even if he and I have rather different ideas about what "useful" means in this case. It can't be *fun* being Speaker of the House these days. There's less chaos in a kindergarten, and at least when you're in charge of a kindergarten, when everyone's cranky, you can make them take a nap.

So now he's done, or will be soon—he's resigning at the end of October as I understand it. I've seen people wondering if the Pope, who spoke to Congress yesterday and whose presence in Congress Boehner has apparently worked toward for years (ironic he got his wish with this particular pope, but even so), might have been an influence on what seems like a sudden decision to resign. I don't suspect directly, no. I don't think the Bishop of Rome pulled him aside and said, "dude, what are you doing? Get out while you can," but I think Boehner may have felt that this particular event was a highlight of his tenure and maybe it was time to go out on a high note, and while he was still young enough (he's 65) to do something else with his life. I think maybe it crystallized his thinking, as in, *why* not *leave now?* It's a valid question.

I don't think Boehner's departure from the Speaker position is going to do the House GOP or the GOP in general any good. I suspect whoever replaces him will be to Boehner's right and more willing to use the House as a bludgeoning tool to get their way, which will be an interesting dynamic coming into an election year, and I use "interesting" in all its connotations. Right now the House GOP is on the verge of shutting down the government over Planned Parenthood; even if they dodge this particular bullet it will likely be by a stop gap measure that means there will likely be another possible government shutdown a few months down the line. The optics of shutting down the government are never good, and it's better-than-even odds that the next House speaker won't have the wit to recognize this. We'll see.

I live in Boehner's district and I'll be very interested to see who replaces him, both short- and long-term. Boehner's been the representative here since 1991 and he's never gotten less than 61% of the vote (his first election), and there hasn't been a Democrat in the OH-8 seat since the Depression. This seat is so safe the Democrats didn't even run someone against him in 2012. Everyone including me assumed that he'd be in that seat until he was rolled out on a gurney. That being the case, I don't think anyone's been lurking in the wings. I mean, I'm sure someone *is*, in some way; I just don't have the slightest idea who it might be. In one sense it doesn't matter, since the GOP could run a dead raccoon in this district and it would still get 60% of the vote. But in another sense, well. Boehner was actually a good fit for OH-8, politically: rock-ribbed Republican rather than unhinged reactionary. I'm mildly worried whoever comes in will be more of the latter than the former.

People have jokingly suggested that now would be a fine time for me to enter public service; my response is thanks, no. I have no ambition to be a US Representative, for many reasons, among them that I would have less time for writing and also because while franking privileges are a compelling perk, overall the pay/perks package is not as good as what I get now. Also, the idea that what I would actually be doing with most of my time is begging for money from people who want me to vote their way, i.e., institutionalized bribe-seeking, depresses the shit out of me. I'm not a fan of the job as it functions today, basically; it seems very far away from what it's supposed to be, which would be me acting as an actual representative of the people who live in the district.

But even if I *were* interested in the job, I'm unelectable in OH-8. I'm not a Democrat, so I don't have that strike against me (I'm registered independent), but I am generally what passes for liberal in the United States. OH-8 is religious and conservative; an agnostic pro-choice dude who believes the rich aren't being taxed enough is gonna be a hard sell. I'm not going to bother to make it. I have other things to do, and I like those other things I have to do. So, sorry, folks: Not running. Try to contain your disappointment.

As for Boehner, I hope that he does something other than become just another lobbyist. He and I don't have a lot in common politically, but he generally seems to be a decent human being who means well and tried to do what he saw as best for his district, his nation and Congress. He's still young enough to do something more with that impulse. I'd like to see him do that.

Trump, and His Jokes, and You

Aug

10

2016

I write funny things professionally, and have done for years. I've made a fair amount of money and even won some awards for funny things I've written. So as a professional writer of funny things I have thoughts on Donald Trump's oblique joke yesterday about how great it would be if a gun nut assassinated Hillary Clinton and/or some of the judges she might appoint. As with many examinations of humor, this will *not* be particularly funny. You have been warned.

1. Of course Trump's comment was a joke, and as someone who has told more than his share of inappropriate jokes to his later regret, I'm pretty sure I can model Trump's brain process to getting there. He's up on stage, he's pissed off that he's losing, he's with a sympathetic crowd that *wants* him to say something punchy, and he has no goddamn filter at all, because why would he, his brand is "I say what I think" and his brand has gotten him this far. So out of the woodwork of his brain comes the clever observation that well, *actually*, some jackass with a gun *could* offer up a lead veto to Clinton and/or her judges, and out it went through his teeth. Trump didn't give it any more thought than that: *pop!* into his head, *push!* out of his mouth. Maybe three tenths of a second from conception to utterance, if that. This is was not a statement he'd been consciously planning months to say.

Was it a joke? Sure. Was it funny? Like most jokes, it depends on whether you're the audience for it. It didn't work for me. Should Trump have said it? Immaterial, since it was said.

Should it be excused as "just a joke"?

Well, but, see. Here's the thing about *that*: There's no such thing as "just a joke," and Trump of all people knows that.

2. The first problem with saying "it's just a joke" is that people very often use that phrase to mean "I get to say/enjoy a horrible thing without penalty." Well, as a professional writer of funny things, I feel perfectly within my rights to call bullshit on that. Jokes don't come out of nowhere. They are the product of a presumably thinking brain just like any other speech, and like any other speech they are susceptible to the same scrutiny and criticism. Just like any other speech the context of the joke is useful, too.

So here's the context of *that* joke: Donald Trump is a man who has pursued the presidency through racism and white nationalism and by insinuating criminal activity on the part of his opponents (or their families), who has encouraged foreign agents to subvert the US election process (another "joke") and who is actively training his base of support—angry and scared white people, many of whom have a nearly-fanatical attachment to their firearms—to consider the election process rigged if it does not produce the result they want. Then, at a political rally, as the GOP candidate for president, while speaking about the 2nd Amendment and arguing how his opponent Hillary Clinton wants to get rid of it—to get rid of his angry white supporters' firearms!—he drops a little joke about how, well, *actually*, they *could* oppose her, nod nod, wink wink.

Trump wasn't making a private joke with friends in the comfort of his own ridiculously baroque home. He wasn't writing satire (which is often not funny) or black humor in the pages of, say, the *New Yorker*. He wasn't on the stage of a comedy club trying out five minutes of edgy new material in front of a half-drunk midnight crowd who are there to see someone else anyway. He wasn't putting it in the comments of his liberal friend's Facebook post about gun control. He wasn't doing any of those things—although even if he *were*, he could still be held accountable for his words. Rather, he was, as the GOP candidate for president, at a rally of his supporters, in a race he is currently far behind in, joking about someone killing off Hillary Clinton, or whomever she appoints as a judge. He wasn't there to make comedy. He was there, quite literally, as a political statement. *That's* the context.

3. *What, politicians can't make jokes?* Well, speaking professionally, it's usually better when they *don't.* They can't all be Ann Richards. Every time Hillary Clinton attempts humor my desire to vote for her goes down a tenth of a percent. I don't want or need my politicians to be funny. I need them to wonk out on unsexy topics like water rights and trade deals, and represent the interests of their constituencies. That's the gig, not killing it for ten minutes at The Comedy Store.

That said, sure, if politicians *can* make jokes, why not? Yuk away. But again, jokes aren't Get Out of Jail Free cards for saying horrible things. And when the jokes are, in fact, saying horrible things, like when the GOP candidate for president pops one off about maybe someone assassinating the Democratic candidate for president because of her alleged position on the 2nd Amendment, it's all right to haul the joke out into the light and begin the utterly unfunny process of picking it apart to see what's really going on there.

Why can't you just let a joke be a joke? Because, to repeat, and as others have noted, it's never *just* a joke. Jokes mean things, just like any other kind of speech. In fact, jokes often have greater *impact*, because jokes aim for the pleasure centers of our brain, not the analytical centers. The *information* of a joke hits in a place where you have fewer defenses against it, and fewer walls barring it from sinking into your overall worldview. This is why, among other things, you probably laugh at things you know you shouldn't laugh at. It's also why you're probably quicker to excuse the content of a joke—*it's just a joke!*—or to minimize the importance of what's being said within one. *How bad can it be if it made me laugh?* And also, *if the joke is saying something horrible, what does it say about me?* You have a vested interest either way in explaining away your reaction.

Trump is not a great politician—indeed, if this election cycle has done anything, it has reminded us that the oft-derided skills of being a great politician are in fact useful and needed—but he is a marvelous bully, and like any gifted bully, he's aware of how to use humor for its manipulative qualities. This is why he mocks his opponents and gives them silly names, why he says outrageous things, planned or unprompted and then immediately wraps them in the rhetoric of humor, and why all his defenders are instructed and prompted to explain away the jokes. *He's not the problem,* you're *the problem if you can't take a joke.* No one wants to be accused of not being able to take a joke.

4. This is where once again I put on my hat as a writer of funny things to tell you the following:

It's okay not to be able to take a joke.

It's okay to think a joke is not funny.

It's okay to focus more on the content of a joke than the delivery.

It's okay to hold a joke to the same standard as any other speech, and to pay attention to the context in which it is delivered.

It's okay to be scared of a joke and the joke-teller. Sometimes that's the right thing to be.

Finally and perhaps most importantly:

Always question the motives of the person who is telling you "it's just a joke."

Why? Because, well, why are they saying that? Sometimes it's because the person is a comedian, trying to convince you they're funny (pro tip: if you have to convince someone you're funny, you're probably not funny to them). Sometimes the person who told the joke realizes they just stepped in it, and is trying to backtrack without making themselves look too much like an asshole. Sometimes the person is gaslighting you, trying to make you doubt yourself, for their own purposes. And sometimes that person is trying to normalize hateful rhetoric—or keep hateful rhetoric normalized—and is trying to make you defensive about seeing it clearly as what it is: hateful.

A person saying "it's just a joke" isn't always an asshole. But assholes are almost always happy to say "it's just a joke" to make it look like the problem here is you. So when someone says "it's just a joke" to you, that's your cue for skepticism. Jokes mean things. Anyone who tells you otherwise either doesn't understand the uses of humor, or is hoping that you don't.

5. You are not automatically a bad person if you laugh at horrible things or find funny a joke whose content, on reflection, is not funny at all. You are a human being, and a skilled communicator—and Trump, for one, is a very skilled communicator—is going to play the changes on you. You might laugh because of the delivery. You might laugh because as a human you like the pleasure of laughing. You might laugh *because* of the context of the joke, or *because* it's subversive, or because the butt of the joke is someone you dislike. You might laugh because the person telling you the joke is someone you admire. You might laugh because it's expected. You might laugh because not laughing might be noticed. You might laugh because honestly you don't know what else to do. You might laugh because it's not safe to do anything else.

Laughing at a horrible joke is not the problem. Excusing that hateful and horrible joke as "just a joke" *is* the problem. The pleasure of humor doesn't mitigate the damage it can do when the hate it offers slips into someone's worldview, or simply reconfirms the hate they already hold. You're not automatically a bad person if you laugh along with hate. You're a bad person if you walk along with it. Humor makes it easy to take that walk. It's up to you to resist moving your feet. The more you resist, the more you'll recognize that hate actually isn't all that funny.

6. Trump made a joke about someone assassinating his political opponent, or the judges she might appoint. Trump's minions and enablers have been scurrying around trying to spin it, or mitigate it, or accuse people of misunderstanding it and *anyway* it was just a throwaway line, *it was just a joke*. But context matters and who is making the joke matters. Trump is a bigot and he's ignorant and he is a buffoon and he has no filter but he is not entirely stupid. He knows when he puts things out into the air that they are heard and that they are taken seriously. Even the jokes. *Especially* the jokes.

Trump wished out loud that someone would assassinate Hillary Clinton because inside, the screaming tantrum-throwing infant that Trump is wants her out of the way, and so does the slightly more grown-up version of him whose business model includes cheating contractors and workers out of their contractually-obliged fees and wages, and so does the 70-year-old version who has spent decades getting his way, who wiped the floor with the laughable opposition he had in the GOP primaries and sees no reason why he should do anything different than before, and is possibly confused as to why it's not working any more, so just *try harder*. Does Trump actively want Clinton *dead?* No.

But *out of the way* covers a whole lot of ground. Trump is a bully and he knows how to phrase a wish. So when that wish came howling out of his id up there on stage yesterday, he wrapped it into a joke and sent it on its way.

Trump made the joke because he knows, better than almost anyone, that there is no such thing as "just a joke." He knows it, and the fact he knows it, and made the joke anyway, should scare the shit out of you.

As should this: When Donald Trump is president, he won't have to make jokes anymore.

LOATHING IS A
STRONG WORD TO
APPLY TO ONE'S SELF

Dec

18

2013

I n a piece over at Salon this week, it's argued that writers have self-loathing "in the blood." Well, I'm a writer, and my blood is self-loathing-free, as is my liver and indeed in any other organ or part of my body (including the brain, which I suspect is ultimately the relevant organ under discussion here). As a result I am more than vaguely annoyed by the declaration above.

This is not to say that on more than one occasion I have not had doubts or concerns about my writing—the thing that writers do when they're in the middle of writing a book and they think to themselves *okay, honestly, I have no idea what I'm doing and that's going to be obvious to anyone who reads this thing* is something that happens to me, oh, a lot. I have concerns about whether my reach exceeds my grasp, whether what I'm writing compares well to what I've written before, and what the response to the work will be. I think this is both normal and probably healthy—the ability to criticize one's own work is often key to having work that doesn't entirely suck.

But none of that is about self-loathing. Self-criticism is "what I am writing right now isn't good, and I need to find a way to make it better." Self-loathing is "what I am writing right now isn't good, I suck, I have always sucked and I have neither the talent nor the ability to write this, I should never have tried and why did I ever think I was any good at writing at all." Even more simply put, it's the difference between "this writing sucks" and "I suck." Personally speaking I think one of these is helpful; the other one really is not. It's also not helpful to confuse the two.

Are there writers who are self-loathing? Absolutely, because there are *people* who are self-loathing, and writers are a subset of people. There are also doctors who are self-loathing, plumbers who are self-loathing, farmers who are self-loathing and so on. There are also writers who are not self-loathing. There are excellent writers who grapple with self-loathing; there are excellent writers who don't (there are mediocre and terrible writers in each category as well, of course). Trying to typify all writers as self-loathing is as useful as typifying all writers as anything, save the base, practical definition of "someone who writes."

Speaking personally, I am not a self-loathing writer primarily because I am not a self-loathing sort of person in general. I have my tics and neuroses, and as noted above I have a healthy regard for my fallibility as a writer, in terms of quality of output (I try not to inflict the bad stuff on the rest of the world). But fundamentally I am okay with myself, and I am fortunate that the construction of my brain doesn't neurochemically incline me toward depression and/or self-loathing.

Also, and this is important, while writing is a very big part of who I am, it is not *absolutely central* to my idea of myself—which is to say, when I have a stretch of poor or indifferent writing, I don't see it as an existential plebiscite on who I am as a human being. It just means I'm writing poorly at the moment. Hopefully I will snap out of it.

Finally, with regard to writing, my ability to do so and its relation to me as a worthwhile human being, the fact that I've been writing professionally for coming on to a quarter of a century now assures me that this is in fact something I can do pretty well. At this point in time any feelings of impostor syndrome (the neurotic underling of self-loathing) would pretty much be a luxury. All that time also reinforces to me the idea that writing is a learned skill and a trade—which is again separate from who I am as a person.

I think people who are writers and who are also the sort to self-loathe can possibly use that self-loathing as a tool in some way, but personally I suspect if you're genuinely deep in the throes of self-loathing, as a writer or whomever, your first stop should be a doctor, to see if that's something that's treatable. It might be easier to deal with the writing that sucks if you're not thinking that therefore, *you* suck.

ME AND
REPUBLICANS

May

13

2015

G. B. Miller asks:

From what I've read, you seem to be progressive Democrat with a distaste for Republicans. Has there/will there be a time where a Republican, on any level, will do something that might momentarily soften your distaste for the Republican party?

Heh.

One, I'm not a Democrat. I've been registered as an independent for as long as I've been a voter. Two, I've voted for Republicans as recently as the last election, for local offices where I believed they were the best-qualified candidates. Three, the last actual politician I donated money to was Jon Huntsman, in the belief that even if I was not a Republican, as a citizen of the US, it behooved me to encourage the Republicans to nominate for president someone who was not ridiculously out there. It didn't do him much good, alas, nor the Republicans.

Four, I'm not at all sure I qualify as a genuine "progressive." I will certainly allow that to folks on the right, I look like a progressive, but then, for a lot of folks on the right, Obama looks like dyed-in-the-wool socialist, rather than what he is, which is a technocratic centrist with just a little lean to the left. Obama being called a socialist causes actual socialists a nasty case of hives, as I understand. With the exception that I was for same-sex marriage well before he was, overall I'm probably a smidge to the right of Obama. As I am fond of saying to people, in the days of yore, the politics I have today would have qualified me to be a "Rockefeller Republican." Which is to say I didn't leave the GOP; the GOP left me. When I was, like, *eleven*.

(If you want another perspective on my politics, ask lefties from outside the United States, i.e., where there *is* still a genuine political left, if I seem like a lefty to them. I suspect most of them would position me as center-to-center-right; in other words, the guy who is wrong in a lot of his politics but doesn't make an ass of himself about it at family gatherings.)

What marks me as a "progressive" these days is the fact I'm for same-sex marriage and am pro-choice, which are positions that could be equally "libertarian," if "libertarian" hadn't somehow transmuted itself into "reactionary conservative" here in the US lately, and the fact that I am both for having the United States have a slightly better social net and infrastructure than it does (which is a "liberal" position) and that it should actually pay for those services/infrastructure rather than deficit finance them (which is a "conservative" position), and that probably the best way to do that is punt up the marginal rate a bit on the high end because those of us on the high end (Hi! I'm the 1%!) can afford it. There are other fiddly details but that's the gist of it.

Bluntly: if that's a "progressive" viewpoint, there's something *very wrong* with the definition of "progressive." In a world where the politics of the moment weren't ridiculously skewed, these positions would be "moderate" at best. Equally bluntly: I'm a well-off, white, middle-aged dude who likes being comfortable and likes his country genially middle-class. I *should not* be seen as *anywhere* near the vanguard of leftist politics in this country. That I am seen to be so really *is* a problem, both for the left and for the right.

The county I live in is overwhelmingly Republican and/or conservative; I get along with nearly everyone here on a day-to-day basis, even if I vote differently than many of them do. I have Republicans and/or conservative friends and family members and business associates; I get along well with them too. By and large they don't have to do anything to make me think better of them; I think well of them as it is.

That said, and to be blunt again, there's very little chance I'll be voting for GOP candidates for jobs above the local level anytime soon, because at the state and national party level, I don't see a lot of rationality when it comes either to individual rights or the proper role of the government with regard to services/infrastructure or taxes. I also think the party's been blinded by frankly incomprehensible hatred of Obama, which almost certainly *does* have a racial element to it, thanks for asking, added on top of a general howling outrage that a Democrat is in the White House at all. I like many Republicans but I actively dislike the policies and strategies (such as they are) of the Republican Party on the state and national levels.

If the GOP ever wants me to vote for it above the local level—and who knows? Maybe they don't!—then they will need to ditch the Gingrich/Atwater philosophy of painting anyone of differing politics as heretics to be burned and never to be negotiated with, and they'll have to have a serious rethink of how they approach taxation and services. I think it's possible to believe in low(ish) taxation and constrained government coupled with a robust private sector while still recognizing that some things really do need to be handled by government, and paid for. I'd also like to see evidence they believe civil rights are indeed for everyone, not just the straight, white and/or embryonic.

But—and this is significant—there is *no* reason for the GOP to change its current strategy. If you've not noticed, it holds both the House and Senate at the national level, and a whole lot of state executive and legislative branches. What it's doing is pretty successful, and when it's not (2008, 2012), the strategy simply to double down and do it harder has not been a bad one for them (2010, 2014). So I don't see the GOP doing anything it needs to do to win my vote—or even to lessen my overall dislike of it—on the state or national level anytime soon.

Which I'm sure they think is fine. They don't, in fact, need my vote. By the time they ever do, I suspect it might be too late for them.

MEET
KEITH JOHNSON

<table>
<tr><td>Jan</td></tr>
<tr><td>**29**</td></tr>
<tr><td>2018</td></tr>
</table>

O ver on Twitter, some foolish person posted the following question, which I will replicate here with all grammatical confabulation intact, because it's necessary for context:

> *As a straight male, how would u feel about your child having a homosexual school teacher?! Who their around 8hours a day!*

This was my response:

> *As a straight male, the best teacher I ever had was a gay man. Among many other things, he taught me the difference between "there," "their" and "they're." His name was Keith Johnson. I would have been absolutely delighted for my daughter to have known him. I sang at his funeral.*

This tweet, boosted by folks like Neil Gaiman, J.K. Rowling and Nick Offerman, has now been seen by over three million people. So now I would like to tell you a little bit about Keith Johnson, the best teacher I ever had.

To begin, in 1980, when he was my sixth grade teacher, I had no idea he was gay. It was 1980, when bluntly it wasn't safe for a teacher to be out (he may have been out to colleagues, but I wasn't aware of it if he was). Also I was eleven years old, and in that time and place, I wouldn't really have known what it meant to be gay. Not that I hadn't heard the word or ones like it, which we flung around as slurs—"that's gay," "don't be a fag," and the game we rather obliviously called "smear the queer," in which someone caught a ball and then everyone else in the game tried to drive them into the ground. But I didn't have a very good idea of why those were slurs, nor how those slurs would have been applied to Keith.

No, in that time and place, Keith was simply "Mr. Johnson"— not *Keith* Johnson, mind you, as the idea of calling a teacher by their first name elicited the sort of holy terror that convinced you that if you were to do so you would promptly burst into retributive flame. "Mr. Johnson" would do. It wasn't until years later that I could even say "Keith" without feeling I stepped over some still-glowing, forbidden line.

Keith's reputation preceded him. At Ben Lomond Elementary's "MGM" ("mentally gifted minors") program, the upper grades went through Mrs. Fox, Mrs. Swirsky and Mr. Johnson, for fourth, fifth and sixth grades. Even in fourth grade you heard about what a hardass Mr. Johnson was, how he didn't suffer fools, and how if you got out of line, you were in for it. He was legendary in a way that elementary school teachers could be: Here was this fearsome leonine visage, and he was *coming for you*. Well, not *coming for you* exactly, but one day you would be in his class, and then you would *feel his wrath*. Sure, you get away with some things in *Mrs. Swirsky's* class. But if you tried that in Mr. Johnson's class? Principal's office. Or *worse*.

Which, when you finally ended up in Keith's class, turned out to be only about 30% true. Certainly, Keith wanted you to pay attention, and if you weren't, he had a boomy baritone voice which would snap you back into line. And if the entire class was lazy or inattentive, then Keith had a phrase that let us know we disappointed him on a fundamental level. "Boy, I'm telling you, *some people*," he would say, loudly and with a slathering of reproach, and then would detail what *some people* would do, and it was clear that *some people* were foolish and silly and would eventually lead lives of regret and disappointment, and the genesis of those regretful lives would be *now*, in *this* moment, when we weren't getting our history projects done in a timely way. And it would work, because obviously we didn't want regretful, disappointing lives, but *also* because we didn't want to disappoint Keith.

Because here was the thing about Keith. Fundamentally, he wasn't frightening, or mean, or an indiscriminate hardass on eleven-year-old kids. He was in fact kind and attentive, and more to the point, he *saw* each of his students in the way teachers are supposed to, and the way the best of teachers do, seemingly by reflex. He saw us, and saw our quirks and flaws, where we needed encouragement and also what kind of encouragement we would need. He saw us as individuals and as a group, and while he always had the same educational goals year in and year out, it became clear he would get us to those goals in ways that *we* could get there.

Being seen by one's teacher, as it turned out, was especially important to me in the sixth grade. My mother was having a bad divorce that left me, my mother and my sister briefly homeless and then shuttling around between houses for the rest of the year. There was little stability, emotionally or physically, in my home life, and it would have been easy—and understandable—for me to fall down a hole and not come out of it for a long time. I didn't because as it happened a number of people stepped up to help save me. One of those was Keith, who in seeing me saw some of the possible paths of my future, and gently but with just the right amount of push, set me on those paths.

I'll give you two examples. The first happened when Keith asked me to write a letter. Every year Keith had his class perform a play (my year it would be "Oliver!" in which I would play the Artful Dodger; I can still sing most of the songs from that play by heart). To pay for it, he would have the class run a small business selling doo-dads to other students and parents. We would do the whole nine yards, including registering the business with the city and issuing stock (and at the end of the year, paying off the stock with dividends, if any), and by naming officers of the corporation.

Among the things Keith had us do was publicity, and one day while explaining the concept of publicity to us, he said one of the things he wanted us to do was contact a local TV station and try to get them to do a segment on us for the five o'clock news—and as he was saying this, he turned to me directly, pointed at me, and said "and I want *you* to write the letter." Why me? He told me later and privately it was because I wrote differently than everyone else in class and he thought I could make the argument in a way that would interest the news crew. Keith was the first person aside from my mother to see that writing was a thing I did—and the first person to say to me that it was a thing I could do *well*, in a way that set me apart. It would be a few years until I decided for myself to become a writer, but I never forgot that Keith saw it first in me.

(Also, he was right: I wrote the letter with his editorial guidance, sent it in to Channel 7 News, and then a couple of months later they called and wanted to do a segment on us. We did an extra run of doo-dads so they could see us in production, and then sold those for a nice profit. And that's how we paid dividends on our stock that year.)

Another example I've detailed elsewhere, when Keith gave me a copy of Ray Bradbury's *The Martian Chronicles*, said to me I would enjoy it, and said to me it was one of his favorite books. For me, this wasn't just a teacher suggesting a book, it was *my* teacher sharing a confidence that was for me alone. And again he was right—*The Martian Chronicles* is in many ways foundational to my understanding of a field that I would eventually come to write in. I can't say I became a science fiction writer because Keith gave me Bradbury's book. But I can say I believe he understood me well enough to believe that it was the right book at the right time for me. And it was.

When I left Keith's class to middle school, I would still drop by after class to chat with him and catch up; he always seemed pleased that I would come to say hello. I wasn't the only former student who would do that—others told me they did it as well—but perhaps I was the most persistent, keeping in touch through high school and then college and then in the early parts of my professional career. Somewhere in there I directly asked him if he were gay, because by that time, several years on, some rumors had begun to circulate among his former students. Keith by this time had retired from teaching and told me it was true, named his partner and seemed perfectly at peace with it, and with me knowing.

By this time Keith was also sick. He was one of the many gay men who contracted HIV in the early days, before it was well understood and before there was a good treatment regimen for the virus. It developed into AIDS and he died of it, as did hundreds of thousands of gay and other Americans (and as thousands still do, even today). I went to his memorial service, as did a few other of his former students, and at his funeral, with the permission of his family and partner, I sang a song I wrote for him.

Keith Johnson was a teacher and I can't claim that I was more special to him than the hundreds of other students who passed through his classroom over the couple of decades he taught. But I think that's the point of him being one of the best teachers I've known: His skills and talents as a teacher were for everyone, and were there for every student who came through his class. I don't think I'm alone in saying he was the best teacher I've had, and I've had some magnificent ones over the years. But he stands alone.

To go back to the original question of how I as a straight male would feel about a homosexual teacher with my child eight hours a day, the answer is: A homosexual teacher was my best teacher, was the right teacher for me at a critical time, and saw me when I could have been lost. It's even possible that in his way Keith Johnson saved me at a time when I most needed saving, simply by being the teacher he was with each of his students. I would have loved to have been able to introduce my daughter, born after he died, to Keith, my teacher and my friend. And I would want my daughter, and for every child, to have a teacher like Keith—one who *saw* her, one who taught her, and one who helped make her more herself, as Keith did with me. How could one *not* wish that for one's child?

And now you know a little more about Keith Johnson, at least from my perspective. He was my best teacher. His memory is a blessing.

THE MORAL
SHAMBLES THAT IS
OUR PRESIDENT

<table>
<tr><td>Aug</td></tr>
<tr><td>13</td></tr>
<tr><td>2017</td></tr>
</table>

Denouncing Nazis and the KKK and violent white supremacists by those names should not be a difficult thing for a president to do, particularly when those groups are the instigators and proximate cause of violence in an American city, and one of their number has rammed his car through a group of counter-protestors, killing one and injuring dozens more. This is a moral gimme—something so obvious and clear and easy that a president should almost *not* get credit for it, any more than he should get credit for putting on pants before he goes to have a press conference.

And yet this president—*our* president, the current President of the United States—couldn't manage it. The best he could manage was to fumble through a condemnation of "many sides," as if those protesting the Nazis and the KKK and the violent white supremacists had equal culpability for the events of the day. He couldn't manage this moral gimme, and when his apparatchiks were given an opportunity to take a mulligan on it, they doubled down instead.

This was a spectacular failure of leadership, the moral equivalent not only of missing a putt with the ball on the lip of the cup, but of taking out your favorite driver and whacking that ball far into the woods. Our president *literally* could not bring himself to say that Nazis and the KKK and violent white supremacists are bad. He sorely wants you to believe he *implied* it. But he couldn't *say* it.

To be clear, when it was announced the president would address the press about Charlottesville, I wasn't expecting much from him. He's not a man to expect much from, in terms of presidential gravitas. But the moral bar here was so low it was *on the ground*, and he tripped over it anyway.

And because he *did*, no one—and certainly not the Nazis and the KKK and the violent white supremacists, who were hoping for the wink and nod that they got here—believes the president actually thinks there's a problem with the Nazis and the KKK and the violent white supremacists. If he finally *does* get around to admitting that they are bad, he'll do it in the same truculent, forced way that he used when he was forced to admit that yeah, sure, maybe Obama was born in the United States after all. An admission that makes it clear it's being compelled rather than volunteered. The Nazis and the KKK and the violent white supremacists will understand what *that* means, too.

Our president, simply put, is a profound moral shambles. He's a racist and sexist himself, he's populated his administration with Nazi sympathizers and white supremacists, and is pursuing policies, from immigration to voting rights, that make white nationalists really very happy. We shouldn't be *surprised* someone like him can't pass from his lips the names of the hate groups that visited Charlottesville, but we can still be disappointed, and very very angry about it. I hate that my baseline expectation for the moral behavior of the President of the United States is "failure," but here we are, and yesterday, as with the previous 200-some days of this administration, gives no indication that this baseline expectation is unfounded.

And more than that. White supremacy is evil. Nazism is evil. The racism and hate we saw in Charlottesville yesterday is evil. The domestic terrorism that happened there yesterday—a man, motivated by racial hate, mowing down innocents—is evil. And none of what happened yesterday *just happened*. It happened because the Nazis and the KKK and the violent white supremacists felt emboldened. They felt emboldened because they believe that one of their own is in the White House, or at least, feel like he's surrounded himself with enough of their own (or enough fellow travelers) that it's all the same from a practical point of view. They believe their time has come round at last, and they believe no one is going to stop them, because one of their own has his hand on the levers of power.

When evil believes you are one of their own, and you have the opportunity to denounce it, and call it out by name, what should you do? And what should we believe of you, if you do not? What should we believe of you, if you do not, and you are President of the United States?

My president won't call out evil by its given name. He *can*. But he won't. I know what I think that means for him. I also know what I think it means for the United States. And I know what it means for me. My president won't call out evil for what it is, but I can do better. And so can you. And so can everybody else. Our country can be better than it is now, and better than the president it has.

MORTALITY

Well, this is a sort of ironic question to address on my birthday, from Theo, who asks:

Do you think about mortality frequently or do you try to put it out of your mind? Do you think it's better to ignore it or jam pack as much as you can into every minute with one eye on the clock?

Well, if I'm going to be right up front about it, I neither frequently think about mortality nor try to put it out of my mind. At this point I've largely made peace with the fact that I will not be immortal and that I will one day die, and also, that there are probably worse things than being dead.

I suspect this is the case because, honestly, I've been dead before—more accurately, not alive, which is what being dead is. However, this particular session of being not alive happened prior to my birth, and we don't call that being "dead" even if that's effectively what it is. Whatever you call it, I was not alive for the first 13.7 billion years or so of the existence of this universe.

How did I feel about it then? Well, I didn't feel *anything* about it. I didn't exist. Not existing—not being alive—didn't bother me; I had no capacity to be bothered about it, or to feel anything else about it. I rather strongly suspect that being dead again will be much the same. It won't bother me, or make me happy, or sad, or anything else. However I feel about not existing prior to nonexistence, and I imagine I will feel *something* about it, will be irrelevant. I'll just be gone. And that will be that.

I should be clear that I *like* existing, actually quite a bit, and am in no rush to *stop* existing. But from experience (so to speak) I know that not existing isn't so bad. It's not something I'm afraid of. I don't fear eternal judgment, or worry that I will miss out on some eternal reward. There's no *eternal*; there's just nothing. Intellectual honesty requires me to note I could be wrong about this, in which case, won't *I* be surprised. But I'm not so worried about being wrong that it's going to cause me to change how I live my life.

Since I'm not exactly afraid of death or preoccupied by the nature of an afterlife, on a day-to-day basis I don't give either a whole lot of thought. I don't hide from it, and when it does cross my mind I'll think about it for an appropriate amount of time. Then I'll move on, because I have enough other things on my plate to keep me busy—I have books to write, and places to go, and people to see and pets to pet. It's a pretty full schedule. And when it's *not* full, that's fine too, since when I'm dead, I won't be able to lie around or nap or zone out, either. I *like* doing nothing every now and again, and now is the only time when I'll be able to do it. So, you know, I'm gonna enjoy it.

I will admit that at least some of my sanguinity regarding death comes from the fact that I feel generally content with my life, which is to say, I have accomplished most of the things I wanted to accomplish when I was younger, and by and large there's not that much about my life that I regret or would change. There is always more to do, of course, and I would be happy for more things to happen before I shuffle off. But honestly, if I get hit by the proverbial bus tomorrow, I don't think anyone would say I hadn't made good use of my time on the planet (well, some people might, but they would be jerks).

In terms of jam packing every single moment—nah. Aside from the notation above that I enjoy doing nothing from time to time, I also tend to be a proponent of quality versus quantity. Being frantic to check things off a list would annoy me after a while. Certainly there are experiences I have not yet had that I would love to have, and I will try to get around to them. But probably not in a wild-eyed sprint against death. Ironically, I don't have time for that.

If you ever get yourself in a spiral about mortality, I would suggest to you that you remember that you, too, didn't exist before now, and that, if you think about it, it probably wasn't that bad when you didn't, even if it does mean you missed the dinosaurs. So future not existing will probably not be too bad, either, and will take care of itself in any event.

With that in mind, you can focus on the part where you *do* exist, and make the most of it, however that works for you. Good luck with that! I'll be doing the same.

My Day
in a
Wheelchair

Apr

22

2015

When I was in Australia earlier this month, I tore a calf muscle and spent several days on crutches and have since been using a cane to get about. The good news is that everything's healing as it should—at this point I'm keeping the cane around as a precautionary measure—so as far as Adventures in Temporary Disability go, this has been likely a best-case scenario.

That said, I did have one relatively brief moment where I got the smallest of glimpses of what I suspect mobility-impaired people go through on a regular basis. It happened when I was traveling back from Australia to the US, and I, in an overabundance of caution, asked for (and got) wheelchair assistance to get around the two airports I was going to be in: Melbourne and Los Angeles.

I will note that initially, I felt weird about asking for a wheelchair at all—my self-image is as an able-bodied person, so even though I was literally hobbling my way around, some part of my brain was "you can *totally* walk around this airport with several heavy bags and a leg injury!" But I decided not to listen to that voice, because that voice was stupid, as reasonable-sounding as it was inside my brain at the time.

And a good thing, because in the case of both Melbourne and Los Angeles, **a)** the airports are huge, and **b)** in LA there was the additional hurdle of customs to go through. If I had had to walk it, I suspect I would still be in Melbourne's airport, subsisting on free wifi and Violet Crumbles. I needed the wheelchair, self-image be damned.

For the record, the first part of the wheelchair experience was pretty sweet and exactly what able-bodied people think when they think disabled people get some sort of awesome superpower: I zipped through security and customs lines super-fast, faster than I had ever done so under my own steam. Also, the Melbourne wheelchair was modern and electric powered and I felt vaguely like Professor X being carted around on it (the Los Angeles wheelchair was probably older than I am and the poor woman they assigned to it could barely push me up ramps. I tipped her hugely at the end). It was just like being a first-class passenger! Only cheaper and I didn't even have to get up!

But then—well. So, in Los Angeles I'm at the baggage carousel and my wheelchair is parked so I can point out my bags to the woman helping me. And of course bags are coming round and people are grabbing them, anxious to get them and get the hell out of the airport, which I can totally understand, since LAX is a terrible airport all the way around.

The thing is, when they're grabbing them, the conveyor belt is still moving, and the people tugging at them are starting to cross into my personal space, shoving into my wheelchair and pushing it around to get at their bags, rather than, say, letting go of the goddamned piece of luggage for just a second to go around me and grab it on the other side. And when they did haul the luggage off the carousel, they managed to smack it across my wheelchair, knocking me about.

The first time it happened, I was, like, whatever. The second time I got annoyed. The third time, the guy hauling the piece of luggage off the carousel actually clocked me in the head with it, at which point I stopped being patient and said "Are you actually *fucking kidding me?*" to him.

At which point the man was entirely mortified and abjectly apologized, because in fact he was probably not a horrible person. He just didn't seem to notice that as a guy in a wheelchair, I was mobility-impaired and couldn't move out of his way like an able-bodied person could. He just didn't factor *me* into his worldview, which at the time was laser-focused on getting his luggage and getting the hell out of Dodge. As a result, he literally battered me. Quite unintentionally, to be clear. But that didn't make my head feel any better in the moment.

I should note that my half hour being shoved about at the baggage carousel (my bags were pretty much the last ones off the plane) does not give me any authority to speak to disabled issues at all. What I am saying, again, is that for a very brief and limited slice of time, I got to experience what it's like to be someone who is disabled and how people—normal, presumably not terrible people—deal with them in their world. It wasn't, shall we say, an entirely positive experience.

It is something, however, I'll remember when I am fully able-bodied again.

My Endorsement
for President, 2016:
Hillary Clinton

Today is the beginning of early voting here in Ohio, which means that it is a good day for me to formally make the following announcement regarding my vote for President of the United States:

I am voting for Hillary Clinton for President of the United States, and I think you should too.

And now, let me explain why, in points that go (roughly) from external to internal, both in a political and personal sense. This entry is long, but this year, I think, longer is probably better.

1. Because she is not Donald Trump. I've written on why I believe Donald Trump is an unmitigated and unprecedented disaster as a presidential candidate, so I don't need to do it again here. But I think it's important to acknowledge that while I am affirmatively voting for Hillary Clinton as president—I want her in the White House—I am also actively and affirmatively voting against Donald Trump. Indeed, even if I wasn't enthusiastically voting *for* Clinton, this year of all years I would pull the lever for her because as the candidate of one of the two major parties, she is the only realistic bulwark against Trump being in office. It's that important that he be denied the presidency.

However, let me go into detail here about one thing. I want to be clear that in voting against Trump, I'm not only voting against him as an individual, although given who he is as an individual—a racist, a misogynist, a liar and a cheat—that would be more than enough. I am also voting against the people who I see as the shock troops of the Trump campaign: the racists, the anti-semites, the religiously intolerant, the sexists and bullies, the toxic stew of hate, stupidity and sociopathy that has tried to pass into respectability with the jazzy new title of "alt-right," but which is just the Klan and the neo-Nazis all over again.

In voting against Trump, I'm voting against the alt-right and larger pool of hate in which they fester, against the people who slur women, blacks, latinos, Jews, Muslims, LGBT folks and others on social media and elsewhere, against the ones who promise them a march to the ovens or a noose over a tree branch or a rape in an alley, against the ones who glory in the fact that Trump's candidacy lends their bigotry mainstream cover, and the ones who, should Trump win, have plans for anyone and everyone who isn't them. I'm voting against the people who believe, when Trump says "Make America great again," it means "Make everyone else afraid again."

To Hell with them, and to Hell with Trump for lifting them up and giving them cover and succor. I don't believe and would not abide the idea that every person who might vote for Trump is the sort of person I describe above. But everyone who votes for Trump has to know that these are the people with whom they ride. I will not ride with them. I will vote against them and Trump, and gladly so. The best way to do that is to vote for Hillary Clinton.

2. Because she is not the GOP candidate. First, the practical: If Trump were to win the presidency, that would likely mean that the House and Senate would remain in GOP hands. Which means that I strongly suspect the first 100 days of a Trump presidency would be a fantastic orgy of the GOP rolling back every single Obama law and policy that it could. Not because doing so would make the lives of Americans better—it manifestly would not—but because they just fucking hate Barack Obama *so much* that giving him the middle finger for a hundred days would fill them with glee. I'm not down with that.

Likewise, not down with the GOP plan to pack the Supreme Court with Scalia clones; there are already two, in the form of Thomas and Alito. That's more than enough for one court, I think.

Both the legislative and the judicial issues outlined above, I would note, would be a disincentive for me to vote for any presidential candidate the GOP might have picked in 2016, especially considering the generally atrocious primary field of candidates, of whom the only one I might have been willing to consider even briefly for my vote would have been John Kasich. But Kasich was too moderate and sensible for the GOP primary voters, which given how conservative Kasich is, is a vaguely terrifying thing.

Second, the philosophical: Look, I'm not a straight-ticket voter. In almost every election I vote for more than a single party, because— here's a wacky idea—I consider each position up for election and who among the listed candidates will be the best for the role. I expect this year I will do the same.

But not on the national level. On the national level I don't think the GOP has earned my vote, nor has it for years. Even before the moment where the GOP primary voters appallingly selected Donald Trump as their standard bearer, the national party's philosophical and political tenets had been long abandoned for the simpler and uglier strategy of "deny Barack Obama everything."

To what purpose? To what end? Well, not for the purpose of actually making the United States a better place for its citizens, or to practice active governance of the nation. From the outside at least—and I rather strongly suspect from the inside as well—it just looked like "sooner or later they *have* to let one of us be president, so let's just throw a fit until then." Fortunately, if you want to call it that, the GOP has spent decades training its electoral base to reward intransigence over actual action to make their lives better, and wasn't above poking at the base's latent (and not-so-latent) bigotry to delegitimize the president.

Trump has given the latter part of the game away—Trump doesn't dog whistle his bigotry, he uses a megaphone—but the other part, the part about the intransigence, I don't see the GOP, as it's currently constituted on the national level, ever letting go of. Let's not pretend that Hillary Clinton will have an easier time with the GOP than Obama did. The GOP already hates her just for being who she is, and it'll be happy to slide the bigoted setting they use on its base from "racism" to "sexism," even if Trump's blown its cover on that. So I expect that the new policy for the GOP will be the same as the old policy, with a new name slotted in: "Deny Hillary Clinton everything."

And that's just not acceptable. I'm not foolish enough to assume the GOP would give a President Hillary Clinton everything she wanted even in the best of times. But there's a difference between an opposition party and an antagonistic party. The former is a participant and perhaps even a partner in governance. The latter, which is what we have, reduces politics down to a football game and in doing so makes life worse for every American. We can argue about how this has come about—training the base, gerrymandering safe districts which incline toward polarization, just plain rampant stupidity—but we can't argue it's not there.

This year of all years the national GOP needs to lose, and it needs to lose so comprehensively that the message is clear: Stop obstructing and start governing again. Now, as it happens, it might lose comprehensively because Trump and the GOP are fighting, and if Trump is going to go down, he might as well take the GOP down with him. Which would be a delightful irony! But just to be sure, and to use *my* vote to make a larger point, I won't be voting for the GOP this year for president or US senator or US representative. I don't imagine it will matter for US representative (my district hasn't gone Democratic since the Great Depression) but for the senate and the presidency, it might help.

3. Because I largely agree with Hillary Clinton's platform and positions. I've mentioned before that had I been born roughly 40 years earlier than I was, I probably would have become what's known as a "Rockefeller Republican," which is to say someone largely to the right on fiscal issues, and largely to the left on social issues. Rockefeller Republicans don't exist anymore, or more accurately, they're best known today as "mainstream Democrats." And, hey, guess which of the two candidates for President of the United States could be described as a "mainstream Democrat"? Why, yes, that's right, it's Hillary Clinton.

So it's not particularly surprising that I find many of her policy positions congenial, both in themselves and in contrast to Trump's positions—that is, when Trump actually has a position that's more than "trust me, it'll be great." As an example, let's take, oh, say, Clinton's tax policy, which essentially tweaks the existing code to make those of us on the top pay a slightly higher amount for our top marginal rate on income and investments, close some corporate loopholes, and essentially leave everyone else alone (or offer them slightly larger tax breaks). It's not sexy, but it's pretty sensible, particularly in contrast to Trump's, which basically gives rich people really big tax cuts and as a result adds trillions to our debt.

"Not sexy, but sensible" in fact describes most of her policies on everything from climate change to farm issues to voting rights to national security, and while I don't necessarily agree with every single thing she proposes right down the line, when I don't, what I *still* generally see is that the policy is based on a cogent reason or rationale in the real world, and not just some angry bellow from a fear-gravid id, which is how a large number of Trump policies come across.

And this is *good*, people. I *want* a policy nerd in the White House, and someone who has had real-world experience with how the political sausage gets made, and who both gets the value of having policies that have some relationship to the world outside their head and has the wherewithal, interest and capability to understand and express them. I'm not under the impression that Clinton will get everything she wants in terms of policy—despite the unbridled optimism on the left due to the events of recent days, I expect the House will stay in GOP hands (but, you know, *prove me wrong!*)—but I like most of what she has, and will likely be happy with whatever she manages to get through Congress.

4. Because I like what I know of Hillary Clinton.

But! But! BenghaziWhitewaterEmailVincentFosterBillIsSkeevy*Gggg-wwwaaa-aaaarrrrgggghhhnnffffnf*—

I'm going to skip over the vast majority of this right now by noting that there are very few people in the world whose personal and public conduct has been so aggressively and punitively investigated, and for so long, as Hillary Clinton, and yet she continues to walk among us, a free woman whose errors, when they have been made, are usually of the venial rather than the mortal sort. Which probably means one of two things: Either this decades-long persecution of Hillary Clinton on the part of her enemies is largely motivated for their own political and financial benefit, or that Hillary Clinton is a criminal mastermind so good at evading the forces of justice that *holy shit* we should be glad that she's finally decided to use her *evil-honed skills* for the *forces of good*. Better give her eight years, just to make sure.

I believe that the vast majority of the bullshit said about Hillary Clinton is just that: bullshit. Hillary Clinton gets shit because apparently she's always been an ambitious woman who is not here for your nonsense. And maybe, like any human who is not here for your nonsense, but especially a *woman* who is not here for your nonsense (and who has gotten more of it *because* she is a woman), she just gets *tired* of the unremitting flood of nonsense she has to deal with every single goddamn day of her life. Maybe she gets tired of being told to smile and when she smiles being told she shouldn't smile. Maybe she gets tired of being called a bitch and a cunt and a demon. Maybe she gets tired of having to be up on a stage with bullies who try to intimidate her with their physical presence in her physical space, and if you think that second presidential debate was the first time *that* happened, look up her senatorial debate just for fun. Maybe she gets tired of it but knows she has to take it and smile, because *that's the deal*.

People, I *flat out fucking admire* Hillary Clinton for having dealt with all that bullshit for 30 years and yet not burning *the whole world down*.

So that's the first thing, and it's *unfair* that it's the first thing, but since that's what gets shoved on you the moment you open your mouth about Hillary Clinton, that's what the first thing has to be.

But let me also tell you that I like her intelligence, her attention to detail, her ability to speak at length about the subjects that matter to her and that she thinks would matter to you, too. I like she doesn't have a problem being the smartest person in the room, even if you do. I like the work that she did on her own, without reference to her husband and his own ambitions. I liked when she said that she wasn't here to bake cookies, and I liked that you could see how much she hated having to bake the cookies when shit blew up around that statement (I like that I believe that in her personal life she probably likes baking cookies just fine, just on her terms, not yours). I like that she tried things and failed at them and picked herself up and kept going and got better at them because of it. I like that she cares about people who aren't just like her. I like that she's ambitious. I like that she's fearless. I like that all the right people hate and loathe her. I like that she plows through them anyway.

There are things I don't like about her too, but not nearly as many, and none of them enough, to reduce my admiration for her for these other things.

I don't expect Hillary Clinton to be perfect, or not to fail, or to be a president whose actions I agree with straight down the line. I've never had that in any president and I think it would be foolish to expect it in her. What I *do* expect, based on what I've known of her since 1992, when she first entered my consciousness, is that she will never not *try*. Try to be a good president, and try to be a president whose administration does the most good for the largest number of Americans. Now, maybe she'll succeed and maybe she won't—it's not all up to her and even if it was, you never know what happens to you in this life. But everything I know about her from the last quarter century convinces me that she has earned this opportunity, perhaps more than anyone else who has ever run for president.

5. Because I like what she represents for our country.
I have written at length about the idea that being a straight white male is living life on the lowest difficulty setting, and if you should ever doubt that it's the case, look at the 2016 election, in which a racist, sexist, ignorant boor of a straight white male, with no experience in public service and no policies he could personally articulate beyond "it'll be great, believe me" went up against a woman who spent the better part of four decades in and around public service, including occupying some of the highest positions in government, and who had exhaustive, detailed policy positions on nearly every point of public interest—*and was ahead of her in some polls* on the day they had their first debate.

If that tape in which Trump bragged about sexual assault hadn't hit the air, the polls might yet still be close. It literally took "grab 'em by the pussy" to get some air between arguably the most qualified candidate ever to run for president, who is a woman, and inarguably the worst major party presidential candidate in living memory, who is a straight, white man. I cannot know that fact and not be confronted by the immense and *absolutely real* privilege straight white men have—and just *how much better* a woman has to be to compete.

I am not voting for Hillary Clinton simply because she is a woman—but at the same time I cannot deny, and *actively celebrate the fact*, that much of what makes Hillary Clinton the person I want to vote for is because she is a woman. Everything that our culture has put on her, all the expectations it has had for her, all the expectations she's had for herself, all the things that she's taken on, or fought against, because she's a woman, *all* of that has shaped the person she is and the character she has, and has become: A person who has talents and flaws, a person I admire, and a person who I want to see in the Oval Office.

When she becomes president, as I believe she will, it won't *only* be because she is a woman. But her experience being a woman will have prepared her for the job and will be integral to how she will be president. Her simply being our first woman president will make her a symbol and an icon and almost certainly in time an inspiration (all of these more than she already is, to be clear), and I am glad for those. But it's how her life and her experiences will bear on the day-to-day aspects of presidency that to me is key, and which I think in time should be what inspires people, as much as if not more than what she represents symbolically. It's something we haven't had yet. It matters to our country, and it matters to me.

And so: with a full heart and with no small amount of joy, I endorse Hillary Clinton for President of the United States.

My Non-Spoilery Review of The Force Awakens

Super-short version: It's not bad! Best since the original trilogy and arguably better than at least one of those. You'll probably have a whole lot of fun with this film.

Non-super-short version: Star Wars is that friend of yours who you haven't seen in a while, who was in a long-term relationship where everything was cool for a while and then things just plain went to hell, and the last time you saw them, they'd kind of hit the bottom. Now you're seeing them again for the first time in years and before they show up you're humming a little mantra that goes *please please please please don't let this be awkward and weird like it was the last time we saw each other.*

And then they show up! And they look *great.* They sound great. You talk to them and slip into the groove with them, and they catch you up on what's been going on in their life, including their new relationship with this fab-sounding person who seems to be doing good things for them. And you suddenly realize that for the first time in years your friend actually seems happy. They're not exactly their old self again—who ever is, after all those years?—but the things you always loved about them are there once more, and you're so happy to see *them* happy again that you almost want to cry.

So, yeah: If you're a Star Wars fan, that's how you're going to feel about *The Force Awakens.*

This is an immense relief, but also, to use the words of a famous Mon Calimarian, it's a trap. Because it's Star Wars, and because you'll have been used to Star Wars films being terrible for so very long, the highly-polished, super-competent and *intentionally entertaining* film that is *The Force Awakens* might feel something like a revelation. Finally, a Star Wars film you don't have to make excuses for! That you *don't* have to mumble something like "well, it's part of a trilogy, you have to wait until the whole thing is done to see the entire structure" to yourself and others in a vain attempt to overlook massive flaws. This is the first Star Wars film *in decades* that you can relax into, and just sit back and enjoy. It's not until the tension of having to pre-emptively rationalize your film choices is lifted that you realize what a burden it has been. The absence of that burden might just feel like greatness.

So: is *The Force Awakens* a great film?

No. It's not on the level of great cinema. It's not on the level of the original *Star Wars* (which I refuse to call *A New Hope* because fuck you George Lucas you're not the boss of me) or of *The Empire Strikes Back*. It's not the best science fiction film of 2015, or even the best new installment in a long-running science fiction film series (say hello to *Fury Road* for both, although *The Martian* and *Ex Machina* are in the running for the former). It's not a great film, and you shouldn't be relieved into thinking it is.

But it *is* a pretty damn good Star Wars film, which at this point in the series is exactly what it needs to be. This shouldn't be overlooked, either.

Things to love (or at least really like): The dialogue, by Lawrence Kasdan, JJ Abrams and Michael Arndt, which for the first time since *Empire* sounds like words that might actually come out of the mouths of actual thinking human beings, and not merely declamatory utterances designed to fill up space. The relationships, of which there are many—more and *more believable* relationships in this one single film than in the entire run of the series to date. The care with which even minor characters are developed and seem like actual people, rather than toy manufacturing opportunities given a line or two in the film as an excuse to make parents buy the action figure for a stocking stuffer. The fact that Daisy Ridley and John Boyega's characters (as well as one other character, who you will know when you see the film) are believably young and act like young people do, i.e., make some questionable choices, without doing stupid things entirely for plot convenience.

In short, most of the best things about this movie relate to the characters in it—and the care which the filmmakers use to make them as real as possible. This is the one thing George Lucas could never manage on his own, partly because he's a leaden writer (Harrison Ford once famously quipped of Lucas' dialogue "You can *type* this shit, George, but you can't *say* it"), but primarily because I just don't think he was that interested in it. He needed characters as chess pieces, not as people. In *The Force Awakens*, we get characters as people, and their game becomes more interesting.

Things not to like? Basically, the several points where the film has to bow to the tropes of the Star Wars universe mostly for plot convenience and fan service. Yes, yes, lasers and explosions and battles and the cute nods to the previous films, they all have to be in there. I get it (trust me, *I* get it). But for me all of that was a sideshow to the characters—and think about that! When was the last time you could say that about a Star Wars film? (*Empire*.) There's also the fact that almost immediately after I left the theater there were a whole bunch of things about the film that I started to pick apart. Trust me, my friends, if you think the nitpickery of the Star Wars universe was positively Talmudic *before*, wait until the dust settles with TFA. There will be nitpickery *galore*.

Here's the important thing about that last bit: On the drive home, I had things I wanted to nitpick—but the operative part of the phrase is "on the drive home." When I was watching the film, I was *in the film*. I wasn't focused on anything other than where I was. And *that*, my friends, is the goal. When I was the creative consultant for *Stargate: Universe*, that was actually my job: To read the scripts early and flag all the things that would throw people out of the story *before* the end credits rolled. It's okay for the audience to be nitpicky, just *afterwards*. Managing that is not as easy as it sounds, and certainly the prequel trilogies never achieved it. TFA does.

Which is a testament to Abrams, his fellow screenwriters and to Disney. When Disney bought Lucasfilm I said that it was "the best thing that could happen, especially if you're a Star Wars fan." I said it because Disney, whatever other flaws it has (and it has many) understands better than almost any other studio that *the audience must be entertained*. You grab the audience, you carry them along for two hours, you keep them busy, and you drop them off at the gift shop when you're done. Disney is *relentless* about this, and they're not stupid about it, either, which is to say, Disney doesn't treat its audience like marks, to be hustled. It treats them as opportunities for a long-term relationship, involving the transfer of cash to Disney.

Cynical? Well, yes. But, look, if what that means is we get good Star Wars films that aren't painful to watch and tell a fun story while we're shoving popcorn into our maws—stories with *lightsabers*—then I'm okay with that. Especially after having slogged through a Star Wars era where the *only* thing of interest was the merchandising. We're getting *more* out of the Star Wars cinematic universe now than we were with Lucas. I don't see this as a bad thing. "By the sweet and merry mouse above, *you will be entertained*," I wrote, when the Disney deal for Lucasfilm was announced.

I was right. I was entertained. And because of the focus on characters in *The Force Awakens*—a focus I expect to continue through Episodes VIII and IX, and in the new "anthology" films—I am optimistic I will continue to be entertained in the Star Wars universe for a good while yet. I can't tell you how giddy that makes me.

I don't need greatness from Star Wars. I just want to have fun with it. And with *The Force Awakens*, I did. I'm glad my friend is back, and happy.

My Personal
Feminism, 2017

```
Aug
22
2017
```

I n the wake of Kai Cole's piece about her former husband Joss Whedon and his infidelity with actresses on his show, and some of the reaction to it, I've been thinking about what it means to be a man in the public sphere who considers himself to be a feminist. Part of this thought process was also spurred on by seeing some of the reaction to the news on Twitter by women who made the point that they were suspicious of men who had feminism as part of their "brand," because that's often hiding less-than-feminist actions.

Well, I've talked before about my own personal feminism here on Whatever. Here in 2017, this is what I think about it:

I consider myself a feminist because fundamentally, I believe that women should have and need to have the same rights, privileges and opportunities that men do—that *I* do—and I think it's worth saying that out loud and working toward that goal. This feminism is part and parcel of believing that *everyone* should have the same rights, privileges and opportunities that I, a straight, white, well-off, gender-conforming man has, not just on paper but in the practical, mundane, day-to-day workings-of-the-world sense. We're not there yet, and as we've seen recently, there are a lot of people who never want to see that happen. I would be ashamed, especially now, not to stand up and be counted out loud as someone who believes in feminism, among all the other things I believe in.

But I am also deeply uncomfortable with feminism being part of my "brand," for several reasons. The first is that I'm aware of my failings and imperfections, and I'm also aware that there are a number of failings and imperfections I'm *not* aware of. With regard to my feminism, I can work on the things I know about and listen when people point out the things I'm not aware of, but the general gist of it is that I'm aware my feminism is imperfect. I am loath to charge in saying *behold, the male feminist!* when I know there are lots of places where I fall down. I'm a feminist, in progress, and suspect I will be until I'm dead.

The second, following on the first, is that I'm also aware feminism doesn't need me as a flagbearer. I'm not and shouldn't be the vanguard of feminism (I mean, if I am, *whoooo* there's trouble). What I can be is support, and occasionally a tank (i.e., someone being an obvious target and taking hits while other people get to work). One of the great gifts of getting older is the realization that you don't have to lead every parade. Sometimes it's enough to march along and have the backs of the people out in front.

The third, which is related to the second as the second is related to the first, is the awareness that I have the privilege of not being performatively feminist. Which is to say that I can—and sometimes do—decide to take a break from actively having to deal with issues and concerns of feminism, because I am busy, or distracted, or tired, or just decide I want to take a breather. My passive feminism is still there, my default belief in the equality of rights and opportunities, but I don't have to *do* anything about it, and the personal consequences for my not engaging are very low.

Having the option to quit the field without penalty, and to engage only when you have interest, means some interesting things, not all of them good. It means, as an example, that you can choose to do only high-profile, high-impact flashy attention-getting things, and not the day-to-day grunt work that other people have to do. It's not at all surprising that the reaction of the latter folks is irritation and frustration that you're getting credit for something they see essentially as stunting for cookies.

I'm not going to deny that I'm aware that I have the ability, within my own little pond, to draw attention to issues and to make things visible by being loud and immovable in only the way someone with my advantages has, and in that way effect change. I try to be useful with that, and to make clear the fact that others have done work I'm essentially pointing to. And I try to do more than just the flashy, attention-getting, cookie-bearing stuff. But at the end of the day I'm aware that I have the *option* to engage, with feminism as with many issues, when other people are *required* to engage if they want their existence to be acknowledged as anything other than background noise. That makes a difference. I don't think I can have feminism as part of my "brand" when I only have to engage with it at my whim.

(There's also a fourth issue here, which is the disconnect between public and private lives. To be very clear, I'm not keeping any affairs— or, really, *anything*—secret from Krissy; we believe in communication and lots of it. But I've also been clear that while my public persona, including on this blog, is me, it's a version of me tuned differently from the me who lives at home with my wife and daughter, away from the rest of the world. I don't know that there's anything in my private life to give someone pause re: feminism, but who knows? There might be. In which case, best to not lead with it as a brand identity.)

I consider myself a feminist. I am also 100% all right with being interrogated on that assertion, and to have people, and especially women, be skeptical until and unless I prove otherwise. I'm also aware that "feminist" is not a level-up—you don't grind until you get the achievement badge and then don't have to think about it ever again. I've said before that if your social consciousness is stuck in 1975, the 21st century is going to be a hard ride, and that continues to be a true thing. You have to keep engaging.

I'm also aware that I'm going to *fail*—that I'll miss a step, or say or do something stupid, or otherwise show my ass, on feminism (among, to be sure, many other issues). And I can pretty much guarantee I'm not always going to take being called on that with initial good grace, because history suggests I'll occasionally screw that up too. I can say that I do try to base my ego not on having to be right, but on doing the right thing. This is why I once did a primer on apologizing: because I need it in my own life.

So, yes. Here in 2017: I am a feminist, imperfectly to be sure but even so. I'm happy for it not to be part of my "brand." I just want it to be part of *me*; of how I treat women, and others, and how I view the world for what it is and should be.

The New Year
and the
Bend of the Arc

As we begin 2017, there is something I've been thinking about, that I'd like for you to consider for the new year. It starts with a famous quote, the best-known version of which is from Martin Luther King, but which goes back to the transcendentalist Theodore Parker. The quote is:

"The arc of the moral universe is long, but it bends toward justice."

In the main I agree with that quote. There are things about it, however, that I think many of us elide.

The first is the word "long." I think both Parker and King understood that moral endeavors can be measured in years, decades and sometimes centuries. This is not an argument toward complacency; indeed I think it's an argument *against* defeatism and fatalism in the face of setbacks and stalemates. We live in moments and days and it's often hard to see past them, and it's easy to believe when we are struck a hard blow that all is lost. All is not lost. The arc is long. Nothing is ever fully decided in the moment or the day. There are years and decades and sometimes centuries yet to go. The arc continues to bend, if we remember that it is long, and that we need to imagine it extending further.

We need to imagine that because of the second thing: The arc is not a natural feature of the universe. It does not magically appear; it is not ordained; it is not inevitable. It exists because people of moral character seek justice, not only for themselves but for every person. Nor is the arc smooth. It's rough and jagged, punctuated in areas by great strides, halting collapses, terrible reverses and forcible wrenching actions. There are those, always, who work to widen the arc, to make that bend toward justice as flat as they can make it, out of fear or greed or hate. They stretch out the arc when they can. If people of moral character forget the arc is not ordained, or become complacent to a vision of a smooth, frictionless bend toward justice, the work to flatten the arc becomes that much easier.

Right now, today, here in 2017, there are those working very industriously to flatten out the arc. They have lately seen little penalty for their hate, or their dissembling, or their disdain or greed; they have contempt for justice other than a cynical appreciation of its features when and only when it is to their advantage; they don't care for anyone or anything outside the close horizon of their own interests. They have won a moment; they have won a day. They will try to win more than that, now, however they can, flattening the arc with hate and fear and greed.

On this day, in this year, in our time: Help to bend the arc back.

As you do, there are things to remember.

Remember the arc is long. It's not one moment or one day or even a year or four years, even when that moment or day or year seems endless.

Remember the arc is not inevitable. It needs you. You are more important than you know, if you don't give in to despair, to complacency, or to apathy. Add to the moral weight that bends the arc toward justice. You can't do it alone, but without you the work becomes that much harder.

Remember that those who are working to flatten the arc hope you give up and give in. They are relying on you to do just that. Disappoint them. Disappoint them in big ways. Disappoint them in small ways. Disappoint them each day, and every day, in all the ways you can. Do not consent to this flattening of the arc.

Remember finally that this arc toward justice never ends. We are human. We are not perfect. We will not arrive at a perfect justice, any more than we will achieve a perfect union. But just as we work toward a *more* perfect union, so too we bend the arc toward justice, knowing the closer we get, the better we and our lives are, as individuals, as communities, as a nation and as a world. This is a life's work, not just work for a moment, or day, or year. You won't see the final result. There isn't one. It doesn't mean the work doesn't matter. It matters. It matters now. It matters for you. It matters for everyone.

It's a new year. There's work to be done. I hope you will do it, and that you find joy in the work.

Happy 2017.

See you on the arc.

Off With Their Comments

Dec

17

2015

*T*he *Toronto Star* newspaper has decided to nix comments on its
Web site. The reason:

> *We have passionate, opinionated readers who are eager to get*
> *involved in conversations about politics, education, municipal issues, sports*
> *and more. You're talking about the news on thestar.com, Facebook, Twitter,*
> *Instagram, Snapchat, Tumblr, LinkedIn and more—and we want to be able to*
> *capture all of these conversations.*
>
> *With that goal, we have turned off commenting on thestar.com effective*
> *Wednesday and instead we'll be promoting and showcasing the comments our*
> *readers share across social media and in their letters and emails to our editors.*

This is a polite and deflect-y way of saying "Our comments are a
raging cesspool filled with the worst that humanity has to offer and you
all make us look bad by smearing your feculent mindpoops on our property, so do it somewhere else and we'll pick the ones we like to highlight."

And you know what? Good for the *Star*. At this late stage in the
evolution of the Internet, it's become widely apparent that, barring committed moderation, comment threads trend quickly toward awful and
vile, and that their ostensible reasons for existing ("free exchange of
ideas," "building community," "keeping eyeballs on the site" etc) are
not just negated but very often undermined by their content. Very few
online sites, news, social or otherwise, benefit commercially or reputa-
tionally from their comment threads. There's a very real and obvious
reason why "NEVER READ THE COMMENTS" is a phrase that has
gained such currency in the online world.

So why *not* just ax them? This is apparently the question that the *Toronto Star* folks asked themselves, and equally apparently could not find a sufficient reason to keep them. Again: Good for them. The site will become marginally more readable, and the newspaper won't have to task some poor sad staffer to moderate the flood of bigots and/or numbskulls and/or spammers who traditionally populate the comment threads of major news sites (and minor ones, and indeed, any site where they are given a chance to thrive). There's no downside.

But what *about* the bigots and/or numbskulls and/or spammers? What of them? Where will they go? Won't their special snowflake voices be silenced? Well, yes, on the *Toronto Star* site. But there is the whole rest of the Internet, and creating one's own outpost to fill with one's own thoughts—and one's own thoughts on the news media—is trivially easy. Look! I'm filling my own site with my own thoughts right now! Now, the drawback to the bigots/numbskulls/spammers is that their thoughts won't get the benefit of being a free rider on the traffic the sites they've attached themselves to; they will have to attract readers on their own in the marketplace of ideas.

But that's not fair! Oh, well. That's life. Also, it is in fact *entirely* fair. As I noted to someone elsewhere on this topic, no one is owed an audience. The audience I have, as an example, comes from a quarter century of writing, including seventeen years(!) on Whatever. You want my audience? The answer is clear: get cracking, folks.

I mentioned on Twitter last night that the world would largely be a better place if all commenting ability were to be vaporized on the Internet, and someone asked me if I would include my own site in that. I said yes, for the general good of humanity, I would be willing to sacrifice my own site's commenting ability (and also, that for the first five years of the site, it did not allow comments, and yet it did just fine). It would be hard, but I'm pretty sure most of the people who I like would keep in touch. Email would still exist.

This *does not* mean, I should note, that I *plan* to get rid of comments on my site. I do actually moderate my comments, and because I do— and because there is in fact a community of people here who care for the quality of the site, often as much as I do—this site is in my mind one of the exceptions to the general rule that comment threads suck. It also helps that this is a very idiosyncratic sort of site; if it was all politics (or all tech or all anything) all the time I suspect it would attract more people committed to trolling and being douchecanoes on particular subjects, and also garner more fly-by commenters. But the site is about whatever is going on in my brain, and my brain skips around a bit. Variety of topics is useful.

But I'll also note that especially over the last few years my patience with comments runs thinner and how I approach them is different. There was a period of time not long ago where I began to dread writing about contentious topics here because I knew it would require me to babysit comment threads, and it would take a whole lot of my time and brain cycles—both of which I could better spend on writing—to plink out obnoxious comments and otherwise act as referee. It genuinely began to affect my overall happiness. I had to change the way I thought about commenting here because of it.

Now I do things like turn off comment threads when I go to sleep, which means I don't wake up dreading coming to my own site to see what some shitty human has posted on it. If I write on a contentious topic but don't feel like refereeing comments, I just plain leave the comments off (which, incidentally, has no measurable effect on how widely a piece is read, as far as I can see). And I'm quicker to mallet comments and punt people out of threads if I decide they're out of line.

Basically, I changed seeing comments as something "of course" and more as "at my pleasure." If I'm not going to be happy they're there, then they won't be.

Which is a point of view I think more people—and more sites—are beginning to take on: What does allowing comments get me? Does it make me happy or not? Will my site be better for them, or not? In the *Toronto Star*'s case, the answer apparently was that the site wasn't better for them, so out they went.

Once more: Good call. I hope more people and sites ask themselves the same questions, and ditch the comments if they don't measure up.

OLIVER SACKS AND PUBLIC INDIVIDUALS AT THE CLOSE

Feb

19

2015

Oliver Sacks has terminal cancer and has decided to say goodbye to the public in the *New York Times*. It's both nicely done and something that's being shared widely in my online social circle. Sacks seems, if not sanguine about the event, at least contented with the path of his life to date. Although it must be recognized that we're seeing an intentionally composed piece of work, which may or may not reflect Sacks actual frame of mind at the news, to the public, at least, he's leaving with some uncommon grace.

And I would imagine that for someone like Sacks, who is a public figure, this is as positive a thing as can be under the circumstances. Public figures are, for better or worse, different than almost everyone else; they are characters in lives beyond their own circle of family and friends, and the narratives of their lives are at least partially offered up by others. When one of them dies suddenly and unexpectedly, the last word on their lives is usually wholly from others—friends and family, and then a host of commentators, who may or may not have been connected with that person's life at all.

Depending on who you are as a person, having certain foreknowledge that your life is quantifiably finite—that you have only months or weeks to live—may not be a thing you want. But if it is a thing you deal with, if you *are* public individual, you have a chance to make your own public exit, and to leave on the terms you set. You won't be the only one having a last word on your life (people will still talk about you after you are dead), but they and everyone else will factor in how you chose to walk off the public stage. And for many people who are in that position, I think that might be a comforting thought.

And what would *I* want? I don't know how well I would handle knowing I was going to die sooner than later—I still like this place and the people in it, and I wouldn't want to leave this party yet—but I suppose if I had to choose I wouldn't mind knowing at least a little in advance. I think I would want to have some parting thoughts before I went, and I would like to be able to manage my public departure before I focused on spending time with family and those I loved. I guess I won't really know until and unless it happens. Like I said, I'd be happy to have to wait a few more decades before having to think about it seriously.

But I am glad that Oliver Sacks, at least, is getting to shape his own moment. I hope he spends his remaining time exactly as he wants. I suspect he will.

ON BEING
AN EGOTISTICAL
JACKASS

May

14

2015

MRAL asks:

There are a lot of people who consider you an egotistical jackass. In your opinion, is this accurate?

Maybe?

Some thoughts on this, in no specific order.

* I certainly have an ego, in the common usage of the term, and don't believe I've ever tried to hide that aspect of my personality. I had an ego well before it was adequately warranted on the basis of my work, and now that I have a track record of work behind me that speaks for itself, it continues well apace. I'm good at what I do, I'm successful at what I do, and I don't have much fake humility about either of those two facts.

So: Ego? You betcha. *Egotistical?* I think I am less egotistical than I was when I was younger, because I have a better understanding of myself and the context of my ego, but I would also cop to still having occasional moments where my self-regard outpaces a healthy understanding of my talents, ability and self. So yes, sure. From time to time I am egotistical. I think whether you see me as overbearingly so depends on what you think about a number of things, including whether you dislike obvious displays of ego and/or dislike me for other reasons as well. I don't think it's *difficult* to see me as egotistical.

* Likewise, I certainly have been a jackass, and am likely to be so again in the future, because none of us are our best selves every single moment of our lives, and from time to time I can be seen not being my best self out in public. Sorry about that. And again, if you are inclined to think less than charitably of me on a regular basis, then, quite obviously, my moments of public jackassery will stand out for you.

* Have I combined the two and been a public egotistical jackass? Oh, almost certainly. Am I an egotistical jackass *all the goddamned time?* I hope not, and try not to be, but it's not really up to me to decide. You have to decide that one for yourself. In your own estimation (or in the estimation of others) the answer might be "Hells yeah, he is, *all the time.*"

* Which is fine.

* But doesn't necessarily mean I should *care*, which, trust me, is a statement that I understand will only confirm my egotistical jackassery to those inclined to see me in that mode. Do understand, however, that I am freely allowed to assess other people, just as they are allowed to freely assess me. A large number of the people who think I am an ego- tistical jackass I assess to be in the "And I Give a Shit What You Think About This or Anything Else Exactly Why Now" category—which again, only confirms their opinion, since if I had any sense I would be *passionately interested* in their assessment. But I'm not! And probably won't ever be! Which just makes them more annoyed still.

* But, I don't know. If you're annoyed that I don't give a shit about your opinion of me, what does that make you?

* The above should be tempered with the realization that your life would be better if there were some people whose opinion you listen to, as regards your behavior and presentation, and that sometimes even someone you don't know might accurately assess when you're being an egotistical jackass in a specific instance. Closing yourself off from *any* opinion that is critical of you or your actions is indeed a very fine way of *actually* ending up being an egotistical jackass all the time. It helps to be self-aware enough to know that you are fallible, both in your actions and in your self-assessment, and it helps to have people you trust who feel comfortable enough with you to call you out when you

show your ass (and it helps if your ego can get out of the way enough for you to listen).

* Obviously, I don't think having an ego is a problem—a healthy self-assessment of skills and abilities is a good thing, in my book, and I don't think you should have to minimize those skills or apologize for them just because someone somewhere might have issues with you for it, for whatever reason. The problem is them, not you. Likewise, I don't think being appropriately rude or dismissive of someone else is a problem, either. It's not usually what I would suggest leading with, when you meet people or interact with them, but sometimes, when all is said and done, there are some people for whom the best response to them or their antics is "You're an asshole. Fuck right off," or some appropriate variation. Sometimes, on the Internet, these folks let you know very quickly when they're not worth your time. Sometimes it takes a little bit more work.

* Related to this, there are some people who really *are* egotistical jackasses all the time, at least in terms of how they deal with other people publicly, and think that's a feature, not a bug. It's okay to feel sorry for them and avoid them whenever possible. There are others who are making jackasses of themselves, whose egos preclude the possibility of them seeing such a thing, despite the worried intervention of friends. It's okay to feel sorry for them, and to avoid them too. There are still others whose egotistical feelings have made them act like jackasses. Once again, okay to be sorry for them, and not to bother with them unless you have to. In the latter two circumstances, you can hope that one day soon they pull their heads out and recognize the errors of their ways. In the former case there's not much to be done, unless you decide you have nothing better to do with the startlingly few moments of your lifespan than to engage with an unrepentant shitheel of a human being. In which case I wish you happiness in your entertainment choices.

* But overall, again, it's worth remembering that none of us—and certainly not *I*—are always our best selves. We have our egotistical moments, our moments of jackassery, our moments of weakness, or neuroticism, or envy, or anger, or pettiness or what have you. They happen

and you deal with them. Owning up to them, acknowledging them and trying to do better the next time is a good thing to try to do. If you can work on that, even if you have been an egotistical jackass (or whatever) at some point, then there's hope that you won't be that all the time. And that's a good thing to move toward.

On the Matter of Empathy For Horrible People

Feb

22

2017

Yesterday I was having a conversation with a friend regarding the implosion of Milo Yiannopoulos, the remarkable two-day period in which the public bigot and Breitbart editor lost a high-profile speaking engagement, a lucrative book contract, and a job, because one of his positions (regarding sexual contact between adults and young teens) finally crossed a line for the horrible clutch of bigots who were keeping him around as their One Gay Friend. The implosion was inevitable—the horrible bigots never really liked him, they just found him *useful,* and suddenly he wasn't useful anymore— and moreover the implosion was karmically appropriate, because Yiannopoulos is a terrible person who became famous for being terrible to others. The dude earned it, and in a very real way it's delightful to see the comeuppance.

While my friend agreed with me that the comeuppance was indeed delicious, he also asked me, essentially: But do you feel even in the tiniest bit *sorry* for Yiannopoulos? Do you have *empathy* for him?

And the answer is: Well, sure. In my opinion Yiannopoulos is clearly emotionally damaged in all sorts of ways and for all sorts of reasons, and it's exhibited itself in a particularly itchy combination of personal self-loathing and a desperate need to feel special, and to have attention. He discovered that playing to a crowd of horrible bigots gave him attention, made him feel special and made him either hate himself less, or at least allowed him to ignore how much he hated himself, so he went with that as long as he could.

And things appeared to be going his way! Trump won, which gave him a more legitimate platform because the horrible bigots he played to were elevated and wanted him to speak at their gathering; he nabbed himself a pretty good book deal with a major publisher; and he got to go on national TV and had hit it off well with the host, even if the other guests told him to go fuck off, which of course played to his strengths as a media personality. It was all coming together!

Then, in roughly 36 hours, all of it was taken away. Not to mention his reputation and standing among much of the crowd that had previously stood behind him. And to top it all off, he lost his professional income. It was all in public, and it happened quick, and in humiliating fashion.

So here's the thing: A damaged soul who thought he had found acceptance, reaching for the goals that he probably thought would finally satisfy him, only to have them (from his point of view) cruelly taken away, all at once, in public?

Again: Sure. I have some empathy there. That all sucks.

BUT

(And you *knew* there was a "but" coming)

Yiannopoulos' damage explains but does not excuse his actions. Lots of people are damaged by life, one way or another. Lots of people crave acceptance and desire fame. Lots of people try to heal themselves through the attention of others. But Yiannopoulos decided to deal with all of that by spouting racist and sexist and transphobic hatred, by lying about his targets and by pointing his passel of online, bigoted followers at people in order to harass and threaten them, and then by laughing at and dismissing as unimportant other people's pain and fear, pain and fear that he caused. It's what he became famous *for*. It was all a lark to him, or so he'd have you believe. Saying so gave him attention and admiration, and if that attention and admiration was from hateful bigots, eh, that'd work for him. Until it didn't.

I can feel empathy for a damaged human being, and understand why he does what he does. I *get* Yiannopoulos. He's not exactly a puzzle. But my (or anyone's) empathy and understanding for him has to be weighed against the damage he's done to others and his reasons for doing so. And the fact is, the damage he's caused others is immense, and the reasons he's done so are self-serving, vain and ultimately wholly insufficient to excuse or mitigate his actions. Empathy and understanding are important, indeed I think critical, when considering the people who have chosen to oppose you. It reminds you they are merely human, and not actually monsters. But they are part, not the whole, of one's consideration of such people; nor does *empathy* automatically convert to *sympathy*. Personally, considered as a whole and including his actions, I don't judge Yiannopoulos deserving of much sympathy. He's earned this moment of his, and in point of fact, he's earned much worse than this. But this will do for a start.

And here's another fact, which is that Yiannopoulos isn't special. There are a lot of damaged people out there on the racist, sexist, bigoted side of things, who have been fucked up by the world in one way or another and who have decided the best way to dig themselves out of that hole is to try to take it out on other people. These are the very people fringe radical and reactionary organizations and would-be leaders seek out; they're susceptible *because* they're damaged and crave acceptance and attention. To get personal here, I look at the bigots who have decided to make me their special enemy and it's not hard to understand why they do what they do, nor to feel empathy for what they have to be going through in their brain. But again, that's weighed against the damage they do to others and try to do to me, and I proceed accordingly.

(Also, a supplementary thought I have, which is that Yiannopoulos is well into his 30s. He's not a child or a young man of whom it could be said that he did not know better. Yiannopoulos may be damaged in various ways, but it doesn't appear that he is not in control of his actions, or doesn't have enough presence of mind to understand right or wrong, even if he apparently doesn't *care* about such things. Yiannopoulos understands what he's doing and why. He owns his choices and actions, and he owns the results of those choices and actions, even when they result, as they did this week, in his downfall.)

So: Empathy and understanding for Yiannopoulos? Sure. Maybe even the smallest soupçon of pity. I think the ability to feel these things for him allows me to say, in full consideration, that he deserves his fall this week from the grace of the horrible and bigoted. And to continue in that vein, I wish for *him* the empathy and understanding to realize just how well he's earned this moment, and to realize how much work he'll have to undertake to atone for the damage he's done to others. I don't expect he'll actually *arrive* at that empathy and understanding, mind you. I don't think he *wants* that. I wish it for him nonetheless.

THE 1% OF
PROBLEMS

Oct

18

2015

Today's Thing About Rich People Appalling the Internet: "Wealth therapy tackles woes of the rich: 'It's really isolating to have lots of money,'" an article in the *Guardian* about therapists who help the rich deal with the apparent loneliness and isolation of having a shitload of money. Here's one of the more choice quotes from the piece:

From the Bible to the Lannisters of Game of Thrones, it's easy to argue that the rich have always been vilified, scorned and envied. But their counsellors argue things have only gotten worse since the financial crisis and the debate over income inequality that has been spurred on by movements like Occupy Wall Street and the Fight for $15 fair wage campaign.

"The Occupy Wall Street movement was a good one and had some important things to say about income inequality, but it singled out the 1% and painted them globally as something negative. It's an -ism," said Jamie Traeger-Muney, a wealth psychologist and founder of the Wealth Legacy Group. "I am not necessarily comparing it to what people of color have to go through, but...it really is making value judgment about a particular group of people as a whole."

The media, she said, is partly to blame for making the rich "feel like they need to hide or feel ashamed".

Oh, lordy, lordy, lordy.

So, point one: Rich people do indeed have problems, and while their problems are problems that most people would *like* to have, because those problems don't generally involve lack of money, it doesn't mean they are not genuine, actual problems that cause stress and unhappiness. I think money can indeed be isolating and strange, especially if you have money and those around you do not; money is inherently powerful and changes power dynamics and how people perceive you. I think rich people also probably need to be able to talk to other people without judgment about their particular and unique set of problems, just like anyone needs to. Otherwise their loneliness and alienation will get worse. It's difficult for many people to imagine a ton of money being a curse, but if you don't know how to deal with what money does to you and other people, sure, it can be a curse.

Point two, holy *fuck* does this article quote absolutely clueless people. "I am not necessarily comparing it to what people of color have to go through, but..." I mean, *wow*. This is the therapist-to-the-rich-people's version of "I'm not saying it's aliens...*but* it's aliens," especially since later in the article she *directly* makes a comparison by encouraging people to replace the word "rich" with "black" to see the problem with how she says people speak of the rich.

Here's a handy pro tip for you: When describing the problems of the rich—who are, statistically speaking here in the US, a very white cohort; the 2010 Census has 96% of the 1% households being white—do *not* bring up in comparison, even to say that you're not *necessarily* comparing them, the problems of people of color. Here's what some of the problems of people of color are, wealth-wise:

The Great Recession, fueled by the crises in the housing and financial markets, was universally hard on the net worth of American families. But even as the economic recovery has begun to mend asset prices, not all households have benefited alike, and wealth inequality has widened along racial and ethnic lines.

The wealth of white households was 13 times the median wealth of black households in 2013, compared with eight times the wealth in 2010, according to a new Pew Research Center analysis of data from the Federal Reserve's Survey of Consumer Finances. Likewise, the wealth of white households is now more than 10 times the wealth of Hispanic households, compared with nine times the wealth in 2010.

So, yeah. This on top of *every single other thing* that people of color in the US have to deal with. One of the reasons the "replace 'rich' with 'black'" formulation rings hollow is because no one who is not utterly delusional believes the average experience of a black person in the US and the average experience of a rich person in the US is anything alike, either in the day-to-day experience or in the power dynamic between those expressing the opinions and those on the receiving end.

Again, I'm sympathetic to the idea that the rich have their problems; everyone does. But I suspect that Ms. Traeger-Muney, whether she wants to own up to it or not, was trying in a sad and clumsy way to appropriate the dynamic of racial inequity to describe the *absolutely entirely different dynamic* of rich people problems, even while denying she was doing it. If you're not *necessarily* comparing them, then don't bring it up at all—it compromises your argument and makes you part of the problem. You help neither people of color nor the 1% by this formulation.

Point three: The media is making "the rich feel like they need to hide or be ashamed"? Really? Huh. She's seeing different media than I'm seeing, at the very least. If you're a horrid little shitlord like Martin Shkreli, who appears so cartoonish as a human being it's amazing that he hasn't actually been photographed diving into a pool of money, a la Scrooge McDuck, then yes, you may feel the media is trying to make you feel ashamed. But it's not *because* Shkreli is rich. It's because he appears by all indications to be a genuinely terrible person, and he appears enabled by money (and his control of it) to be a genuinely terrible person in ways that affect innocent others.

Indeed that's the hallmark of what rich appear to be castigated for in the media: they're doing terrible or clueless things, often to other people, and use their money to further those ends, or use the money to insulate themselves from the consequences. Even the fictional very rich noted in the article are like that. People don't dislike the Lannisters in *Game of Thrones* because they're rich. They dislike them because they're a family of sadistic schemers who will absolutely cut off your head or have you gored by boars or *whatever* if you get in their joyless, unhappy way. The single *good* thing about the Lannisters is that they're rich; they famously always pay their debts. It's everything else about them that's the problem.

So, yes. If you're very rich and you're acting like an asshole—using your money to rise prices on parasite-treating drugs or blocking access to a public beach near your house or trying to buy an election or shutting off electricity to grandmothers during a heatwave to make money on the margins or cutting off the head of the Hand of the King even though you agreed to spare him and let him take the black—people are going to not like you very much. People tend not to like assholes. This should not be a surprise.

More generally, the rich also have the circumstance of getting manifestly richer in an era in the US and the Western world in which literally everyone else is seeing their real incomes drop, sometimes by negligible amounts (in the upper heights of the middle class) and by more noticeable amounts the further down you go. Should this make the rich anxious? Probably, because if they're decent human beings they will recognize the increasing inequity of wealth is no good for anyone in the long run, because it's already giving rise to systematic problems that will take generations to correct. Should they be *fearful?* You know what, if the heads of the rich are not already on spikes after 2008, it seems unlikely they ever will be, so I'm gonna go with "no."

In my observation of things, neither people nor the media seem to dislike people either becoming or being rich. I can speak to this a little bit personally: after my multi-year, multi-book deal was announced earlier this year, I'd say 99% of the response to it, in the media and out of it, was "cool, well done" (1% was the usual people who dislike me continuing to dislike me, and, you know: HA HA HA sucks to be them). I know people who are worth substantially more than I am; there doesn't seem to be a reflexive dislike of them, either. If anything, the media and people in general are tuned to like and admire wealth and those who have it. It's that particularly American version of the Protestant Work Ethic which says that in the US there are two types of people: The rich and those who aren't rich yet. You have to work hard (no pun intended) to make people dislike you when you are rich. It's much easier—again, speaking from experience—for people to dislike you because you are poor.

So, yeah, no: I'm not inclined to believe the media is particularly hard on the rich.

Yet again, this is not say the rich don't have problems, including alienation, loneliness and anxiousness. I'm sure many do, and I'm also sure that for many rich people having their wealth be their initial outwardly defining characteristic is not a happy one. It's okay to have some sympathy for the rich. But it's also okay to recognize that the problems of the rich are their own set of problems, often unlike the problems that most people have or, honestly, will ever have. They are the 1% of problems.

PEOPLE ARE THE
PROBLEM AND
THEY PRETTY MUCH
ALWAYS WILL BE

Sep

27

2014

Today noted skeptic PZ Myers ruminated about the problems he has with the atheist movement here in the US, much of which, from my point of view, boils down to "the problem is that there are *people* in it."

Which, I will hastily note, is *not* me snarking. People are hierarchical, status-sensitive and in many ways fundamentally conservative creatures. We crave structure, hate disruption and are wary of outsiders and change. And some people are just plain rotten people, and those people are widely distributed. I'm not entirely sure why the atheist movement (and/or the various public examples of it) would be at all different. And given the larger society in which the atheist movement in the US exists, it's not entirely surprising that things play out as Myers notes:

Too many atheists turn out to be just as shallow as the fervent faithful I rail against. Too many see atheism as another useless difference they can use to excuse discrimination against others they are already prejudiced against. I used to have this illusion that an atheist society would be more tolerant, that under it government and education would be secular, but the churches would still exist, if people wanted to attend them—a sort of Scandinavian ideal. But no, what I'm fast learning is that tolerance isn't automatically a property of abandoning the false tribe of religion, but is more a reflection of the greater culture it is embedded in. Atheists can still hold a "kill the wogs" mentality while babbling about the wonders of science; people who regard women as servile appliances for their gratification don't seem to become suddenly enlightened once the scales of faith fall from their eyes.

Shorter, reductive version: Atheists are as perfectly capable of being complete assholes as anyone else; becoming an atheist will not, in itself, keep one from being a complete asshole. This isn't surprising; what would be surprising, in fact, is if it did. Because that would be a first, in the history of all humans and all of their congregations, regardless of how, and around what, these congregations formed.

This is why, incidentally, the phrase "we're supposed to be *better* than that," drives me crazy, when it's used as a way to argue against a group of people laying down certain official guidelines in how to deal with each other, most recently in dealing with harassment issues. Sure, okay, you're *supposed* to be better than that, but you know what? You're *not*, because you're all human. Having one thing in common, whether it be a belief or enthusiasm or hobby or political mission, does not make you *immune*, individually or as a class, to all the other ridiculous social baggage humans carry with them all the time. The belief that it does or *should*, among other things, creates within any assemblage the space for assholes to thrive and prey on other people.

I am agnostic of an atheistic sort (I don't believe based on the scientific evidence that the universe needed a creator but as a technicality I'm aware I can neither prove nor disprove that one existed), and quite a lot of my friends are also agnostic or atheist. But they are not my friends because they are agnostic or atheist, nor are they better people because they are agnostic or atheist. They are people who are good and are atheist/agnostic. In some cases becoming atheist/agnostic helped them to become good people, by helping them to abandon ideologies that led them to treat people poorly. In other cases, they were good people, who also came to believe the universe didn't need a god in it to exist.

Conversely, there are people who believe the same things I do, with regard to the existence of god, who I judge to be absolute shitcanoes. Sometimes they were already shitcanoes, and sometimes they have decided their atheist/agnostic beliefs allow them—or even demand them—to be absolute shitcanoes to others. They're terrible people and I want nothing to do with them. I'm okay with calling them out for being terrible people.

You don't get credit with me simply for believing something I believe. You get credit for how you deal with other human beings.

I think internalizing the fact that no opinion/belief/enthusiasm inoculates either you or anyone else from the baser aspects of the human condition, or the larger social milieu in which we all exist, is probably a very smart thing to do. It helps manage the disappointment when the cool new group you find yourself with is eventually revealed to be full of flawed and fallible human beings, and it helps to free you from the initial desire to rationalize shitty behavior within a group merely for the sake of identity politics. And on the rare occasions when everyone in the group is actually good and decent, it allows you to appreciate just how nice that really is.

A Personal History of Libraries

Feb

23

2013

The first library I ever remember visiting was the library in Red Bluff, California. I was five at the time, and living with my aunt while my mother was recovering from surgery. I remember the children's area of the library, and in my recollection of the place today, the rows of books went all the way up to the ceiling. I remember specifically, although not by name, a picture book I pulled down from the rows, about children leaping for the moon. It was explained to me that I could take the book home—and not just *that* book, but *any* book I wanted in the *entire* library. I remember thinking, in a five-year-old's vocabulary, *how unbelievably perfect*. I took home a book about stars, which started a life-long love of astronomy.

The second library I have a strong memory of was the Covina Public Library, in my then hometown of Covina, California. My mother and then-stepfather worked all day and I would walk or bike to the library most afternoons, and read magazines and look through reference and trivia books. I also remember specifically spending a lot of time with a book about dragons.

I remember the library at Ben Lomond Elementary School, also in Covina. It was there I first made the acquaintance of Robert Heinlein, in a library-bound edition of *Farmer in the Sky*. It was the start of a beautiful relationship.

At the West Covina library, I discovered that one could borrow LPs and listen to them at turntables in the library! I remember sitting in a chair, next to a turntable, headphones on, listening to Bill Cosby LPs and giggling as quietly as I could (it *was* a library) while simultaneously flipping through a Time-Life book called *The Planets*, written by one Carl Sagan.

The library in Glendora was where I stayed in the afternoons when my now-divorced mother worked. I would sit just outside the kids' area, eating Jujyfruit candies (you could buy a whole big box for 49 cents at the Ralph's just down the street), reading what were called "juvies" then and are called "Young Adult" books now. It was the first place I was exposed to a real live computer: A TRS-80 Model III. I remember programming the computer in BASIC to play simple games. It was there I met Mykal Burns, who was (and remains) one of my best friends. I also met—*actually* met, not just in a book—Ray Bradbury there, which to me was something like meeting a wizard.

The library at Sandburg Middle School is where I would be in the early morning before school started, reading science fiction and rushing through my homework. It was also the scene of some of my greatest junior high triumphs, as I participated in school-wide "science bees" staged there, for the Red team (the school divided alphabetically into colors), and would single-handedly *utterly slaughter* entire opposing teams. All those years of checking out trivia and science books paid off with a vengeance.

At the Thomas Jackson Library at the Webb Schools of California I met Dorothy Parker, Robert Benchley, James Thurber, Harold Ross— heck, the whole of the Algonquin Round Table—plus Ben Hecht, H.L. Mencken, P.J. O'Rourke, Molly Ivins and Hunter S. Thompson, Tom Stoppard and George Bernard Shaw. In the science fiction section I was introduced to Robert Silverberg, Larry Niven and Ursula K. LeGuin. Here was where I discovered many of the writing idols of my youth.

The University of Chicago unsurprisingly had many libraries; the one I spent the most time in was the Harper Library, where the University kept most of its fiction. The space these days would remind people of Hogwarts, I suppose; at the time I thought of it like a cathedral, filled with books, and also, very comfortable cushions to read (and, sometimes, nap) on.

When I left the University of Chicago, my relationship with libraries changed, because my position in life changed. I had a job and money, and for me that meant I could *buy* books. So I did: I bought new books by the authors I was introduced to in the library, and bought the old books that I'd checked out so many times *from* the library, because now I could afford to own them. I bought books on the subjects I first became interested in by wandering through the library stacks. I bought as gifts the books I had grown to love and wanted others to love, too. I had become a fervent buyer of books because libraries made it easy to become a fervent reader of books—to make them a necessary part of my life. For about a decade I didn't use the library much, because I was in the bookstore. It was a natural progression.

I remember the library in Sterling, Virginia, because that was where I lived when I got my contract for the very first book I would have published: a book on online finance. As part of my research for writing the book, I went to the library and checked out just about every book on finance they had, to see how those authors had written on the subject, and to make sure I didn't have any obvious gaps in my own knowledge of the subject. When it was published I went back to the library and was delighted to find my new book there too. And it had even been checked out! More than once! I felt like a real author.

Finally I arrive at my present library, the one in Bradford, Ohio. It's a small library, but then, Bradford is a small community, of about 1,800. For that community, the library holds books, and movies, magazines and music; it has Internet access, which folks here use to look for jobs and to keep in contact with friends and family around the county, state and country. It hosts local meetings and events, has story times and reading groups, is a place where kids can hang out after school while their parents work, and generally functions as libraries always have: A focal point and center of gravity for the community—a place where a community knows it *is* a community, in point of fact, and not just a collection of houses and streets.

I don't use my local library like I used libraries when I was younger. But I *want* my local library, in no small part because I recognize that I am fortunate not to *need* my local library—but others do, and my connection with humanity extends beyond the front door of my house. My life was indisputably improved because those before me decided to put those libraries there. It would be stupid and selfish and shortsighted of me to declare, after having wrung all I could from them, that they serve no further purpose, or that the times have changed so much that they are obsolete. My library is used every single day that it is open, by the people who live here, children to senior citizens. They use the building, they use the Internet, they use the books. This is, as it happens, the exact opposite of what "obsolete" means. I am glad my library is here and I am glad to support it.

Every time I publish a new book—every time—the first hardcover copy goes to my wife and the second goes to the Bradford library. First because it makes me happy to do it: I love the idea of my book being in *my* library. Second because that means the library doesn't have to spend money to buy my book, and can then use it to buy the book of another author—a small but nice way of paying it forward. Third because I wouldn't be a writer without libraries, hard stop, end of story. Which means I wouldn't have the life I have without libraries, hard stop, end of story.

I am, in no small part, the sum of what all those libraries I have listed above have made me. When I give my books to my local library, it's my way of saying: Thank you. For all of it.

And also: Please stay.

POLICE AND ME
AND
PHILANDO CASTILE

Here's the thing: I've been pulled over by the police before, mostly because I'm speeding, but at least once because of a broken tail light. When I'm speeding, I usually know that I've been speeding, so when the police officer asks me if I know why I was pulled over, I say "probably because I was speeding. You caught me, write me up." I do it because I know there's a good chance he'll be so tickled by me not even trying to evade the ticket that he'll just let me off with a warning. One time I was speeding on the freeway, and when the cop pulled me over, I asked if I could speak to him outside the car. He allowed me to get out of the car, and when he did, I leaned in close and said, "the people with me in the car have not stopped arguing since I picked them up. I need a break from them. Write me up, and please, take a *long time* doing it." The cop laughed, didn't write me up, and chatted with me for about five minutes to give me breathing space from the squabbling in the car.

I have never once been afraid of being pulled over by the cops in my car. I have never once been afraid of the cops when they have approached me for anything. It does not occur to me to be afraid of the cops. Why would it? When I have been pulled over by the cops, the worst that will happen to me is that I will be cited for speeding—which is, when it happens, an entirely fair call on the part of the cop, because I usually *was* speeding. I have literally been pulled over by the cops with an *actual skinhead neo-Nazi* in my car—and *there's* a story for you, long and complicated, and mostly aside from the point at the moment so I'll skip it for now—and the neo-Nazi was literally biting his tongue so he wouldn't scream *fuck yooooooou, PIIIIIIIG* at the cop at the top of his lungs. I sat there and chatted with the cop about me speeding, and he let me off with a warning and I went on my way, neo-Nazi with bulging neck veins apoplectic in the passenger seat beside me.

So I repeat: I have never once been afraid of being pulled over by the cops in my car. I have never once been afraid of the cops when they have approached me for anything. It does not occur to me to be afraid of the cops.

Nor, I rather strongly suspect, does it occur to anyone who looks like me—white, male, visibly part of the mainstream of American culture—to be afraid of the cops. The only time we *are* afraid of the cops is when, say, we've got a dime bag and the car smells of skunkweed. Or when in fact we've had more to drink than we should have. Or we have that unlicensed gun poking out from underneath the passenger seat. Basically, when we are doing something that's against the law, and we can get in trouble for it, and the cop would be perfectly within their rights to take us to jail for it.

This is why, I suspect, when so many people who look like me, white and/or male, and visibly part of the mainstream of American culture, hear about a black person being gunned down by a cop, in their car or out of it, immediately go to "well, what did they do to deserve it?" Because, in the somewhat unlikely event of one of *us* being arrested by a cop, much less gunned down by one, we know *damn well* that dude did *something* stupid to warrant the cop taking that action. My own lived experience of 47 years, and the lived experience of nearly every other person who looks like me that I know, confirms that fact. I'm not going to get stick from a cop unless *I* did something to get that stick.

Now, here's what I know so far about Philando Castile, which is what anyone at this point knows: This 32-year-old guy who worked at an elementary school was, with his girlfriend, pulled over for a broken tail light, and was in the act of complying with police instructions and *volunteered information* to the police officer that he had a gun, which he was *licensed to carry*, when the police officer shot him. It's not a huge stretch of the imagination to suppose that the *reason* Castile told the police officer he had a firearm was so the officer wouldn't see it, panic, and shoot him. But it didn't matter, and he was shot anyway, and died. He died, by all indications, despite doing exactly what he was *supposed* to do—complying with police instructions, and doing what he could to defray any potential problems.

I have been pulled over by the police. I have had a broken tail light. I have complied with police instructions. And while I don't travel with a firearm in my car on most days, if I had one in the car and was pulled over, you're damn right I'd let the cop know about it, especially if it was on my person. Why wouldn't I? I don't want to give the cop any surprises. And I am just about 99.9% certain, in that situation, if I were doing all those things, I wouldn't suddenly find myself shot, dying in that car.

But then, I'm white, and Philando Castile wasn't.

I posted this tweet last night, about the announcement that Philando Castile had died:

Jesus.

https://twitter.com/jennifermayerle/status/750908509139693572

And the *first* comment was from a guy just like me, white, middle-aged, clearly in the mainstream, who responded, "Jumping to conclusions again, John? Maybe we need more time on this one. Guy said he had a gun and reached inside his coat."

Leaving aside the data point that according Diamond Reynolds, her boyfriend was reaching for his wallet in compliance with officer instructions, and leaving aside the data point that she maintains that Castile was informing the police officer about the gun so *he would know it was there* and presumably not be alarmed by it, all I said was one simple word: "Jesus." Shock that Philando Castile died. Nothing else—I didn't comment on whether I thought the shooting was justified or not. I didn't comment on the color of Castile or of the police officer. I didn't make a statement on who was at fault, or of my general feelings about police, or of anything else. Just, "Jesus."

And the first comment, from a white, middle-aged, mainstream dude, is reaching for a rationalization for the cop for shooting Philando Castile.

The most charitable explanation I can give for that fellow is what I mentioned above: For him, and for me, and for the folks who look like us, the *only* way we'd get shot is if *we* were doing something that would get us shot.

But I also know, with high levels of certainty, that someone who looks like me merely informing a cop that we have a gun would be unlikely to get us shot. I mean, hell. Aside from anything else I've mentioned here, I live in rural America. You think a non-trivial percentage of people here *don't* have guns on them? Even when they're pulled over by cops? It's also worth noting, as I say the above, that the racial composition of my county is 98% white. If my neighbors or I get pulled over and inform a cop, in the process of complying with their instructions, that we have guns, we're very likely to live. Not everyone can say the same.

I'm not saying the fellow who made the comment to my tweet is actively racist. He's probably not, any more than I am. But we live in a racist society, and some of that racism gets exhibited in how our police forces deal with us. I have a very different experience of the police than my friends and fellow citizens who don't look like me. It's an experience different enough that while I understand intellectually that there are people who are afraid of the police, just as a default setting, and it's something I see again and again as minority friends of mine vent and rage on social media, I still can't *feel* it. I am not afraid of the police. I never have been. I have never had to be. I probably will never have to be. That doesn't mean that my friends are wrong.

The police officer who shot Philando Castile wouldn't have known that Castile worked in a school, and was by all indications well-liked in his community, *but even that* is placing the burden of exculpation on the man who got shot. In the same situation, pulled over with the same broken tail light, telling the cop the same things, with the cop knowing exactly as much about me as he did about Castile, I still don't get shot. Of that I feel certain. Nor should I be. *Why* should I be? Even if you hate the idea of people being able to conceal carry weapons, if someone is following the law, they shouldn't be shot for carrying that weapon.

The cop made a threat assessment and decided to shoot. A man is dead for it, one who, by all indications, complied with the officer's instructions and acted to keep the officer aware of his situation, so there would be no surprises. And I know that because the man is dead by the cop's hand (and by his weapon), there will be people, many of whom will look like me, who will look to find fault with Philando Castile, with what he did or said, something, *anything*, to justify the shooting. And it's possible that what we know now is not the complete story, and that Castile *did* do something, *anything*, that made the cop in question shoot to kill.

But, two things here. First: would that something, anything, be enough to kill *me*, if I did it? I would like to bluntly and rather racistly suggest that the standard for policing in this country not be how the police treat black men, but how they treat white men, and specifically, white men like *me*, me who has no fear of police because he has never had cause to fear the police, and never been made by the police to fear them. By all indications, there was no reason for this police officer to fear Philando Castile any more than he would have to fear me. We know this now. But in the moment, I suggest in the same situation, I would still be alive where Castile is dead, and we need to ask why. The officer who shot Castile may not be racist any more than I or the fellow who commented back to me on Twitter likely is. But we live in a racist society, and the ambient racism steeps into each of us whether we acknowledge it or not.

Second: If you're one of the folks looking for something, anything to excuse the shooting of Philando Castile, as a matter of intellectual honesty you should consider the possibility that you're wrong, and that Castile, in fact, did nothing to warrant his death, and that the officer shot him, needlessly. And when you entertain that notion, you should also ask yourself why Castile is dead anyway. If your answer to that question is entirely devoid of anything having to do with the fact that Philando Castile was a black man, you should probably try again.

I am not afraid of the cops. Never have been. Probably will never have to be. That is a luxury and privilege not everyone gets to have. I'm glad I have it. I want more people to have it, too. We're not there yet. We can't pretend we are.

The Poverty
"State of Mind"

May

25

2017

Ben Carson, our HUD Secretary of somewhat dubious expertise, recently burbled on about how he thinks that "poverty, to a large extent, is a state of mind," a statement which earned him some well-justified push-back and which prompted several people, knowing of my general thoughts about poverty, to wonder if I had any thoughts on the matter.

My thought on poverty in the United State being a "state of mind" is that what it really is, to a rather *larger* extent, is a lack of access—to money, to education, to opportunities, to adequate housing, to networks of expertise and help, among many other things, and most importantly (and as often a consequence of all the others noted and more) to the *margin of safety* that people who are not in poverty have when any individual thing knocks them off their stride.

It's the last of these, in my opinion, that illustrates the gormlessness of Carson's thoughts on poverty. You can have the most can-do spirit in the world, but your *state of mind* doesn't mean jack when confronted with, say, a broken-down car you can't afford to repair, which means that you can't get to your job, which means that the job goes out the window, putting you at risk of not being able to pay the rent (or other bills), increasing the possibility of putting your family out on the street, making it more difficult for your kids to get and maintain an education. Your "can-do" spirit doesn't mean shit to a worn-out timing belt or transmission. Your "can-do" spirit doesn't mean shit to the landlord who decides to raise a rent you can barely afford, because he knows he can get more from someone else. Your "can-do" spirit doesn't mean shit to the ice outside your home you slip and fracture your arm on when you head off to your second job. Your *state of mind* is not telekinetic. It can't fix things that are out of your control, and which by dint of poverty you have no immediate way of addressing. When you're poor, so *many* things are out of your control.

Conversely, if you have margin, your "state of mind" matters even *less*—because you have the ability to address problems as they arise. It doesn't matter what my *state of mind* is if my car stops working; I can afford to have it taken to the shop and fixed. My state of mind is not relevant when I crack my arm; I have good health insurance with a low deductible. My state of mind is neither here nor there to my housing situation; my mortgage is paid off. My margin is considerable and will be regardless of what state my mind is in.

Yes, you might say, but *you*, John Scalzi, have an industrious state of mind! Well, that's debatable (more on that later), but even if it is true, is it *more* industrious than the person who works two shitty jobs because they have no other choice? Am I more industrious than, say, my mother, who cleaned people's houses and worked on a telephone exchange while I was growing up, so that I could eat and have a roof over my head? My mother, who barely cracked a five-figure salary while I grew up, worked as hard as hell. Tell me her "state of mind" was less industrious than mine is now, and I'll laugh my ass off at you. Tell me any number of people in the small, blue-collar town I live in, who make significantly less than I do, and who are one slip on the ice away from tumbling down the poverty hole, have a "state of mind" substantially less industrious than my own, and I'll likely tell you to go fuck yourself.

I happen to be one of those people who went from poverty to wealth, and because I am, I can tell you where "state of mind" lies on the list of things that have mattered in getting me where I am. It is on the list, to be sure. But it's not number one. Number one is access to opportunity, which I got when my mother—*not* me—decided to chance having me apply to Webb, a private boarding school that cost more than she made in a year (I was a scholarship kid), with immense resources that allowed me entree into a social stratum I might not have otherwise had access to.

Number two is a network of people—mostly teachers at first—who went out of their way to foster me and nurture my intellect and creativity when they saw it in me. Number three is luck: being in the right place at the right time more than once, whether I "deserved" the break I was getting or not. Number four is my creativity, my own innate talents, which I then had to cultivate. Number five are the breaks I got in our culture that other people, who are not me, might not have gotten. Number six would be Krissy, my wife and my partner in life, who has skills and abilities complementary to mine, which has made getting ahead easier and building out our family's margins much simpler than if I had to do it on my own.

Number seven—not even in the top five!—I would say is my "state of mind," my desire and determination to make something of myself. And let's be clear: this "state of mind" has not been an "always on" thing. There have been lots of times I was perfectly happy to float, or fuck around, or be passive, because times and opportunities allowed me to be so. There have been times when I have been depressed or apathetic and not interested in doing anything, and I didn't—but still got along *just fine* because of my margin of safety. There have been times I have been overwhelmed and barely able to make any decisions at all. "State of mind" is a changeable thing, and importantly can be deeply influenced by one's own circumstances. It's much easier to have a positive "state of mind" when you know that no one thing is likely to knock your entire life askew. It's easier not to give in to fatalism when not everything has the potential to ruin everything else. It's easier to not feel like nothing you do matters, when you have the ability to solve many of your problems with a simple application of money.

I have seen people with what I'm sure Carson would describe as the correct "state of mind" fail over and over again because their legs are kicked out from under them in one way or another, and who never seem to make it no matter how hard they try. I've seen people who definitely *don't* have the right "state of mind" succeed and even thrive—have seen them fail *upward*—because on balance other things broke their way. "State of mind" as a predictive factor of economic mobility is, bluntly, anecdotal bullshit, something to pull out of your ass while ignoring the mountains of evidence showing that economic mobility in the United States is becoming more difficult to come by. It's not "state of mind" that's the issue. It's long-term systematic inequality, inequality that's getting worse as we go along. Ignoring or eliding the latter and pinning poverty "to a large extent" on the former means you're giving everyone and everything else that contributes to poverty in the United States—from racism to inertia to greed—a free pass.

I'm well aware that Carson has his own anecdotal rags-to-riches story, as I do; we both even have mothers who sacrificed for us so we could succeed. Good for him! I applaud him and his effort to get where he is now. But this doesn't make his story any more than what it is, or what mine is—a single story, not necessarily easily replicated at large. Certainly *my* story isn't easily replicated; not every poor kid can be given a break by a private boarding school catering to the scions of wealth and privilege. I think it's fine if Carson or anyone else wants to lecture or opine on the poverty "state of mind." But until and unless our country makes an effort to address all the other long-term issues surrounding poverty, Carson's opinion on the matter is bullshit.

Control for opportunity. Control for access. Control for *margin*. And *then* come back to me about "state of mind," as it regards poverty. I'll be waiting, Dr. Carson.

PRONOUNS

Bebe asks:

My younger child, a sophomore in college, has asked me to use "they" "them" as their preferred pronouns. I live in a very liberal and gender-choice aware New England college town, and I still find this difficult to consistently comply with. Sometimes my English major brain rebels at using plurals for a single person, sometimes I just don't want to have that conversation with a stranger, especially one who has already stated views that suggest they have no sympathy for the preferences and realities of others. Sometimes I'm just tired and it's hard to keep it all straight. So, what do you think of gender neutral pronouns? Can you suggest something...better than they, them? Am I being disrespectful of my child by failing to consistently respect and comply with their request? And how would you, or an older, female, Southern version of you respond to the boor who immediately brings up Caitlyn Jenner and insists on calling "him" "Bruce"? And, since you love writing questions, have I used too many """"'s in this question?

Small things first: The number of quotation marks seems fine to me, and as far as "they" "them" and "their" are concerned, not only is there a long history of their being used as singular pronouns, it's something that's rapidly becoming standard usage. When you feel weird about using them for singular usage, just remember a lot of commonly-accepted grammar rules were invented fairly recently as a way for the status-anxious to feel better about how they used the English language. And, you know, that's just stupid. Good grammar is that which makes the language clear, not that which makes it clear someone else isn't following arbitrary rules.

As for how I feel about gender-neutral pronouns: I'm for 'em, and specifically I like "they," "them" and "their." One, I already know the words, which means that they're easier for me to incorporate into my daily usage than other gender-neutral pronouns which have been more recently invented or drafted into service; two, I've already used "they" "them" and "their" as gender-neutral singular (and plural!) pronouns for years; they're already part of my personal style guide.

I prefer them, in fact, to "he or she," both because it's a less awkward construction and because I know more people now who neither identify as "he" nor "she." Inasmuch as "he or she" is meant to be an inclusive construction, when you know people who identify as neither (or both, or either on a sliding scale contingent on factors, or *whatever*), then you realize it's not actually as inclusive as it's meant to be. In which case: Hey! "They" offers a really easy solution.

When someone asks you to refer to them by a particular set of pronouns and you're reluctant to comply, are you being disrespectful? Yup! Self-identity is important, and refusing to accept someone else's identity for your own reasons will be taken to mean that you dislike or disagree with their choices about who they are. And this is your right, but it means you're saying that your choices in this regard are more important than the choices of the person who has to live with their own identity every single moment of their lives.

Which is a hell of a thing to say. Are you sure you want to say that? And how would you feel if someone made that choice about you? I identify as male (and cis-gender), and my pronouns are of the "he" set. If someone consistently and purposefully used a set I didn't identify with, I'd want to know why. And here's the thing: generally speaking, when someone *does* misgender me, they're doing it specifically to be disrespectful. I have assholes out there who use the "she" set of pronouns when referring to me because in their minds, it's a terrible insult to call a man a woman, and this is a sign of their contempt.

Now, as it happens, I'm not insulted by the "she" set of pronouns being used for me, because I don't believe being a woman is an inferior state of being. It's not *correct*, but it's not an insult. But my point of view on the matter doesn't change the fact that the misgendering is *intended* to be disrespectful and an insult. Likewise, the boor calling Caitlyn Jenner "Bruce" and "him" is almost certainly being disrespectful. Bless their heart.

So, yes: Not using someone's preferred set of pronouns is disrespectful.

With that said, let me share a personal story here. In the reasonably recent past, a friend of mine who went by one set of pronouns let it be known that from that point forward, they would like to be known by another set. When I read that, I wrote to them that I would be happy to comply, and also, because I had been using a different set of pronouns for them literally all the time I had known them before, it's possible that from time to time, and despite my intent, I might fuck up and use the previous set. If I did, first, sorry about that and I would try better, and second, please call it out if they saw me do it, because I didn't want them to think it was intentional, and I wanted them to know it was all right to correct me and to expect an apology. Thus I let them know I respected who they are, that I was also fallible, and that when I failed them, I wanted to do better going forward.

People aren't perfect. We'll all screw up from time to time and fail the people we know, the people we like, and the people we love. It's okay to acknowledge that will happen even as we work to accommodate the people we know, like and love. I do find in my experience that if you acknowledge that you might mess up but will consciously work to improve when you do, you end up messing up less over time, and when you do, people are generally more willing to be understanding.

So: Use people's preferred pronouns. If you unintentionally screw up, correct yourself, apologize if you feel you should, and try to do better from there on out.

Let me also note that the pronoun thing is one of the best current examples of both the culture and individuals being on a journey, and that even people who mean well, or who want to do what's best, can still be behind the curve. I'm not where I am with pronouns—and all the aspects of gender and identity that the pronoun issue is semaphore for—because one day I woke up and decided I was going to be cheerfully progressive on the issue. In fact, it wasn't all *that* long ago that I would have argued about what the "real" identity of someone was, and whether it was bounded by their genetics, and whether just because *you* wanted to use one set of pronouns, that other people should then be obliged to accept your request, and so on.

What's changed over time with me? Well, some of it is simply knowledge—knowing more people who are trans and genderfluid, and learning more about science and culture, which over time convinced me that a binary understanding of gender is woefully incomplete, and that maybe my own stances should reflect that.

But as much as that—and even more than that—was the question of who I was, and who I wanted to be in respect to others. Simply put, a strong person, a person who is good and kind and righteous, does not need to demand that *other* people have to shoehorn their self-identity to someone else's expectation. A strong person, a person who is good and kind and righteous, says to the other person "tell me who you are" and accepts the fact of what they're told.

Which is not to say I *am* a strong or good or kind or righteous person. As noted above, I'm as fallible as the next person, imperfect and otherwise still trundling on the karmic wheel of suffering. But I know who I *want* to be, and who I want to be is not someone who freaks out about other people's gender identity (or their sexuality, or their cultural identity and so on). So I work on not doing those things.

Am I perfect about this? Nope: See above story about me acknowledging that I would probably screw up a friend's gender identity. And likewise, people who want to do better can just be starting on this particular path, and will screw up, and fumble and otherwise be imperfect. That's okay, just as it's okay for people to get exasperated and frustrated and angry when their identity is imperfectly understood or accepted, even by the people who hope to be good people. I would get exasperated and frustrated and angry too, if I were in their shoes. I wouldn't feel at all shy about saying so, either.

In any event: Yes, when someone tells you what their pronouns are, use them, won't you? It doesn't seem too much to ask. It requires nothing from you but practice. In return you acknowledge who they are as human beings. And with that simple recognition of their identity, you, too, acknowledge who you are as a human being. That matters, too.

PUNCHING NAZIS

I t's time to begin this year's Reader Request Week, and let's start with something *punchy*, shall we? Janne Peltonen asks:

What do you think of the whole 'punching Nazis in the face' phenomenon? I found it very confusing. It seemed to me to be mostly about performance ('let's show the power-hungry extremists that we resist') but is that reason enough to cross the line to actual physical political violence?

Well, I have two answers for that.

One: the starchy old Believer in the Actual First Amendment me believes that even Nazis have the right to peaceful assembly, physically unmolested, and that indeed this is the very *essence* of the First Amendment: that even the morally repulsive have a right to trot out their fetid wares in the public marketplace and see who wants to buy them, and that everyone else's job is to make sure other people see those shitty ideas they're peddling for what they are. Constitutionally speaking, provided the Nazis are peacefully assembling, people should not be punching Nazis *just* for being Nazis, and having Nazi views.

Two: I find it positively *delightful* people out there *are* punching Nazis, and could watch (for example) pathetic wannaNazi shitball Richard Spencer get punched for *hours*. And have! My understanding is this weekend Spencer got himself punched up again, and once more I find this utterly delightful. Nazis being punched will never not bring a smile to my face. Go get punched some more, Spencer! You certainly deserve it, you mountainous pile of crap.

"But Scalzi," I hear you say, "how can you think both that Nazis should have the right to peaceably assemble, *and* that it's delightful when Nazis get punched? Isn't that a contradiction? Doesn't that make you a complete hypocrite?"

Short answer: Yes!

Longer answer: I recognize that there's a difference between what I believe is correct intellectually and philosophically, and what makes me feel good emotionally. Intellectually and philosophically, I stand foursquare with the First Amendment, and the right of *even Nazis* to have their spot in the political conversation of the nation. Emotionally, I find Nazis, whatever you want to call them—today we're calling them "alt-right," although that appellation is already past its "sell-by" date and no doubt some of the more marketing-savvy in that crowd are already casting about for a new label to brand their strain of racist fascism—repulsive, and the whiny, privileged, smugly awful, college dorm devil's advocate alt-right variation of it particularly annoying. They're assholes. So when one of their number gets punched, I feel pretty good about it, like I would when *any* asshole who deserves a punching gets what they deserve.

Are these two positions reconcilable? Well, I don't know that they *have* to be reconcilable. There are lots of gaps between the things I believe intellectually and the things I feel emotionally. I know intellectually speaking that broccoli is nutritionally better for me than gummi worms, but emotionally gummi worms make me happier. I know intellectually speaking my preference for Levi's over Lee jeans is pointless as they are essentially the same product with the same intent, but emotionally I don't want to be seen in Lee jeans because they're not *me*. Intellectually there is no superiority of the music of Journey over, say, that of Big and Rich, but I know which band's greatest hits album emotionally affects me more.

Do these positions need to be reconciled? I don't necessarily think so. I acknowledge them and accept the dichotomy. Now, there is an argument here that there's a difference between preferring gummi bears to broccoli, and believing Nazis have a First Amendment right to assembly and yet still being happy with them being punched. I wouldn't disagree, although I note in this formulation, it's a difference in degree, not kind. Fundamentally, I think we all have various places where we recognize and should acknowledge we have a gap between what we believe is correct intellectually (or philosophically, or morally), and what feels good to us emotionally.

This is one of mine. Nazis' right to peaceable assembly is guaranteed under the First Amendment and they should not be punched merely for existing and being Nazis, *and* when they *do* get punched in public for being fucking Nazis, I feel *just fine* about it.

Now: Should there be consequences for the person who is battering the Nazi? Sure; they should be prosecuted for battery, assuming they are caught, and if convicted, they should do their time. On the flip side: Is it possible my intellectual and philosophical position re: the First Amendment right of Nazis to be in the public discourse is grounded in the fact that as a well-off straight white dude, I'm near last on the list of people that (specific obsessed and envious loser stalkers aside) the Nazis or other bigots are likely going to have a problem with? Again, sure. It's easy for me to be sanguine about bigots and racists when I'm not directly in their line of fire. I don't *feel* the same level of threat—and I don't factually *have* the same level of threat—from them that other people do. It's *easy* to say "even the hateful have a place in the discourse" when the hate isn't focused on you, or is likely ever to be in a very serious way, and that is a thing I don't think people like me appreciate on a gut level. We are free riders, in a very real sense, regarding the intellectual question of how the principle of free speech interacts with a philosophy founded on the idea that *you* are less than human, and deserve less than full human rights.

And yes, we here in the US *are* in a moment right now, thank you Trump voters, where everyone who *isn't* a well-off straight white male can be seriously asking themselves whether this administration and its enablers actually believe they *should* get all the rights someone like I have as a matter of course. *I'm* not the one who is going to be asked to give over his phone and passwords coming back into the US. *I'm* not the one whose ability to control what happens to his body is being questioned, again. *I'm* not the one whose ability to pee in safety is being hauled up for discussion. *I'm* not the one who will have any difficulty being able to jump through state-erected hoops in order to vote. And so on. The Trump administration has racists, sexists and bigots whispering into the president's ear (and the president himself is a real piece of work on these scores as well). So many people who kept their active racism, sexism and bigotry under a rock are now gleefully exulting in it. Is it a threat? Is it a threat that needs to be met with a punch or two? Not for *me*. I think other people might have a different thought on it, and an argument that the threat to them isn't just one that exists in their *feelings*.

I think the next obvious question here is (and one I think that's implied): Would *I* punch a Nazi? Unprompted, probably not. If one was coming at me or people near me with the intent to start a fight, I would feel fine defending myself or those near me. But again, that's not peaceable assembly, now, is it? We move off the First Amendment square there, into another area entirely. Short of that, I'm not likely to be the one to throw the first punch. I might *think* about it, and how fun it would be. But I'll stick to enjoying the YouTube videos. They are indeed lovely.

A Q&A
FOR THE
POST-WEINSTEIN ERA

```
Nov
12
2017
```

(Note: this piece contains general discussion of sexual harassment and assault, so heads up on that.)

Hey there! As most of you know, I'm a dude. And like most dudes, I've been watching this whole post-Weinstein era we're in with some interest. And because I am reasonably well-known on the internet for talking about *things*, I've had people, mostly dudes, contact me via social media and email with various questions about what's going on and my opinions on these topics. So, let me go ahead and address several of them at once, with the help of my fictional interlocutor. Say hello, fictional interlocutor!

Uh, hello.

Let's get started, shall we.

I… I just want it on the record that I'm deeply uncomfortable with these topics.

Of course you are! You're a dude! What's the first question?

I'm worried that someone might call me out for having been a harassing piece of shit at some point in my past.

Well, let me ask you: Were you, in the past, in fact, a harassing piece of shit?

Maybe?

I'm gonna take that as a "yes."

I wish you wouldn't.

Too late! And here's the thing: If in fact at some point in the past you were a harassing piece of shit to someone, probably to a woman but really, to *anyone*, then you deserve to be called out on your actions.

But I hardly even remember the incident!

Ah, but the question is not whether *you* remember it, but if the person you harassed does. And you know what? When you're harassed, it kinda *sticks in your brain*. For example, did I ever tell you that some dude once pinched my ass when I was in the supermarket? When I was, like, 11?

What? No.

God's honest truth. I was standing at the supermarket magazine rack, looking at a video game magazine, when suddenly I feel my ass getting pinched. I turn, and here's the creepy old bald dude, who must have been like sixty, walking by. And he turns around to see me looking at him, because clearly he's the only one who could have pinched my ass, and you know what that creepy chucklefuck does? He *winks* at me. And then he goes off and he does his shopping, or whatever.

What did you do?

I didn't do anything. I was eleven at the time, it didn't occur to me that there was anything *to* do. So I thought "what a creepy old dude" to myself, and went back to reading my magazine. As far as sexual harassment involving an 11-year-old goes, it really was—well, I don't want to say a "*best* case scenario," so let's call it a "*least damaging* case scenario."

But here's the thing about *that*: Even now I remember the event, in detail, from where I was to the creepy wink and smile that dude had on his face. If I can remember *that*, for an event that took all of three seconds and otherwise hasn't had a substantial impact on my life, you better goddamn *believe* anyone who you did worse to remembers what you did. They remember. In *detail*. Read the accounts of those coming forward with their stories. There's often a lot of specificity in them. There's a reason for that.

If you don't remember (or barely do), it's possibly because the event wasn't *trauma* for you. The person you harassed almost certainly has a different perspective on the event.

But it was a different time!

Ah, yes, the Harvey Weinstein defense of "I grew up in the 60s and 70s and it was a different time then." I mean, it didn't really work for Weinstein, now, did it? Partly because in his case claiming that things were different *then* doesn't excuse being an assaulting piece of shit *now*, and it's clear he was harassing and assaulting women right up until everything blew up in his face. But also partly because, who gives a shit if it was a different time? If you raped someone in 1973, you still *raped* them, you *asshole*. Or in 1983. Or 1993. Or 2003. Or 2013. Or *now*. There's never been a time that rape and assault and harassment *haven't* been rape and assault and harassment.

Yes, but now there's consequences!

Well, yes, there are. There's no statute of limitations on consequences, which apparently comes as an unhappy surprise to a lot of dudes. A lot of the mewling about this is, "well, it was *so* long ago." It might be! But your actions almost certainly had consequences for the person you harassed (or assaulted, or raped) and may have altered the course of their life—caused them to change their career or quit a job to avoid you, or given them psychological or physical damage.

There were *always* consequences to your actions. It's just that now *you* might have to share in them.

I'm a better person now!

Great! Did you ever make amends to the person you harassed or assaulted? Apologized, publicly or privately? Taken responsibility for your actions in some way? Worked to make right the trespasses you have made against others, to the extent that they wanted or allowed you too? Spoken to others, particularly those who love/like/are in business with you, publicly or privately, about your past transgressions so they aren't blindsided by your past?

Not as *such*.

Aaaaah, so you were just hoping it would all just go away and you would never have to think about it again.

Pretty much.

Well, surprise! You're certainly thinking about it *now*.

Let's say that before someone else outs me, I decide to out myself and admit I was a harassing piece of shit at one time in my life. What then?

I don't know. Try it and find out. I mean, I'll applaud your honesty, as long as it's backed by actual repentance and effort to change and make right what you've done in the past. But, you know. Unless you're that creepy chucklefuck who pinched my ass 36 years ago (and you're probably not, I'm guessing he's dead by now), I'm not the one to be asking about this, because I'm not the one you've wronged.

Can't we have, like, a truth and reconciliation commission?

Pardon?

You know! Like they did in South Africa, where everyone admits the horrible things they did and everyone gets amnesty.

What an *interesting* idea. Now, you do realize that particular commission was created after the fall of apartheid, by a government largely constituted by the victims of apartheid, yes?

I'm not following you.

What I'm saying is that before we get to a sexual harassment truth and reconciliation committee, basically the patriarchy will have to be dismantled and then it will be up to those running the new system to administer such a commission. How does that work for you?

Uh...

Dude, I'm *totally* ready to ditch the patriarchy if you are!

Let me think about that for a while.

Do that. In the meantime, yeah. You're not getting off the hook.

So if I come out and admit to being a harassing shit, I'll likely get thumped on. But if I don't admit it and it comes out anyway, I'll likely get thumped on.

Sounds about right.

Neither of those really sounds appealing.

Maybe you should have thought of that *before* you decided to be a harassing piece of shit.

I will say this: sorting out your own shit is always existentially better than waiting for other people to sort it out for you. There's a small but telling difference between "I did this shit, and I was wrong, and I want to do better" and "Now that you've *found out* I did this shit, let me just say I was wrong, and I want to do better." Neither is going to be a cake walk, I expect. But then, you were a harassing piece of shit. You don't deserve cake for that.

Can I change the topic, a bit, *please*?

Sure. What's up?

Let's say that I didn't *mean* to sexually harass anyone, but someone says I did or said something that made them feel harassed and uncomfortable. What then?

One, an actual apology is good. Two, don't do it again to them or anyone else.

But why should I apologize? I didn't mean to do it!

Okay, and? Look, let me be blunt with you: That person calling you out on a behavior that made them feel unsafe? They're doing you a *favor.* If your behavior, intentional or not, is creepy enough that someone was compelled to say something to you about it, there are probably others who thought the same thing but didn't say it—or didn't say it to *you.* So the person actually saying it is like a person who pulls you aside and says "Dude, your breath smells like a cat shat on your uvula, maybe partake in a *mint*," except instead of halitosis they're talking about you skeeving everybody out with your words and/or actions. Thank them! In that context, a sincere apology is an *excellent* thank you, followed by adjusting your behavior.

But why should *I* change the way *I* do things? If they have a problem with how I say or do things, it's their problem, not mine.

Fine, don't.

Wait, what?

Dude, I'm not the boss of you. If you want to continue to make people uncomfortable with your presence and actions, then follow your bliss. Just don't expect to have a whole lot of friends who aren't complete assholes. Also, be aware that if you keep that shit up, there's an excellent chance that sooner or later five or six people are going to speak out about you and your asshole actions, all at the same time, and then you'll be in the same boat as the "actual" harassers, i.e., being an *actual* harasser, because you didn't think you had to *learn*.

Which is fine! Really, it's fine. Go ahead, do that, it's fine. Totally fine.

Okay, but what about if I've never done anything bad to anyone and I *still* get accused of harassing someone?

Well, either you did it and you didn't know, in which case, see above, or, rarely, the other person is lying.

Yes! They're lying! Yes! That!

My dude, aside from the actual fact that a woman accusing a man of harassment has her life turned into such a shitshow that the bar for her choosing to tell her story is almost unspeakably high (and therefore not fertile ground for lying), I want you to consider a singular and depressing fact, which is that nearly every woman you know has *actual dudes* who've harassed them. They will go after *them*, rather than outright lying about *you*. I'm not saying that people *don't* get falsely accused of sexual assault and harassment. I *am* saying it's pretty rare. Rare enough that when someone comes forward with a harassment claim, it's worth taking seriously.

But still—

Also, you know? As someone who has jerks falsely calling him a rapist for purely malicious reasons (because I wrote a satirical piece on the subject, an alt-right weenie thought it was me admitting something, and then when it was pointed out I wasn't just decided to go with it *anyway*), allow me to suggest that people see through bullshit pretty quickly.

Fine. But I'm worried that I will try to let someone know I'm interested in them and they'll think I'm harassing them.

So you're saying your dating strategy is indistinguishable from harassment?

Dude, I don't even *know* anymore.

Maybe it's worth the time to find out and fix it if it is. I'm not, shall we say, active in the dating scene, but it seems to me that communication, consent and the active ability to take "no" for an answer will go a long way.

I'm just worried that every woman defaults into thinking I'm a creep until proven otherwise.

They might! Not just you, to be clear. Every dude.

Doesn't that bother you? That every woman might start off thinking you could be a creep?

Well, you know. Pretty much every woman I know has been harassed or assaulted or been the recipient of unwanted sexual attention from dudes simply for *existing*. I know a fair number of men, mostly gay or bi but some not, in the same boat. I know relatively few trans and non-binary folks (although I suspect I know more than many folks), but I know sexual harassment and assault, primarily by men, is a huge issue in that community. Not only men sexually harass and assault, and as they say, not all men sexually harass and assault. But men are the large majority of those people who *do* sexually harass and assault. And, alas, the ones that do that shit don't walk around with a neon light saying "Harassing chucklefuck" blinking over their head for easy identification.

So in point of fact I'm fine with women (and others) who I meet for the first time holding in their mind the idea I might be a creeper. I might be! They don't know! I'm fine with doing the work to make them comfortable with me (the "work" in this case generally meaning "being respectful and kind," which honestly isn't *that* hard), and with the idea that they might never be entirely comfortable with me in this respect. I'd like to live in the world where every dude is not seen as a potential harassing creep, but we're not there yet, because, as the events of the last few weeks have made abundantly clear, there are still a shitload of harassing creeps out there.

You want not to be seen as a potential creep right off? Great! Do the work among men to bring the ratio of harassing shitheads *way* down. Don't ask others to do the work that you want to see the benefit of.

One last question.

Sure.

What do you do when a friend or someone you admire, or whose work you admire, is outed as a harasser or abuser?

You mean, besides be sad and probably very pissed off at them?

Yes.

With people I admire, I think it's obvious that I would probably stop admiring them. With regard to people whose work I admire, it would put the work in a different context and at that point I'd have to see how

I felt about it. In both cases, I don't find it difficult to hold two thoughts about someone in my head—that someone can be an admirable talent in their field *and* a harassing piece of shit, or that a particular book/movie/song can be amazing *and* the person who created it a terrible human.

With that said, someone being outed as a harassing/assaulting piece of shit makes it much less likely I will support their future work, since I generally prefer not to give money to people who sexually harass and assault people. To be blunt, there's a category of work I file under "to be enjoyed after the creator is dead." That's where a lot of work is being sent these days.

With people I consider friends, well, look: I have standards for friends, and one of those standards is treating other people with basic human respect. Sexually assaulting or harassing other people is a pretty solid indication that you don't respect that person, or the group of people they are a part of. My friends are all grown-ups and they live in 2017; they should know better. If they don't, well. That's a problem for me.

People I know as acquaintances or casual friends I don't have a problem casting off; I have lots of other, less problematic acquaintances. I am fortunate that none of my very good friends has been shown to be an assaulter or harasser. If one ever is, that's going to be a thing. One because they managed to keep it from me for so long, which calls into question the nature of our relationship. Two because I'm going to have to ask myself if there's *anything* there in the long path of our friendship that will make it worth salvaging. Maybe there is, although at the moment I don't know what it might be. I'm not in a rush to find out.

So, this has been a long entry.

Yes it has. We've covered a lot of ground. I want to note that some of the ground I'm covering here has also been covered by women, so if it sounds familiar, that's why. And if it's all new to you, maybe you should read and listen to more women, my dude.

Any last pieces of advice?

Sure. Dudes, don't be a harassing piece of shit, don't accept other dudes being harassing pieces of shit, and when women (and others) tell you that someone has harassed or assaulted them, believe them.

This is all pretty simple. And yet.

TRUMP IS A RACIST. STOP PRETENDING OTHERWISE.

<table>
<tr><td>Jan</td></tr>
<tr><td>12</td></tr>
<tr><td>2018</td></tr>
</table>

Here in January of 2018, this is the deal: I'm gonna judge you if you can't admit openly and without reservation that Donald Trump is a racist. Not *just* racist, which is to say, he has some defense in the idea that we live in a racist society so we all participate in its racism whether we like it or not, but *a* racist, as in, he's actively prejudiced against non-white people and groups, as evidenced by his words and actions, both before he was president but especially since then. If you can't admit this here in January of 2018, when the evidence of his racism is piled up grossly upon the floor in full view of everyone down to the cats, then I'm going to go ahead and judge you for it. It's *long* past time, folks.

(He's also sexist and religiously bigoted and transphobic and classist, among many other bigotries, but let's go ahead and save those for another time.)

Mind you, people *are* still going out of their way to pretend that the president's comments yesterday about "shithole" countries isn't *really* racist ("Well, they *are* shithole countries, not that I know anything about them, which conveniently means I can elide the centuries of racist colonialism and exploitation countries including the United States have engaged in to help make them so") or how immediately contrasting those "shithole" countries with Norway isn't racist ("There are brown people in Norway too, just ask Anders Breivik") or when all else fails trying to change the conversation to be about whether the word "shithole" was actually used (it was), rather than acknowledging

Trump's entire position in the conversation was racist and "shithole" was just the juicy soundbite.

But *we* don't have to be those people. Trump said a racist thing and he wants to keep people from these "shithole" countries from immigrating to the United States (as opposed to people from Norway) because he's a racist. There are *other* reasons he doesn't want them here, to be sure (Trump also hates poor people, as an example, and many of the immigrants are liable to be poor when they arrive), but none of those mitigates or obviates the racism. That it's there *too* doesn't subtract or divide its vileness. It adds and multiplies it.

At this point, there's nothing to be gained by pretending that Trump isn't a racist. Rather, the opposite: The willingness to deny Trump's active, obvious and unsubtle racism suggests not just passive complicity in his racism, but an active participation in it. Trump's folks in the White House yesterday suggested that his "shithole" comment would resonate with his base, which to be clear, is an explicit acknowledgement by the White House that it considers his base to be just as racist as Trump himself. If you consider yourself part of Trump's base, you now get the chance to indicate whether or not you are as much of a racist as Trump.

And maybe you are! We do know that while not all Trump voters consider themselves racist, nearly everyone who considers themselves a racist voted for Trump. Maybe you're one of the people who celebrates Trump's clear and unambiguous racism. But if you *don't* in fact consider yourself a confirmed and unapologetic racist, now is a fine time to make that clear. Even if you supported Trump before, it's not too late to get off that rapidly-derailing train and to tuck-and-roll yourself clear of the continuing association with the man and his active racism.

And here's the first test of it: Do you believe Trump is a racist? At this point it's really a "yes" or "no" question, with no waffling qualifications needed. If you answer anything other than "Yes," to that, well. You should really ask yourself why. And in the meantime, expect to be judged. By me, as noted. But, I strongly suspect, by others as well.

Raising
Strong Women

May
12
2015

This question was asked by JRed:

What advice do you have for raising a strong woman in today's world*? Our daughter just turned one, and I want her to grow up to know who she is and what she wants, and to not take crap from anyone. But it's overwhelming when society seems to have 10,000 conflicting messages about what those qualities even mean for women, much less how to cultivate them. I realize this topic might set you up for the haters, but my husband and I would love your thoughts. *OK, let's narrow "the world" to the United States.

I can't give a recipe for this other than what we've done with regard to our own daughter, but inasmuch as I expect that's what you're asking, here's how we've done it.

(Disclaimers early: I'm not a perfect parent. Neither is Krissy. Any suggestion that we are should be treated with skepticism. Likewise, take into account who we are and the conditions of our life, i.e., we have a whole lot of advantages, and by association, so does our daughter. Also, this is not meant to be an exhaustive and complete list. Also, I am not a perfect feminist. And so on. Got it? Okay.)

1. Give your daughter a strong woman as a role model. In our case, this would be Krissy, Athena's mother. Krissy is intelligent, strong, organized, opinionated, clearly used to being in charge of her own life, and doesn't take shit from anyone while at the same time being kind and loving. When this sort of woman is your mother, then every day of your life you have that as your primary definition of what being a woman is and can be. This is a good baseline to work from. How Krissy is a strong woman is not the only way to be one, mind you. But she definitively *is* one. A woman's role model for a strong woman, likewise, does not have to be her mother (and to be clear Krissy is not Athena's only role model in this regard). But if you can have a strong woman in the house, I think it probably helps. Likewise:

2. Let your daughter see the man in her house treating women with respect and as equals. That would be me, in our house. Athena has always seen her mother and me in a relationship where not only are we loving to each other, but we treat each other with respect, and she can see many places where her mother is the lead in our partnership (because of skill or inclination or other reasons) and I not only acknowledge that fact, but am pleased about it. Nor is this lead role always in "traditional" male/female tasks and roles. Again, in a day-to-day sense, our daughter sees the two of us in our relationship with each other, and that becomes her baseline of expectation of how men and women together treat each other. We *don't* treat each other as we do because our daughter is watching—we treated each other that way long before she came along. But our daughter receives the benefit of seeing that relationship dynamic. But while we're on the subject of men:

3. Let your daughter see the man in her house have good relationships with women who are not his spouse and (again) treat them with respect and as equals. I don't think it's enough for Athena only to see the respect with which I treat her mother; it's also useful to see me interact with other women and see how I treat them as well. The reason it's important is that Krissy is my wife, and that spousal dynamic is always going to be its own thing. So she needs to see me with my women friends, my women colleagues, and even how I respond to women I don't even know. Once again, the day-to-day experience of that sets her baseline of what behavior she should expect from men, when they talk to and interact with women. And once again, I don't treat women with respect *because* my daughter is watching; I treat them with respect because people deserve respect. It's still important that my daughter sees it.

None of the above points, it should be noted, are things that should be called out for praise or are meant to be cookie-bearing activities—this is simply about what you do with your life on a day-to-day basis, which your kid will see and pick up on by osmosis. Parents are their kids' first teachers, and kids watch and learn even when you don't think you're teaching them. You're always teaching them. They're always watching you.

Moving on.

4. Give your daughter appropriate agency. Here's a small example, which I've noted here before: As soon as Athena was old enough to understand it, I've always gotten her permission before posting pictures, or talking about things she's done, here and other places online. Why? One, again, simple respect, but two, I wanted her to understand from a very early age that she should have a right *and expectation* that her wishes and opinions would be listened to and followed and taken seriously. You've never seen a picture or anecdote here about her after the age of about four, that she didn't sign off on. It's a small thing, but on the other hand, it's also a concrete example to her that she is being respected. From me, a man. In time that becomes a baseline expectation. If it's not met elsewhere, she'll know something is off. Related to this:

5. Treat your daughter as a thinking human. This is not the same thing as treating your kid as "an adult," which is a brag I sometimes hear: "We've always treated our children like adults." Well, that's dumb; kids aren't adults and depending on their age, there's a whole lot of mental and physical development between where they are now and where they will be as grown-ups. What I think is more important is to realize that every step of the way your child has a brain, and it's working, and you address that brain with respect. Which means your child learns to trust that you are dealing with them fairly, even (especially) when you are being the parent. Again, it's about the expectations you're offering your kid: To be taken seriously, to be heard, and to be appreciated.

6. Point out cultural nonsense as it happens (in an age appropriate way). Culture sends 10,000 conflicting messages, but it doesn't mean that those messages have to be received unmediated. We very early on taught Athena how to recognize when she was being sold to, when someone was asserting something that wasn't true, and in particular regard to the question at hand, when she was being exposed to sexist bullshit. We didn't necessarily make a big production of it—*stop everything! It's time for a lesson!*—but calling things out does a couple of things. One, it trains your kid not to uncritically accept what culture is pushing on them; two, it makes them aware that culture's messages don't *have* to apply to them, and that they're free to make up their own minds.

7. Back your daughter up. Back her up when she wants to try things. Back her up when she succeeds. Back her up when she fails. Back her up when she's confronted by people who try to make her into something society expects rather than what she's interested in. Back her up when she needs information. Back her up when she tells you how she's feeling. Back her up when one of the less pleasant messages society is trying to send her manages to hit home. Back her up when people give her shit, just for being a woman. Back her up when she fights back. *Back her up.* Be the solid ground your kid plants her feet in to push against all the bullshit. She's going to need it. She's going to need it a lot.

8. Do all of the above without needing to get credit for it. Kids are self-centered, in the worst and best ways. They don't always get what their parents do for them until a whole lot later. That's fine. The goal isn't a Parent of the Year ribbon. The goal is a daughter who is strong, capable and her own person. Help make one of those, and it's a pretty good bet eventually she'll figure out what you did for her.

So, that's how we're doing it on our end. Maybe some of this will be useful for you, too.

The Reputational Reset, Or Not

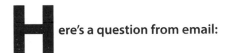ere's a question from email:

If you fuck up, how long should you have to spend in the wilderness before you're allowed to come back?

I mean, I think it *depends*, don't you?

I suspect this question is asked in reference to the #MeToo movement, in which prominent men who have sexually coerced, assaulted and harassed women (and others) have been called into account and have, to varying degrees, been banished. But while the answer to this question in reference to those men feels relatively simple (i.e., "to hell with them"), in a larger and more general sense, the question of when (and if!) to no longer factor transgressions that people have made against you or others into your view of them is one I've wrestled with personally. Because, you know. Over the years, people have gotten themselves onto my personal shit list, and from time to time it's worth revisiting that list to see whether those people should be paroled from it.

And as it happens, in thinking about this I've realized that over the years I've mostly unconsciously developed an informal rule for taking people off my personal shit list. You know how it takes seven years to take a bankruptcy off your credit report? For me, and *generally* speaking, it takes roughly ten years before I stop counting what I personally consider a major fuck up against you.

Why ten years? Because ten years is enough time not only to see if you've *learned*, but to see if you've incorporated that learning into your actual life. Like so: Have you recognized the error of your ways? Have you accepted responsibility for your actions? Have you (when allowed) made amends to the people you've wronged? Have you avoided minimizing or excusing your actions, and avoided trying to place the blame for them on others? Have you not repeated the same bad action again, or with others? If the answer to all of the above is "yes," and for ten years running, then, fine. We probably all get to move on. If not, then not, and every time the answer to one of the questions above is "no," well, then. The ten-year clock resets.

(I also tend to credit this retroactively: We just met and I learn you fucked up a decade ago, realized your error, worked to fix it, and didn't do the same fuck up again? Fine, the decade clock for you has already run down.)

I think this is a reasonably good informal general rule (for me) because, look: People can and do change, and people can and do work to rebuild their lives so they can be a better version of themselves. I feel it's not *unreasonable*, after an appropriate amount of time and evidence of work done, to credit people with effort and assume they have gotten themselves right. Maybe that's optimistic of me, but I think optimism isn't a bad thing to practice with people.

That said, I'm not especially squishy about these things. I don't, for example, equate absence of bad action with contrition. I think there are a lot of harassers out there who have stopped harassing not because they recognize the error of their actions, but simply because they just can't get away with it anymore. And, yeah. You don't get credit for *that*, bucko. This is a wagon it's supremely easy to fall off of.

While I'm at this: not holding something against you is not the same as pretending a thing had not been been done; or more simply, forgiving is not forgetting. I don't tend to forget. Oh, and: Not holding something against you anymore isn't the same as *liking* you. Just because I no longer hold a previous bad action against you, it doesn't make us friends. That's an entirely separate process.

(Likewise, I can and have liked people who I think have fucked up, and can hold their fuck up against them, even as sometimes I have helped them recover from that fuck up. What can I say, people are complicated sometimes.)

(That said, it's *very* rare I do that. Specifically I tend to drop people I have determined have willingly transgressed against me, because life is short and I don't have time for assholes in my life anymore. So, you know. If you go out of your way to fuck with me, don't think having been a friend will have much weight on that score. Friends don't go out of their way to fuck with you.)

(Gosh, *that* just got dark, didn't it.)

I should also note that for me this formulation generally works better for people you know in your own life than in the world of celebrity and notability, if for no other reason than it's easier to see people doing the work to right themselves when they're in your personal sphere of social perception. It *can* work with celebrities and notable people, I guess, if you're super-invested in them, on the grounds that some people know more about celebrities and their lives than they know about their neighbors. I'm usually not *that* invested, so my practice with celebrities tends to be a bit more ruthless—out they go, generally speaking. There are always more celebrities and people making cool things to enjoy, and people to move into positions of power. I do have a small stack of celebrities on my "possibly enjoy again after they're dead" list, but while they're alive they won't get another penny or another moment of my time. That seems reasonable to me.

At this point it's fair to ask whether I would be comfortable with people holding the same standards against me, should they determine that I've fucked up or transgressed. The answer is: Well, I probably *should*, shouldn't I? I'm not special, after all: I've fucked up, and transgressed against people, and otherwise people have made their own determinations about whether or not I'm worth their time. I've frequently apologized for my actions, made amends when I could and when allowed, and have continually made efforts to be a better person, with varying but hopefully positive results.

How much credit I get for that, if any, is up to any individual person. *I* have an informal rule for all this, but it's not to say *my* informal rule will work for anyone else. Everyone gets to make their own rules about who to forgive, and when, and if, and who gets to be in their life. There are probably some people who will be happy never to see me again, for whatever reason, and that's fine. I prefer not to inflict myself on people who want nothing to do with me.

(And as for the "celebrity" portion of that as an author—well, I mean, *definitely* don't buy my stuff if you think I'm a terrible person.)

So this is generally how it works for me. I give credit for work done, but I also don't grade easily, or on a curve. Whether this sort of formulation works for you will depend on a whole bunch of factors, mostly related to you. It's okay if it doesn't, or if you have some other formulation entirely. The thing about all of this is, it's personal.

A SEASON
IN THE SHOW

This last weekend I had an enjoyable time at the Confusion science fiction convention, which is no surprise, as I usually do—it's one of the reasons I've gone back to it now for nine years running. I mostly hung out in the bar and talked to writers, doing the usual combination of business talk and complete idiocy, as writers generally do at conventions when they chat with each other.

One evening I talked to a couple of different authors about writing careers and the ups and downs careers have, and how from time to time we're all filled with frustration with them, especially during a downturn. We all want to be on award lists; we all want to have bestsellers. If those things don't happen we can wonder if what we're doing matters much at all. As we were talking about it I came up with a metaphor which I thought was useful, in terms of talking about careers. Not entirely surprisingly, it involves baseball.

In baseball, getting into the major leagues is called "going to the show." When you get to the show, what that means is that your skills are advanced enough that you can play at the highest levels—you're one of the top 750 people who play the sport. Even the lowliest major leaguer has skills and abilities that can impress.

Not every player in the major league is going to play in the All Star Game; not every player in the major league is going to go the World Series. Some years will be better than others. You can have a career year one year and be in danger of being dropped the next. Sometimes a player will be traded. Sometimes a player will be sent to the minors and will have to fight their way back into the show. Some will be instant stars. Some of those stars will fade. Some will never be more than journeymen, going from team to team and hoping to be seen as utility players, working whatever position there's a need for. Some of these utility players, with the right team and coaching, might find everything clicks and be propelled into the game's front ranks.

Thing is: You never know. You only know what's going to happen by playing the game. The longer you play in The Show, the more chances you get to make things happen for yourself.

Being published (by major publishers primarily, but with some notable exceptions) is like being in The Show. It means that you're working at the top levels of your field—just having a book out there in the world means you've got skills that distinguish you from the mass of people who hope to be where you are. It's an accomplishment in itself.

But as with major league players in their idiom, not every author is going to be an instant, obvious success. Not every book is going to get into the bestseller lists. Not every book is going to get nominated for an award. Some writers have instant hits; some have to keep at it for years, slowly building an audience of readers. Some authors will never hit it big; some that do hit it big will have it happen just once. Sometimes authors will be dropped from their publishers and need to find another one. Sometimes they will have to use a different name to get published again (and sometimes they will be a hit under that different name). Sometimes the book an author thinks is their best will sink while something they think as inconsequential is a major hit.

Once again: You never know. No one knows. But as long as you keep publishing, you get to keep making chances for yourself.

An example, you say. Okay: Once upon a time, there was a young author who started publishing in, oh, let's say, 1970. Within a couple of years this writer started making a name for himself and getting nominated for awards, winning his first major award five years later. He starts writing novels but they don't do fantastically well, and one of them does so poorly (by the writer's own admission) that less than a decade and a half after his fiction writing career began, the writer assumes it's over and moves on to other related fields to support himself.

Nevertheless, two decades after his first story is published, this writer decides to try again with another novel. It's published more than a quarter century into this writer's career and is a success. The fourth book in the series, published almost a decade later, is a number one *New York Times* hardcover bestseller. So is the fifth. A television show based on the series becomes one of the most popular and talked about shows in the medium, now forty-four years into this writer's career.

I am obviously speaking of George RR Martin here. His career was up; his career was down. He was finished as a novelist; he's currently arguably the most famous novelist alive. Who knows what will happen tomorrow.

Will you, as a writer, become like George RR Martin? Probably not. But you might find your own measure of success, so long as you keep showing up. Maybe you have the sort of career where at the end of it all you've done is published a bunch of novels that have sold just well enough to allow you to get that next contract. Which means that *you've published a bunch of novels*, i.e., stories that previously existed only inside your head are now out there in the world. You've done a thing, and had a career, that millions of people have only *dreamed* of. You made it to The Show, and that's a hell of a thing.

So, writers, just keep writing. Every time you publish is another season in The Show. And maybe you'll be a bestseller and maybe you won't. Maybe you'll get an award and maybe you won't. You never know. It's fun to find out.

A SHORT REVIEW OF GHOSTBUSTERS AND A LONGER PUMMEL OF MANBOYS

Jul

17

2016

What I thought of the new *Ghostbusters*: I liked it, and would happily rewatch it. It's definitely the second-best Ghostbusters movie, and much closer to the original in terms of enjoyment than the willfully forgotten *Ghostbusters 2*. There are legitimate criticisms to make of it: the plot is rote to the point of being slapdash, the action scenes are merely adequate, and Paul Feig is no Ivan Reitman, in terms of creating comedic ambiance. But the film got the two big things right: It has a crackerjack cast that's great individually and together, and it has all the one-liners you can eat. And now that the origin story of these particular Ghostbusters is out of the way, I'm ready for the sequel.

But what about the Ghostbusters being all women?!??!?? Yes they were, and it was good. If you can't enjoy Melissa McCarthy, Kristen Wiig, Kate McKinnon and Leslie Jones snarking it up while zapping ghosts with proton streams, one, the problem is you, not them, and two, no really, what the *fuck* is wrong with you. The actors and the characters had chemistry with one another and I would have happily watched these Ghostbusters eat lunch, just to listen to them zap on one another. And in particular I want to be McKinnon's Holtzmann when I grow up; Holtzmann is brilliant and spectrum-y and yet pretty much social anxiety-free and I honestly can't see any sort of super-nerd *not* wanting to cosplay the shit out of her forever and ever, amen.

BUT THEY'VE RUINED MY CHILDHOOD BY BEING WOMEN, wails a certain, entitled subset of male nerd on the Internet. Well, *good*, you pathetic little shitballs. If your entire childhood can be irrevocably destroyed by four women with proton packs, your childhood clearly sucked and it needs to go up in hearty, crackling flames. Now you are free, boys, free! Enjoy the *now*. Honestly, I don't think it's entirely a coincidence that one of the weakest parts of this film is its villain, who (very minor spoiler) is literally a basement-dwelling man-boy just itchin' to make the world pay for not making him its king, as he is so clearly meant to be. These feculent lads are annoying enough in the real world. It's difficult to make them any more interesting on screen.

But this is just the latest chapter of man-boys whining about women in science fiction culture: Oh noes! Mad Max has womens in it! Yes, and *Fury Road* was stunning, arguably the best film of its franchise and of 2015, and was improbably but fittingly nominated for Best Picture at the Academy Awards. Oh noes! Star Wars has womens in it! Yes, and *The Force Awakens* was pretty damn good, the best Star Wars film since *Empire*, was the highest grossing film of 2015 and of all time in the domestic box office (not accounting for inflation. Accounting for inflation, it's #11. #1 counting inflation? That super-manly epic, *Gone With the Wind*).

And now, Oh noes! *Ghostbusters* has womens in it! Yes, and it's been well-reviewed and at $46 million, is the highest grossing opening for its director or any of its stars and perfectly in line with studio estimates for the weekend. Notably, all the surviving principals of the original film make cameos, suggesting they are fine with passing the torch (Harold Ramis is honored in the film too, which is a lovely touch), and Ivan Reitman and Dan Aykroyd are producers of the film. If your childhood has been ruined, boys, then your alleged heroes happily did some of the kicking.

I'm an 80s kid; my youth is not forever stained by a *Ghostbusters* remake, any more than it was stained by remakes of *Robocop* or *Point Break* or *Poltergeist* or *Endless Love* or *The Karate Kid* or *Clash of the Titans* or *Footloose* or *Total Recall* and on and on. I think most of these remakes were *unnecessary*, and I don't think most of them were particularly good, or as good as their originals, and I question why film companies bother, aside from the "all the originals were made before the global movie market matured and there's money on the table that can be exploited with these existing brands," which is, of course, its own excuse.

But after a certain and hopefully relatively *early* point in your life, you realize remakes are just a thing the film industry *does*—the first Frankenstein film listed on imdb was made in 1910, and the most recent, 2015, and Universal (maker of the classic 1931 version) is planning yet another reboot in 2018 or 2019—and maybe you get over yourself and your opinion that your childhood is culturally inviolate, especially from the entities that actually, you know, own the properties you've invested so much of your psyche into. It's fine to roll your eyes when someone announces yet another remake, tweet "UGH WHYYYYYY" and then go about your life. But if it causes you *genuine emotional upheaval*, maybe a reconfigure of your life is not out of the question.

(Not, mind you, that I think these shitboys are genuinely that invested in *Ghostbusters*, per se; they're invested in manprivilege and, as noted above, would have wailed their anguished testeria onto Reddit and 4chan regardless of which cultural property had women "suddenly" show up in it. This is particularly ironic with anything regarding science fiction, which arguably got its successful start in Western culture through the graces of Mary Shelley. Women have *always* been in it, dudes. Deal.)

The happy news in this case is that, whether or not this *Ghostbusters* reboot was *necessary*, it's pretty good, and fun to watch. That's the best argument for it. I'm looking forward to more.

SOME MUSINGS ON AVENGERS: INFINITY WAR

Apr

30

2018

I liked *Avengers: Infinity War* and in many ways it's a technical cinematic (excuse the pun) marvel—it's not an easy job to integrate this many storylines, characters and stars into a single movie and both give them all enough space to do their thing, and still keep the film hurtling inevitably toward a climax. In this regard, this film's cinematic predecessors aren't so much other superhero films as the Cecil De Mille-style biblical epics, the kind where big name stars were dropped in for even the smallest roles, and part of the experience was watching, say, Vincent Price vamp about as a ridiculously incongruent ancient Egyptian. This is that, except that the gods are played by Australians and Brits, and the plague in this case is Josh Brolin, underneath some impressive CGI.

But as impressively well put together as it is—and it *is*; after this, *Civil War* and *The Winter Soldier*, I'm perfectly willing to say that the Russo brothers are possibly the most adept action directors we have working in film right now—and as enjoyable and exciting as the film is in the moment (which, bluntly, is its remit as a superhero film: to keep you munching your popcorn delightedly as events transpire onscreen), the film suffers and for me is ultimately unsatisfying. Not for anything the film itself does or doesn't do; again, this is an extraordinarily competent film, and enjoyable on every level, and a more than satisfactory funnel into which to pour the entire official Marvel universe to date. It suffers not because of what it does, but because of what I know.

And what do I know?

(and here is where I put the **spoiler warning**, so if you haven't seen the film, go no further)

(although honestly since the film made $250 million domestically and $630 million worldwide in its first weekend, there doesn't seem like there's anyone who hasn't seen this film by this point)

(even so, once again: **spoiler warning**)

(okay, that's enough parenthetical grafs for right now)

What I know is that there's no friggin' way Spider-Man and Black Panther, to name just two, go out like punks.

This isn't a question of story, this is a question of economics. *Black Panther* grossed $688 million in the US and $1.3 billion worldwide; even if a *Black Panther 2* made half that (and it seems unlikely it would make *just* half that), it would still be one of the top five grossing films of its year. If you think Disney, of all companies, is going to leave that sort of money on the table, you are officially *super* high. Likewise, if you think Marvel is going to let Spider-Man, still their biggest and most well-known superhero, despite years of fumbling at the hands of Sony, lie fallow after they've just now reintegrated him into the official Marvel universe (and his most recent film did $880 million business worldwide), then, again, you are supremely buzzed, my friend.

Additionally, I'm well aware that on the Marvel schedule, there is another Avengers film, originally called *Infinity War, Part 2*. It's not called that anymore, but it's not because *Infinity War* was meant to be its own stand-alone film in the Marvel continuity, or because the next Avengers film isn't going to be *Infinity War, Part 2*; they just want to give it a cooler title. This was always going to be a film that was going to end on a cliff-hanger.

Knowing what I know about Marvel and Disney's business, here's what I felt when Black Panther turned into dust at the end of *Infinity War*, not for anything he did, but simply because he was part of the unlucky half of the thinking universe that fell under Thanos' curse:

lol, yeah, okay there, Marvel.

Likewise with Spider-Man; likewise with two-thirds of the Guardians of the Galaxy, and so on.

Again, to be clear: This is not the fault of *Avengers: Infinity War*. It hit its marks and hit them well, and the internal logic of the film holds up. Viewed from the inside of the film, the filmmakers didn't shy away from what was necessary—they killed a shitload of characters, not only to illustrate the stakes, but to make the point of what Thanos' scheme means to everyone in the universe. It does just about everything right within its own framework. I could quibble at points here and there, but not with the overall film.

But *Infinity War* doesn't exist only within its own framework; it exists as part of an overall business plan for Marvel and Disney. And, leaving aside the simple fact that comic book universes aren't exactly a sterling model of *finality* in even the best of times, Marvel and Disney aren't going to deprive themselves of consistent money-makers. Not just in the cinema but in merchandising, licensing and all other sorts of ancillary revenue streams.

And that, simply, lowers the stakes. People who were congratulating the Marvel universe for going all Game of Thrones on their characters misapprehend this fact about the films' corporate masters. When George RR Martin kills someone, they (mostly) stay dead; there's real risk there. In the case of Marvel, and of *Infinity War*, meh. They'll be back. Most likely, they'll *all* be back (yes, even Loki. As if they would waste *that* fan favorite).

So, while I very much enjoyed *Infinity War*, and would highly recommend it on its own merits, in a fundamental way I left the theater unengaged with it. It's because I knew, more than in any other film in the Marvel universe to date, that its stakes were false. I mean, I could be wrong. I would be *delighted* to be wrong. But I know Disney, and I know Marvel, and I know their release schedule, and I know basic economics. And I know if you're one of the largest entertainment companies on the planet, you don't wipe out that sort of value, just for the sake of a single film, and one splash of box office income. It's just not smart.

And thus the irony here is that the real *Infinity War* spoiler for me was not a list of who lived and who died in the film, but a release schedule, and a company philosophy.

SPEECH, CONVERSATION, DEBATE, ENGAGEMENT, COMMUNICATION

Sep

16

2013

Some thoughts on each.

1. As a general concept, freedom of speech includes the right to decide how and when to speak, and to whom.

2. This freedom of speech also includes the right to choose *not* to speak, and not to speak to whomever, including to you.

3. No one is obliged to have a conversation with you.

4. If they are having a conversation with you, they are not obliged to give you the conversation you wanted or expected to have.

5. If you challenge someone to a "debate," they are not obliged to have a debate with you.

6. If they do not debate you, this does not mean you win. You can't win a debate the other party has not agreed to.

7. Not all engagement is useful or fruitful, either for the participants or for the observers. Sometimes the best course of action is not to engage.

8. If people do not engage you, it is not necessarily because they are afraid to engage you. Maybe they don't have the time, or interest. Maybe they think you're too ignorant to engage, either on the specific topic or in matters of rhetoric. Maybe they don't want to either implicitly or explicitly let you share in their credibility. Maybe they think you're an asshole, and want nothing to do with you. Maybe it's combination of some or all of the above. They may or may not tell you why.

9. Communication is not always confrontation. Confrontation is not always communication. If you see communication as an opportunity to fight, you may find yourself without opponents. No, this doesn't mean you "win," either.

10. People will communicate as they will. Outside of your own spaces, you have no power to control or compel them. Attempts to dictate the terms of their communication may be ignored. Attempts to demand they comply to your terms for communication will make you look like a child, stamping a foot.

That should be enough for a start.

Steubenville and CNN and the Rest

Mar

19

2013

Various news organizations, CNN and Fox most notably, have been catching all sorts of crap on my Twitter and Facebook feeds for being unduly handwringing about the fate of the two Ohio teenage boys who raped a drunk and unconscious girl and then found themselves found guilty (actually "delinquent," which is the juvenile crimes version of guilty) of the rape. The boys were called good kids and excellent students who now faced very different lives because of the verdict. Not much was said about the girl who was raped, although I am led to understand Fox at least partially outed her identity. The combination of these things inspired various levels of rage among the social media set.

And, well. The social media set is right. From the CNN clips I saw, it was as if there was a "passive voice" version of events—*look what's being done to these poor boys*—without a corresponding emphasis on the fact that what was being done to the boys was a direct consequence of *what they did*, namely, rape a drunk and unconscious young woman who could not consent to their actions. This wasn't a Kafkaesque moment in American jurisprudence, in which these two kids were hauled up in front of a judge for something they didn't do; they *did* rape someone. The best (in the sense of "least egregious") thing you could say is that these boys didn't *understand* that their actions made them rapists. But that doesn't make them innocent of rape, and moreover if they were good kids and students, it seems doubtful they had *not* learned at some point that sticking your fingers into a woman while she's too drunk to consent is a thing one should not do. Even if one wanted to argue that's not rape (which would be incorrect by Ohio law, which is the relevant standard here), it's still physical battery of a specially egregious sort. It's hard to formulate a scenario in which a good kid who is a good student doesn't know that fact.

I think it's reasonable to be sad these two young men did not have the good sense not to do what they did. I think it's reasonable to lament that those around these young men did not or could not make them understand that the actions they took were rape before they took those actions. I think it's fine to note that because of their actions, these kids won't have the future they would have had if they chosen not to take those actions. What you don't do is imply that two young people found guilty of rape were victims of tragic circumstance. They weren't the victims of tragic circumstance; they were the authors of it.

Outside of the news organizations in question, there have been lots of comments that want to find some way to make the girl who was raped share in the blame of her rape, the most obvious of which is the "well, what was she doing drinking so much she lost consciousness?" sort. These comments imply (and in some cases, state explicitly) that if you drink so much you can't think straight then you kind of deserve what's coming to you. It should be obvious why this sort of thinking is full of stupid, but as it's apparently not, let's go over this again:

1. One's own poor judgment does not excuse the poor judgment of others.

2. Nothing excuses rape.

Toward the first, yes, it was not a good idea for the girl to drink so much (presuming she did, and was not roofied, or given drinks stronger than she wanted, or all sorts of other scenarios of that sort). This is *separate and independent* from the fact that it was not a good idea for two boys to rape someone too drunk to give consent. Attempting to link the two is an attempt to suggest causality ("Because the girl was drunk, she was raped"). The causality is easy to infer, but it's wrong, both legally and morally. The young woman was drunk; *separately and independently* two young men raped a woman unable to consent to their actions. The young woman should not have been that drunk, perhaps, but her being that drunk does not mean that she invited, should have expected or should bear without complaint, being raped.

There are folks who respond to this with something along the line of "yeah, but if you taunt a bear, you shouldn't be surprised when your arm gets torn off." The correct response to this is that human beings aren't bears. We expect more from human beings and have systems in place to deal with them when they choose not to act humanely to other people. Any response of "Yeah, but…" essentially reduces humans to dumb animals. It's okay to expect more from humans than that they are dumb animals.

Toward the second, there is no social, legal or moral action in which sexual assault is a reasonable end result, period, end of sentence. Which means that everyone trying to shift blame to the girl for her rape are wrong, and also means that everyone out there going "Hurr hurr those doodz are going to get it in the ass in jail for sure" are wrong, too. The two boys who raped the girl shouldn't themselves be raped. If you're confused as to why this is, please refer to point one.

The two young men who raped the young woman are solely responsible for their actions, and are being punished for their actions. It's a shame they did what they did. But they did do it. It's a point not to be forgotten, by CNN, by the people trying to include the young woman in the blame, or by anyone else.

SUDDENLY, NOSTALGIA

```
Aug
16
2014
```

Back in the wild and wooly days of the World Wide Web, I hung around on a newsgroup called alt.society.generation-x, where I made a number of online friends, some of whom became real world friends, with whom I kept in contact, sporadically, over the years. One of those was Douglas Lathrop, a fellow writer who very recently sold a novel, not his first written (very few "first" novels are first novels), but the first to be picked up by a publisher.

Not too long ago Doug fell and ended up in the hospital, and in part because of other long-term factors relating to his health, he didn't recover. He passed away today.

And I'm kicking myself because a couple of weeks ago I was in San Diego, during Comic-Con, and as I was crossing the street, he was crossing the street, too, going the other way. And we were in the middle of a cross walk and there were probably a couple hundred other people and we moved past each other too quickly, and I thought to myself, *huh, I'll have to tell Doug I saw him in the cross walk,* and then I walked off to whatever it was I was doing next, which I can't remember now.

I wish I would have taken that moment in the cross walk to say hello. It was the last time I'll see my friend in this world. I should have said hello. I didn't. I'm going to regret that forever now.

I was supposed to be writing in the novel this morning, but in the aftermath of Doug passing away I found myself wandering through some of the archives of the alt.society.generation-x newsgroup and getting a little depressed and nostalgic in a way that I don't frequently get.

I'm not a notably nostalgic person, in part because I don't feel the best part of my life is in the past, but it definitely hit me this morning, and I had to spend a little bit of time figuring out why.

The closest I can come to it is that asg-x is the one thing in my past that is really in the past. My high school and college, for example, are still there and still have people running through them—they are living entities, and even though my time in them gets increasingly further away in the rearview mirror, I know each new group of people who have the experience of going there has some consanguinity of experience with me. Not exactly *my* experience, but we're still connected by the same common thread.

asg-x, on the other hand, is tied into a very specific time—from 1993, when it was created, to about 1999—during which the USENET was still a common place for people exploring the Internet to find and read and use. USENET's moment is over; there are people who still use it, but they're the people who've *been* using it. It's hard to find now and it's not bringing in new people. And asg-x, the newsgroup, is definitively dead—there's nothing new there now but spam posts, either containing dance music lists or political rants.

There's a finite group of people who experienced what asg-x was, when asg-x was something at all. There's a finite group of people for whom asg-x was a community, and for whom it was *their* community, with all the little tics and quirks, positive and negative, that a community has. We're all that there will ever be, basically. Doug's passing is a reminder that this small and finite community is in the process of shrinking, inexorably, through the simple passage of time. There's going to be a point, hopefully several decades from now, when the last person who ever attended a "tingle" will pass from the planet, and then that will be it. The end of the asg-x community.

To be clear, it's a small thing, and a community that was significant mainly for the people who were in it. But even so, within that community, friendships were made, people fell in love (and some of them even got married and had children), laughs were had, arguments were posited, gatherings planned, memories created and milestones celebrated. It was real and it happened, and now its moment is gone and to a very real extent nothing will ever be quite like it again. There's no way of getting back there. There's no there there anymore.

And that's fine. Some things are finite—well, in the long term sense of things *everything* is finite, it's just some things are finite *faster*—and asg-x is one of those things. I'm not going to wish it were suddenly 1996 all over again and everyone was back on USENET, with a flood of new newsgroups of their own (although I can just imagine what alt.society.THANKS.OBAMA would look like). I'm all right with asg-x having its time, and that time being over.

But now I understand why people are nostalgic. It's your brain trying to express a moment, and recognizing that the only people who would ever truly get what you're trying to express were the ones who were there, and they already know.

THAT
NEW YORK
MAGAZINE COVER

```
Jul
27
2015
```

(New York magazine did a cover featuring thirty-five women who had accused Bill Cosby of sexual assault. These were my thoughts on it.)

So, that's a hell of a magazine cover. As of this writing the *New York* magazine site itself is down because of a hacker attack; the hacker in question alleges this has nothing to do with Bill Cosby. Interesting timing nonetheless.

A friend of mine tweeted a comment last night that said "power corrupts" and I tweeted back something snarky about that; turns out she was tweeting about Bill Cosby and I missed the context, so I apologized and deleted my tweet. Turns out I am just as susceptible to the failure mode of clever as anyone else.

But I had additional thoughts on her comment. I think it's true that power corrupts, or that it can. I also think it's true that power *reveals*—which is to say, that with some men and women, it's not that having power weakens their will or leads them into temptation, but rather that power allows them to indulge in the things that they've always wanted to do. They didn't need to be corrupted. They needed only the means to do what they willed, which power provided.

Ultimately, however, it doesn't matter if power corrupted or revealed Bill Cosby's nature. I don't imagine it matters to the women who were sexually assaulted whether Cosby gave into temptation or indulged in his will, or both. At the end of the day they were still raped by him. And at the end of the day, for decades, they were told there was no point in telling anyone about it because no one would believe them. Corrupted or revealed, Bill Cosby's power protected him, until it didn't. I am absolutely sure that the irony of what kicked the Fall of Cosby into high gear was Hannibal Buress, another man, calling Bill Cosby out on stage was not lost on these women, or women in general. The information was out there; women had been saying these things for years. They still needed a man to say it in order to have the world pay attention.

I'm not sad for Bill Cosby. He raped women, he did it for decades, and now everyone knows he did it. He deserves condemnation for it, and he deserves to see his reputation destroyed (he also deserves jail time, which at this point he is unlikely to receive. But I think for a person like Bill Cosby, the destruction of his reputation is probably no less painful than time in a cell). The man was and is a genius, and his comedy mattered to me; I remember being a kid listening to his comedy albums at the West Covina public library and trying (and failing) not to laugh out loud in a place where you weren't supposed to make a lot of noise. *Bill Cosby: Himself* was one of my favorite comedy concert films. And by the time *Himself* was released, Cosby had assaulted 22 of the 35 women featured on that *New York* cover. Bill Cosby is a genius; Bill Cosby is a rapist of women. The former does not excuse the latter and never should have.

I *am* sad we are still in a place where women aren't believed when they come forward about sexual assault, and that it's such a matter of fact of our culture that *The Onion* can satirize it. I'm sad and sorry for the women who had to wait until a man came forward to call out Cosby in order for the cultural tiller to shift in their direction. Anita Sarkeesian—who knows something about the bullshit women have to put up with in order to speak—and others have said that one of the most radical things you can do is believe women when they talk about their experiences. It seems like a dramatic statement until you take a hard look at that *New York* magazine cover, and the thirty-five women there, bearing witness to sexual assaults over four decades, finally being believed in some cases fifty years later. You realize it's not dramatic at all.

There Shall Your Heart Be Also

Lately I've been thinking about Matthew, chapter six, and how it applies to me and my life.

Matthew, chapter six, for those of you who do not know, has Jesus midstream in the Sermon of the Mount, talking about giving to the poor, and praying and being pious. The gist of it is simple: if you do good things in order to be seen by other people doing good things, then that is your only compensation; God will reward you no further. But if you do them quietly and without any fuss, then God will indeed reward you in full, in heaven. The summation of this line of thinking is in verse 21: "For where your treasure is, there shall your heart be also." In other words: You are what you value.

I am an agnostic of the "I'm almost certain God does not exist, but intellectual honesty requires me to admit I just don't know" stripe, so in an obvious, literal sense Matthew 6 can't do much for me. I don't pray, and for the good works I do here in this world, I don't expect compensation in the next, because I don't believe there is a next world. Here and now is all we have.

But I know wisdom when I see it, and the underlying wisdom of Matthew 6 is universally applicable. It asks *why* one does good works: Is it to be seen doing good works, or because good works are *in themselves* are worth doing, regardless of public reward? Is it more important to be a good person or to be *seen* as a good person? The answers to these questions point to who you are.

I struggle with this because one of my failings is a desire for recognition (hello, I'm a writer). I like to be seen and I like to be seen doing things of value. I like the response I get from them; I like being known as a good guy. I can even argue that there is value in me being seen doing good "out loud," as it were. In the science fiction and fantasy community, for example, I am a "big name." My actions can be multiplicative. By being seen doing good, I can sometimes cause more good to happen. It's a cool thing to be able to do.

But it's a rationalization that avoids the actual question of *why* I choose to do good things. Am I doing it because I am doing what I feel is correct moral action? Am I doing it because I enjoy people telling me I am a good guy, and the one sure way to do that is to be seen being a "good guy"? At the end of the day, what is at the root of my drive to do good?

It's easy to argue that in one sense it doesn't matter. The homeless guy you give new shoes to doesn't care whether you're doing it to look good to others, to God or to yourself. What he cares about is the new shoes. And that's a solid point to make. Actions matter in themselves. Good can result from actions undertaken for selfish reasons, or through vanity.

But I do think it matters, or at least it matters to me. There's a line out there that says "Character is who you are when no one else is watching." You are who you decide to be and how you choose to act, even when there is no penalty or reward outside of your own sense of self. I am vain; I like being seen doing good things. Separately, I have pride that when I choose to do good out loud, that it can make a difference in my community. But I *also* want to be the person who would do good things even if only I ever knew what I had done. I want to be the person who can choose to make life better for others even if those people never know. I want to have the moral courage to do right action for itself. I want to know that, stripped of vanity and pride, I will still choose to *do* good, and thus *be* good. I want to believe that I can be the better image of myself I hold in my head.

And that's why Matthew chapter six turns over and over in my mind. It speaks to me because it speaks to how I live my life and who I want to be. It reminds me that it is difficult to strip away the ego and see right action as its own reward. It reminds me that even when I do good work out loud that the focus should be *what* I am doing, not that *I* am doing it. It reminds me that it's fair when people question my motives. It reminds me how much work I have left to do on myself.

And I do have work to do. I am a flawed human being. I am vain. I am proud. I seek approval. I want to be seen as good. Matthew chapter six reminds me how much better it would be to actually *be* good, first and always. It is the treasure, wherein hopefully one day I may find my heart.

These Are a Few
Of My Favorite
Things, On Tiers

Aug

19

2013

I get asked a lot about what my favorite book/movie/album/ creatively generated object might be (or my favorite author/ filmmaker/musician/creative type), and I find as I go along in life I get progressively more annoyed with the question. This is usually not the fault of the person asking the question, who is generally trying to make innocuous conversation and is doing so by opening up a socially-approved line of trivial conversation.

It is, however, the fault of the question itself, which is unsophisticated, naive and annoying. Like most people over the age of twelve, who both had time to expand their creative palates and who recognize that life is not always a zero-sum *Highlander*-like experience, in which There Can Be Only One, I don't have a single favorite book, or movie, or album, etc, or a favorite author or filmmaker or musician, or so on. I like a lot of different things (and artists) almost equally for reasons that are often *not* equivalent or comparable.

What I have instead—and what I suspect most people have—are personal tiers: general landings of favor in which the works/creators are held at a mostly equivalent level of esteem. For works of creativity, these tiers *basically* look like this:

First tier: The works of art that, for lack of a better term, regenerate me: I take them in and they make me feel like a better person for having gone through them.

Second tier: Works that I enjoy a lot and happily reconsume when the mood strikes me.

Third tier: Good once, could enjoy again, but probably won't go out of my way to do so.

Fourth tier: Once was enough for all time.

Fifth tier: Mildly annoyed that I spent my time with it.

Sixth tier: Deeply annoyed some of the precious few moments in which I exist as a conscious being in this universe have been wasted on this crap.

For the artists themselves, it looks like this:

First tier: I consider these folks as my personal artistic pantheon.

Second tier: These folks are very reliable purveyors of entertainment that works for me for one or more reasons.

Third tier: Good at what they do; some of their work also speaks to me.

Fourth tier: Good at what they do, but what they do isn't my thing.

Fifth tier: Not very good at what they do, but they make other people happy, so, meh.

Sixth tier: Abstractly okay with the concept that these people are allowed to express themselves in a manner that looks like creativity if you don't think about it too hard, but honestly, what the hell.

Even here, "tier" does not capture the complexity of the thinking about these things, since the tiers themselves have plateaus, slopes and fractal surface features, reflecting that I like different things for different reasons. The objects and people in the tiers are likewise often in motion, moving up and down the tiers as my personal tastes, interests and experience change (or whether, for example, I've listened to/read/watched that particular thing too many times recently). Likewise, first tier artists can create lower tier output; lower tier artists have created works I unreservedly place on my top tier of creative experiences. And so on.

The point is that on the first tier of things, both with artists and with output, it becomes difficult (or difficult for me, anyway) to accurately quantify how or whether one is better than other. My top tier of movies, for example, contains both *Tootsie* and *Stop Making Sense*. One is a comedy and one is a concert film. One has great acting performances and one has great musical performances. One makes me laugh, and the other makes me dance. Likewise, among writers, I enjoy ee cummings and H.L. Mencken for reasons that have almost nothing to do with each other. If you come in and say to me "Yeah, but if you *had* to choose one over the other, which would you choose?" I would look at you like you were dense.

(The "yeah, but if you *had* to choose" questions drive me up a wall, too. Because I immediately get sidetracked into the why. *Why* do I have to choose? What circumstances of fate have led me only to be able to pick one book/movie/album, etc? I want to know why civilization has collapsed to the point (or whatever other circumstances occur) where I only get one thing. Because that seems kinda *crucial* to me. Really, in a situation like that, focusing only on that one book/movie/album seems the ultimate in wasting brain cycles on inappropriate trivia. This is especially the case now that we live in a world where I can carry ten thousand songs, an equal number of books and a couple of hundred movies with me at all times.)

(Also note that my *favorite* works/creators are not necessarily the *best* works/creators by any sort of critical and/or popular consensus. *Citizen Kane* is generally considered one of the greatest films of all time, and I do not disagree with that assessment one bit. It is possibly the Best Film Ever. But I don't often feel like going out of my way to see it; it's not on my personal First Tier. Likewise, Bob Dylan is both indisputably one of the most important musical figures in the last 60 years and on my fourth tier of artists; I like nearly all his stuff better when it's covered by someone else. Personal taste is a weird and wonky thing.)

All of this is a very long way of saying that asking me what my favorite thing is, is not likely to get you the answer you want, unless the answer you want is a sour, exasperated look and a long, drawn out sigh (and if that is the answer you want, you're a bad person and *I don't like you*). On the other hand, if you ask me what some of my *top tier* books/ music/movies are, then you might get a more interesting answer, especially interesting because then you get to try to figure out what it means that someone would like both *Tootsie* and *Stop Making Sense* almost equally as much. You're well on your way to a psychological profile right there.

A Thing
Not to Do When
You're Smart

In the various recent kerfuffles surrounding science fiction and its awards, there have been a couple of people (and their spouses, declaiming about their beloved) who have been slapping down Mensa cards as proof that they (or their spouse) are smart. Let me just say this about that:

Oh, my sweet summer children. Just *don't*.

If you want to be in Mensa, that's fine. Everyone needs hobbies and associations, and if this is the direction you want to go with yours, then you do you. Not my flavor, but then, lots of hobbies and associations aren't my flavor.

That said:

1. Literally no one outside of Mensa gives a shit about your Mensa card. No one is impressed that you belong to an organization that has among its membership people who believe that because they can ace a test, they are therefore broadly intellectually superior to everyone else.

2. Your Mensa membership does not imply or suggest that you are the smartest person in the room. Leaving aside the point that the intelligence that Mensa values is a narrow and specialized sort, a large number of people who *can* join Mensa, don't, for various reasons, including the idea that belonging to a group that glories in its supposed intellectual superiority is more than vaguely obnoxious.

3. Your need to bring up the fact you have a Mensa card suggests nothing other than it's really really *really* important to you for people to know you're smart, and that you believe external accreditation of this supposed top-tier intelligence is more persuasive than, say, the establishment of your intelligence through your actions, demeanor, or personality. Which is to say: It shows you're insecure.

4. Your Mensa card does not mean you know how to argue. Your Mensa card does not mean you do not make errors or lapses in judgment. Your Mensa card is not a "get out of jail free" card when someone pokes holes in your thesis. Your Mensa card does not mean that you can't be racist or sexist or otherwise bigoted. You may not say "I have a Mensa card, therefore my logic is irrefutable." Your Mensa card will not save you from Dunning-Kruger syndrome, and if you think it will, then you are *exactly* who the Dunning-Kruger syndrome was meant to describe. You Mensa card will not keep you from being called out for acting stupidly, or doing stupid things.

5. Your Mensa card does not immunize you from being a complete, raging asshole.

In short, it's not actually *smart* to flash your Mensa card, and if you *were* smart, you'd know not to do it. If you have to resort to waving your Mensa card around to establish your intelligence, you're signaling that you have no other way to do it. And you don't have to be a genius to know what that actually means about you.

THIS NEW
AMERICA

Jun

29

2015

I was in the airport last Friday when the Supreme Court ruling on same-sex marriage came down, and one of the first thoughts I had on that was, "Looks like I picked the right week to go to San Francisco." And you know what? I was right! The city was, verily, bedecked in rainbow flags and happiness. After my events at the American Library Association conference on Saturday I went with friends to City Hall, where the pride celebration was in full swing, and watched people being happy, all over the place (plus occasional hippie nudity, because San Francisco). It's very rare to be in the right place at the right time, when history is actually and genuinely happening around you. But I was, and I was delighted in the happy circumstance that put me there.

I'm even more delighted that my country is now a better place than it was at 9:59am on June 26, when a minority of states still didn't allow gays and lesbians the simple, basic right of marrying the person whom they loved and wished to spend their life with. Those days are now gone, thankfully, despite a few pockets of resistance, which I don't suspect will last very long. Texas, as an example, is a place where the Attorney General is telling county clerks they may defy the Supreme Court; it's also a place where two octogenarian men, together for more than 50 years, became the first same-sex couple to wed in Dallas County. Who do you think history, and Texas, will celebrate more: The two men confirming their decades-long love to each other, or the government official symbolically standing in front of the courthouse door to oppose their right to confirm that love?

Bluntly: Texas Attorney General Ken Paxton is going down in history as a bigot. So will Texas' governor and lieutenant governor. So will Ted Cruz, Mike Huckabee and all the other politicians (and would-be politicians) who are thumping around now, pretending not to understand what it is that the Supreme Court does, or the legitimacy of its rulings under the Constitution, and pretending that their religion makes that feigned lack of understanding all right. Dan Patrick, the Texas Lieutenant Governor, has said "I would rather be on the wrong side of history than on the wrong side of my faith and my beliefs." Well, Mr. Patrick, you're not only definitely on the wrong side of history, but you're also on the wrong side of your professed faith. Jesus never once said "be a bigot in my name." If you believe He did, you might want to recheck your Bible. That admonition is not there, although the admonition to love your neighbor as yourself is.

On a related topic, a *Time* magazine article by Rod Dreher on orthodox Christians being "exiles in our own country" struck me as a bit dramatic. Not being in step with the mainstream of American life and opinion does not make you an exile, especially when you suffer no estrangement under the law. When the mainstream of American life did not include the idea that same-sex marriage was a viable thing, which was an opinion different than mine, *I* was not in exile in my own country—although same-sex couples may have been, as the law estranged them from the rights they should have had under the Constitution, now affirmed by the Supreme Court. The affirmation of those rights did not and does not take away rights from anyone who believes same-sex marriage is wrong. You may still believe they're wrong; you just can't stop those couples from getting legally married. Unless you think it *should* be your right to deprive others of their rights, everything's the same for you as it was before. And if you *do* believe it's your right to deprive others of their rights, then you're a bigot, whether you cloak it in religion or not.

I suspect that this is the thing Dreher is really worried about, whether he's aware of it or not—that the perception of certain religious sects will change from them being depositories of rectitude to cisterns of intolerance. Well, this is a fair concern, isn't it? Over the last twenty years in particular, nearly every American learned that someone they cared about or even loved—a family member, a friend, a co-worker or neighbor or a person they admired—was not straight, or 100% conforming to society's ideas of gender. Over the last two decades, Americans decided it was more important to tell those people they still loved them and that they deserved the same rights as everyone else, than it was to listen to those people who said, through their words and actions, that these people we loved represented some sort of threat. Your mom is not a threat to America, if she happens to be gay or bisexual. Nor is your dad. Nor your sibling, or your best friend, or Doug from Accounting or Jillian down the street or Ellen DeGeneres. Who are you going to choose to stand with? Your sister, or some dude at a pulpit demanding we believe the bowels of Hell will empty if she marries her girlfriend? Your sister's girlfriend is awesome! That guy is a jerk!

Which is the thing: the religious sects terrified that they will now lose their moral standing lost that standing long before, when they said, in so many words, in so many actions, that the people we love and know and know to be good, and their desire to have the same rights as everyone else, are what's wrong with America. Dreher laments we now live in a "post-Christian" America, but he's wrong. The Americans who are standing with their loved ones and neighbors are in fact doing exactly what Jesus asked them to do, when he said that we should love each other as we love ourselves. It's possible, however, that we live in a post-accepting-bigotry-cloaking-itself-in-the-raiments-of-Christ America. And, you know. I can live in that America just fine.

Regardless, the America we do live in now lets any one person marry any other person who they love. I like this America. I am glad I live in it.

THOUGHTS
AND PRAYERS

Jun

12

2016

Aman goes into an immigration services center in Binghamton New York, blocks the exit in the back with his car, goes through the front door with handguns, body armor and ammunition. He shoots the receptionists and opens fire on a citizenship class. He murders thirteen. This is horrific. I offer my thoughts and prayers.

A psychiatrist trained to help others with the stress of combat goes to Ft. Hood, the army base at which he is stationed, and opens fire on his fellow soldiers and some civilians, too. Another thirteen people are murdered there. Three are killed charging the shooter. Words cannot express my sorrow. I offer my thoughts and prayers.

A professor is denied tenure at the University of Alabama at Huntsville. She goes to a department faculty meeting and in that conference room pulls out a nine-millimeter handgun and shoots six people, three of whom she manages to murder. Those people were just doing their jobs and what happened to them is terrible. I don't want to have to think about it any further. I offer my thoughts and prayers.

A truck driver in Manchester, Connecticut comes out of a company disciplinary hearing for allegedly stealing beer and starts shooting up his place of work. He murders eight people, calls his mother and tells her about it, and then shoots himself. Gun control discussions are a mess in this country and they never go anywhere productive, there's no middle ground, and they make me tired thinking about them. I offer my thoughts and prayers.

In Tucson, Arizona, a member of Congress is meeting with her con-stituents in the parking lot of a supermarket, and a 22-year-old man comes up and shoots her straight in the head. A representative to Congress, can you believe that! She somehow survives, but he murders six others, ranging in age from nine to 79. That's quite a range. Surely the attempted assassination of a US Representative will start a substantive discussion by someone. In the meantime, I offer my thoughts and prayers.

Seal Beach, California, where a man and a woman are having a cus-tody dispute. His solution: Enter his wife's place of work, a hair salon, and open fire on anyone there. He murders his ex-wife and seven other people, including one man not even in the salon. He is in his car in the parking lot outside the salon. Bad luck. Here's an interesting thing: there is a sort of magical power to saying that you offer your thoughts and prayers.

Oakland, California, and at a small Christian college, a man who had been expelled for behavioral and anger management problems decides that he's going to find an administrator he has issues with. He doesn't find her, so instead grabs a secretary, enters a classroom and orders the students there to line against a wall. Some refuse. He shoots, reloads and shoots some more. Seven people are murdered. The shooter later says he's sorry. The magical power of saying that you offer your thoughts and prayers is that once you do it, you're not required to do anything *other* than to offer your thoughts and prayers.

In Aurora, Colorado, a midnight audience of Batman fans are half an hour into the final installment of Christopher Nolan's superhero tril-ogy when a man enters the theater, clad in protective armor, sets off two gas canisters and starts shooting. Some audience members think this is a stunt tied into the film. It's not a stunt, and the shooter, armed with an assault rife, a shotgun and a glock, murders a dozen people, ten of whom die right there in the theater. When police visit the shooter's home, they find it rigged with explosives. The shooter placed a camera to record what happens if the police just barge in. Saying "thoughts and prayers" is performative, which is to say that just in saying it, you've performed an action. Prayers leave your mind and go to God. It is a blessed, holy and as such apparently *sufficient* thing, to offer your thoughts and prayers.

Sunday morning, and in Oak Creek, Wisconsin, members of the Sikh temple there have gathered for services and meditation and are preparing a communal meal when a white supremacist and Army veteran starts shooting, murdering six and wounding a police officer before killing himself. Did you know that Sikhs are often confused by the unknowing and possibly uncaring for being Muslim, and that the excuse of "I thought they were Muslims" is itself a sign of racial hatred? Mind you, there are people who will say to you that it's not enough, only to offer your thoughts and prayers.

In Minneapolis, a man is called into an office by his supervisor and told he is losing his job. The man replies, "Oh, really?" and pulls out a handgun, shooting the supervisor after a struggle for the weapon, eventually murdering five others before killing himself. Indeed, people particularly expect more from lawmakers, who have the ability to call hearings and allow government studies and even change laws, rather than only to offer their thoughts and prayers.

Brookfield, Wisconsin, another hair salon, another estranged couple. The wife seeks a restraining order when the husband threatens to burn her with acid and set her on fire with gasoline. He does neither. He does, however, murder her, along with two other women. Witnesses say the wife tried to protect the others before she died. But again, even if you're a lawmaker, with the ability to do things that could have concrete impact, you might argue that your responsibility to women being murdered by husbands, workers murdered by co-workers, religious minorities murdered by bigots, soldiers murdered by other soldiers, innocents murdered by those who are not, ends when you, in a tweet, Facebook post or press release, offer your thoughts and prayers.

A man enters an elementary school in Newtown, Connecticut, and with a Bushmaster XM15-E2S carbine rifle, murders twenty children, all of whom are either six or seven years old.

We pause here a moment to think about that.

Twenty children. Ages six, or seven.

And here maybe you think to yourself, *this is it*. This is the place and time where thoughts and prayers in fact aren't enough, where those who only offer their thoughts and prayers recognize that others see them in their inaction, see that the convenient self-absolution of thoughts and prayers, that the magical abnegation thoughts and prayers offer, is no longer *sufficient*, is no longer proper, is no longer just or moral, or even offers the appearance of morality.

We pause here a moment, and wait to see what happens next.

And then they come. One after another.

I offer my thoughts and prayers.

And it keeps going.

Five murdered in Santa Monica, California by a gunman. I offer my thoughts and prayers.

Twelve murdered in a running firefight through the Washington Navy Yard in DC. Like a ritual, I offer my thoughts and prayers.

Ft. Hood, Texas again, for another three murdered. Like a litany, I offer my thoughts and prayers.

Six murdered in Isla Vista, California. Violence against women is horrible, and I offer my thoughts and prayers.

Nine murdered in Charleston, South Carolina. It's unspeakable that violence against black Americans has happened like this, and I offer my thoughts and prayers.

Five murdered in Chattanooga, Tennessee. Muslims should answer for the crimes of this person, even if they do not know him or would in any way condone the action, and I offer my thoughts and prayers.

Nine murdered in Roseburg, Oregon. I offer my thoughts and prayers.

Three murdered in Colorado Springs, Colorado. Thoughts and prayers.

Fourteen murdered in San Bernardino. Thoughts. Prayers.

Fifty murdered in Orlando.

Fifty people, in a gay club, by a shooter who his father says was disgusted by the sight of two men kissing, and who news reports now tell us had pledged allegiance to ISIS.

And what do we do now, I wonder, when the victims are who they are and the perpetrator is who he is, the situation is ripe for posturing, and there's a phrase to be used that allows one to assert maximum public virtue with minimum personal effort or responsibility?

What do we do now, when thoughts and prayers are easy, and everything else is hard?

Here is the thing: In the aftermath of terrible violence, offer thoughts, and prayers, if it is your desire to do so.

Then offer more than thoughts and prayers. Ask for more than thoughts and prayers. Vote for more than thoughts and prayers. Help those for whom thoughts and prayers are the start of their responsibilities, not the abdication of them. And as for the others, you may politely remind them of Matthew 6:5-6, and perhaps also Matthew 7:21-23. Perhaps they will see themselves in the words there. Perhaps not. They're worth thinking on regardless.

"I offer my thoughts and prayers."

Thank you.

It's not enough.

It never was.

What more do you have to offer?

THOUGHTS ON
A WRINKLE IN TIME

Mar

11

2018

"So, why were you crying through the entire film?"
—my daughter Athena, who was mildly concerned.

There are several answers to this, most of which boil down to the fact that I am a father who remembers being the ten-year-old boy who fell in love with Madeleine L'Engle's book, and the movie engaged both of these states. I cried because the casting and performance of Meg (played by Storm Reid) is immensely good—such a stubborn, willful, doubt-filled girl—and because I could see both myself as a child and my daughter in her. I cried because I remember being a fatherless child and being a father who would never want to leave his daughter. I cried because the film has empathy not only for bright but difficult children but for all children, and because it wants so much for Meg to see herself, just as I would want to be seen and would want my own child to see her value. I cried because I remembered being lost like Meg was lost, and remembered everyone who helped me find myself, as everyone in this film does so for Meg, and as I hope I have helped my own daughter become who she is meant to be.

I cried because this film has an enormous amount of empathy, as the book did, and that essential core remains intact, even as the film takes liberties with the source material. It would have to, 56 years after the book's initial publication, to speak to the audience it's intended to speak to, which is *not* me, a 48-year-old white dude, although it clearly and so obviously did. I cried because this film gets the book right, because it *sees* the book, just as the book saw me when I came to it almost four decades ago, and has seen so many other children since. Director Ava DuVernay's love of the material, and her willingness to put the work into it to make it speak today, is self-evident and appreciated.

It is not a perfect film, in itself or in its adaptation of the source material. Lots is truncated, changed and elided, some new stuff is put in to middling effect. The commercial needs of a $100 million film mean that some tropey elements get past the gate, and on more than one occasion the special effects become the tail wagging the dog. In the end I didn't see much of this as a problem. The film is not perfect, and also, this is a film *about* faults, and how our own faults ultimately may give us power to save ourselves and others. While I'm not going to say this film's faults ultimately give it power, I can say that none of the film's faults are that important to me when the film's core is solid, and intact, and so powerfully on point. It's not perfect, nor does it have to be to work.

(And, you may ask, what do I think about the film's multicultural and feminine viewpoint and aesthetic? I think it works very well, and it's a reminder that things that are not designed specifically for one in mind may still speak *significantly and specifically* to one, if one is open to it. I would not have imagined *A Wrinkle in Time* the way DuVernay has—I seriously doubt I *could have* imagined it this way—and yet there I was crying my eyes out all the same. *I do not need* the world to be imagined as I would have imagined it. I want the world and the things in it to exceed my imagination, to show me things I cannot make for myself but can take into myself, hold precious, and make my imagination that much wider from that point forward. As I noted before, this movie was not, I think, made *for* me, and still here I am, loving it as much as I do.)

Should you see this film? Well, I think you should. I also think you should see it on a big screen, because it's visually impressive enough to warrant it and because films still have their most potent power on a big screen, in front of an audience. Maybe it won't have the same effect on you that it had on me—in fact, it probably won't, because you are not me. But I'm willing to believe it will have *some* effect. Whatever that effect is, it'll be worth getting yourself to a theater for, and maybe taking a kid or two along with you, too.

As for me, I can honestly say that I don't think I've been this affected by a film in years. Part of that is because I loved the book as a child, but I've loved other books before, and their adaptations, and yet didn't spend their entire running time in tears. I think, in the end, it's what Ava DuVernay, her team and her actors (especially Storm Reid) brought to it: Empathy, joy, optimism and their own point of view that brings *A Wrinkle in Time* into modern times. No one needs me to tell them that DuVernay is a major director; that much was evident with *Selma* and *13th*. What I can say is that DuVernay, rare among directors, is now someone whose vision I trust—not to give me what I think I want, but to give me what I didn't know I needed, until she showed it to me.

I knew I was probably going to like *A Wrinkle in Time*. I didn't know I was going to love it this much. I certainly didn't know I was going to find myself crying all the way through it. That's on DuVernay and her team. And for that, I say: Ava DuVernay, thank you. I don't think it's possible for your film to have moved me more than it has.

20 Years

Twenty years ago today, Krissy and I were married. We stood up in front of friends and family, said our vows (and they were our vows, as we wrote them), and formally began our time together, making a life between us.

In that twenty years, there has never been a single day where I have not had cause to reflect on how much better my life is because Krissy is with me and is my partner. There has never been a single day where I did not reflect on the ways my life would be different, and a lesser life, without her in it. There has never been a single day where I have not been frankly amazed that a woman so capable, so loving and so gorgeous has chosen to be with me.

There has never been a single day in those twenty years that I have not told her that I love her.

More than a decade ago, I wrote "Marriage is work. It never stops being work. It never *should*." I stand by that observation. Krissy and I were in love the day we were married and are in love now, twenty years later. But that love is not a default state of being. It is a choice we make every day, and work follows that choice. Work is the proof of that choice. Love is the result of that work. Love gives us another day together, and the opportunity to make that choice once more.

As we have, day in, day out. Every single day, for twenty years. It is why we said "I do," when we made our vows. It's why we say "I do," symbolically, each day of our lives together. There is no greater work that I have accomplished than this, and is a work that is impossible for me to have done alone. I can only do this work with someone else. With Krissy, in point of fact. It is a life's work. My life, and hers, and ours.

There has never been a single day that I have had cause to doubt or regret the choice we made, twenty years ago today, to love each other that day and every day since. There has never been a single day that I would not, in front of family and friends and all the world, do it again, all over again. There has never been a single day in those twenty years where I have not. I am every day the groom to her bride. Every day the man who stood with her and said, with her, I do.

I do. Yes. Today and every day.

I love you, Kristine. I do.

2017, WORD COUNTS AND WRITING PROCESS

oday I wrote 1,850 words on *Head On*, my novel which is coming out next year. In any year previous to 2017, 1,850 words from me in a single day would be an okay day—slightly below my general average of 2,000 or so that I can reliably pump out on a daily basis, but not so far below that I would worry about it. The 2k daily goal is fungible. Some days I'll get 1,850 words, some days I'll get 2,300, and over time it all comes out in the wash. I get a novel done in roughly three or four months, a span of time which leaves room for false starts, snipping out dead ends, and otherwise revising and fixing the novel as I go along.

Here in 2017, 1,850 words on the novel in a day—1,850 usable words—is an actual goddamned miracle. I started *Head On* in January with the plan to be done in the first half of the year, to leave the rest of the year open for other projects, including getting a head start on the next book in the Interdependency series. And here we are in October and I'm still not done, and generally speaking I've been lucky if I've gotten a few hundred usable words out of a writing day. I have never had as hard a time writing a novel as I have had with this one.

Not because this particular book is hard to write. The novel, which is the sequel to *Lock In*, is *complicated*—it's got a mysterious death and lots of twisty and turny bits—but I've done complicated before. Complicated is not inherently difficult to write. It just takes attention to detail, which normally I'm able to do just fine. When I write on it— when I have those stretches of being able to write—it all works. The plot flows well, the characters are doing their thing, and everything chugs along. What I'm writing is good. There's just so much less of it than usually happens for me.

I'm not trying to be mysterious about what it is about 2017 that is different. The answer is obvious: Trump is president, and he's a peevish bigoted incompetent surrounded by the same, and he's wreaking havoc on large stretches of the American experience, both in his own person and by the chaos he invites. But to say "well, *Trump*," is not really to give an answer with regard to what's different. We've had terrible presidents before—George W. Bush springs to mind—and yet my ability to create work was not notably impacted. When Dubya was in office I wrote five novels. The Dubya era was a crappy time for America (recall the wars and the Great Recession) but from the point of view of productivity, it was just fine for me.

The thing is, the Trump era is a different kind of awful. It is, bluntly, *unremitting* awfulness. The man has been in office for nine months at this point and there is rarely a week or month where things have not been historically crappy, a feculent stew of Trump's shittiness as a human and as a president, his epically corrupt and immoral administration, and the rise of worse elements of America finally feeling free to say, hey, in fact, they *do* hate Jews and gays and brown people. Maybe other people can focus when Shitty America is large and in charge, but I'm finding it difficult to do.

Here's one way to put it: Twelve years ago, when Hurricane Katrina hit and the US Government flubbed its response and hundreds died, I was so angry and upset that I almost vomited in sadness and anger. It's not an exaggeration, by the way—I literally felt like throwing up for a couple days straight. I eventually had to write "Being Poor" because it was either do that or go crazy. That was a week of feeling generally awful, and it wrecked me for another week after that. It took two weeks for me to get back on track with the novel I was writing at the time.

Got it? Okay, listen: 2017 has been me feeling like I felt when Katrina hit *every single fucking month of this year.*

Because, well. Pick a month, guys. Every month of 2017 has been a *treat.* Travel bans, white supremacists marching, awful health care repeals that just wouldn't die, and not one, not two, but *three* historically massive hurricanes and the scouring of Puerto Rico. Russia. Fucking *Russia*, man. Not to mention Spicer, Scaramucci, Flynn, Price, Bannon, Gorka and the rest of that ridiculous cast. Any one of those is enough to get me (and not just me, lots of people) spun up and distracted. And it's not just any one of these things. It's that all of these things *keep on happening*. When you're already spun up, it doesn't take all that much more energy to stay spun up and distracted.

Well, just unplug! Well, see. Here's the thing about that: I have. And I've found out it doesn't really work like it used to. The world gets in anyway, because the world is in worse shape and wants you to know. It's not just a matter of unplugging from social media, although it does help to get away from that. But short of building a Faraday cage around my house and then never, ever leaving it, the news of the day arrives.

Now, I want to be clear: It's not just the news. It really is also *me*. I have never not been politically engaged—remember I wrote an opinion column when I worked in newspapers, and that I was writing here on Whatever for years before *Old Man's War* was published. It's *hard* for me to disengage; more than, I suspect, many other people. In a very real sense, this is part of who I am and what I do. I find it difficult to walk away from it, because I know it doesn't stop just because I'm not paying attention to it.

(And also, while we're on the subject, let's talk about the fact that even if it *is* hard for me to tune this shit out, I *could* tune it out, with relatively little penalty to me. In Trump's America, if you're a straight white rich dude, none of his bullshit is aimed at you personally. Meanwhile lots of people I know *can't* tune it out, because the bullshit is aimed right at them. It's not accurate to say I feel guilt about this. It is accurate to say that I feel uncomfortable not standing with my friends and others who don't have the luxury I have, of tuning out when it's inconvenient to be tuned in. Note also this is *also* about me—I know folks who have to tune out in order to stay outside of a depression spiral, and I encourage them to do so. This about my own struggle with this stuff, not anyone else's.)

What 2017 has been doing for me is making me realize that I can't do work in the same way I used to. It's too hard to tune out what's going on in the world, and because of it I have to make some changes—to my workflow, to my understanding of what's a good writing day, and in allocating time to get work done. In effect, I have to learn how to change my swing in order to work effectively in this chaotic new environment. It's taken me longer to figure this out than I would have liked; I've spent a lot of time this year trying to make the old workflow function rather than reconfiguring my process to the new facts on the ground. Part of this was, simply, hoping things would settle down and get back to normal. But it's October 2017 and it's time to face the fact that, at least as far as my writing process goes, the old "normal" is gone.

Why am I talking about this right now? Basically, because I know it's not just me. I know a lot of writers have seen their process take a hit here in 2017. It's hard to focus when the world is on fire, and with novelists in particular, I suspect that sometimes it's hard to focus when you've got the suspicion that your fiction is almost frivolous in the context of what's going on right now. Well, and maybe it is. But, speaking as someone who spent an hour retweeting pet pictures today to break up the horror of mass shooting news in people's tweetstreams, sometimes frivolity helps. And for all writers (and probably other creative people as well), knowing that you're not the only one having a fucked-up world messing with your process might make you feel less alone.

(Yes, yes, Scalzi, solidarity with writers and all, but what does this mean for *Head On?* From the reader point of view: Nothing. The book will be written in ample time for the April release date. And it will be excellent—like I said earlier, what I'm writing is *good*. It's just slower this time.)

So, yeah, writers: this gig is harder here in 2017. It's not just you. And I feel you. I really do.

THE UNIVERSITY OF CHICAGO, TRIGGER WARNINGS AND SAFE SPACES

Aug
28
2016

Last week the University of Chicago caused a bit of an uproar by sending out a letter to incoming students telling them not to expect intellectual safe spaces or trigger warnings when it came to critical inquiry. This caused celebration in some quarters and consternation in others, in both cases in no small part to the use of the phrases "safe spaces" and "trigger warnings," which are apprehended in different ways by different general audiences, cutting roughly but not exclusively along US liberal/conservative lines.

I am a University of Chicago graduate, and having come out of its classically liberal educational ethos, I have some thoughts on the letter, and on the general matter of intellectual inquiry, and on safe spaces and trigger warnings and so on and so forth. Note that a lot of this follows on (and may repeat) what I've written about free speech and other related topics before, so some of this may seem familiar to you.

1. In a very general sense, as a graduate, what I understood the University of Chicago letter to mean is this: "When you get here, your previous notions are going to be confronted and challenged and sometimes this process might be deeply uncomfortable for you. We find this to be a feature, not a bug." Which I find to be a largely unobjectionable sentiment, when it comes to education and the development of the individual. You have to be confronted, you have to be challenged, and you have to learn the skills that allow you to robustly defend your point of view and to abandon that point of view when it is not tenable, and come to a new understanding through the process. This is all very

Hegelian—thesis, antithesis, synthesis—which means it's very Chicago, where Hegel might as well be the school mascot.

2. I thought the Dean of Students did a less than 100% excellent job in conveying this particular point, choosing to spice up his letter to the kids with lingo to show how he's hip and with it, or *something*, in the process letting shouty people drag the letter out and wave it about for their own purposes. So, yeah, well done, there, dean. Additionally, I'm not entirely sure that that message in that particular letter was necessary. This is the University of Chicago, guys. Is anyone who actually *intends* to attend unaware that the university prides itself on rigorous examination, discussion and debate? Basically, I found the letter a bit silly. If I were an instructor (or an editor), I would have sent it back with the instruction to tone down the posturing and just get to the meat of the letter sooner.

3. I think it's good and fine and necessary that an education requires confronting one's own thoughts and beliefs, subjecting them to the crucible of inquiry and discussion, and thus tempering the quality of one's own beliefs as a result. What is equally important—and what in my experience Chicago was good at, and a thing not conveyed very well by the letter—is that those leading these excursions, the professors and other instructors, work the room. Which means not only leading discussion but also focusing and shaping it and creating an environment in which every student can be a component of the discussion. Which can mean anything from making sure a couple of egotistical loudmouths don't just drone on every goddamn class session, to drawing out those students who might otherwise feel like there's no percentage in making their own points. You can only robustly interrogate beliefs and assumptions when everyone who is there to learn knows they can speak. That's on the instructors, and professors, and on the University as a whole. I believe Chicago does that—or did, when I was there—and that's something I wish was better articulated.

4. Likewise, the educational process is more (and better) than some sort of Intellectual Thunderdome where the validity of a point of view is decided solely through trial by combat. Robust interrogation of one's point of view by others is a thing, and a *necessary* thing, but is not the *only* thing. There are all sorts of ways to learn, to acquire knowledge, assess and reassess one's ground assumptions, and come to a better understanding of the world therein. My Chicago experience had a lot of me squaring off against some other student—or a professor! Screw you, Dr. Whoever! I have points I'm gonna make and *I will fight you on them*—but just as much if not more of my education was spent doing other things, from quiet reading to co-operative participation to just shutting up and letting someone more knowledgeable and experienced than I was show me something I didn't already know.

5. Over on Twitter the other day I noted the following:

> *The conservatives gloating about @uchicago's "No Safe Spaces" policy don't appear to think it will apply to them, too, the dear wee lads.*

Which made a lot of conservatives on Twitter really rather foamy, bloviating about how *they* never ask for safe spaces, harumph harumph, *gwaaaaaaaar*. Which I found pretty funny. First because I found it non-responsive to the point that Chicago's policy means that all points of view will be open to interrogation, which will include conservative points of view that new students might bring in. Having seen more than a couple of young conservatives at Chicago walk into a moving fan blade of people as smart as they were, with better command of facts and rhetoric, and coming out rather upset and angry with the experience, I'm not at all convinced every young conservative is ready to have their own baseline assumptions challenged. I expect some will assume Chicago is an implictly "safe space" for them, like, as it happens, most of the rest of their world. Which of course is the point: when (some) conservatives like to brag that they never ask for safe spaces, that's very much like a fish bragging that it never asks for water.

Let me suggest a radical idea (which is to say, it's not really radical at all), which is that the ability to take a challenge to one's fundamental precepts of the world, and the enthusiasm to engage with those who oppose those precepts, is largely orthogonal to one's political views. There are liberal-minded folks who love to walk into a room full of people ready to hate them and bellow, *bring it, suckas*; there are conservatives who are the most special of special snowflakes who ever wafted down, weeping precious and icy tears. And vice-versa, and the same no matter where one plots one's self on a multi-dimensional political chart.

I might suggest a salient difference between liberals and conservatives in this regard is that many of the groups that traditionally comprise the liberal coalition—minorities, women, LGBTQ+—don't have the baseline assumption of safety in the world that generally white, generally straight conservatives do. This makes it easier for (some) conservatives to pretend that they don't in fact expect to have their worldview coddled and allowed for every bit as much as they accuse liberals of doing. And when they run into a buzzsaw that shreds their worldview—as they will at Chicago, almost guaranteed—their perhaps previously unrealized assumption that Chicago was "safe" for them, intellectually, is going into the hopper.

6. With respect to the University of Chicago specifically, it's been suggested that one reason for the letter is a bit of institutional territory marking (see this *Vox* article http://www.vox.com/2016/8/26/12657684/chicago-safe-spaces-trigger-warnings-letter) basically telling the kids that the sort of protesting that works at other schools isn't going to fly at Chicago, so don't even bother. While I'm not at all convinced that this is really what the letter was about, it is *absolutely true* that institutionally speaking the University of Chicago doesn't take kindly to protesting. When I attended Chicago, I wrote an in-depth series of articles about when, in the 1960s, Chicago students, like other students at elite universities, took over the administration building as a protest (in the case of Chicago, for a popular teacher being dropped). Chicago's response, basically, was to wait out the protesters, discipline a stack of the students for being a nuisance, and then never speak about it again (the teacher was not rehired, either). This last year, the president of the student government at Chicago barely escaped with his degree after he allowed students into the administration building for a different protest (seriously, don't screw with the administration building. They get annoyed and they will punish you).

But again, I don't think the letter was a warning so much as a poorly expressed declaration of intellectual intent. *Yes, the school and/or students will occasionally bring in people to speak whom you hate. No, your protests won't stop it. Deal.* Which again is a very Chicago thing to do.

7. How do I personally feel about safe spaces and trigger warnings in a general sense? With regard to the latter, I think they're fine, and often courteous. I think the world has come to a place where we understand people have their various sensitivities, and if it would be a kindness to give people a heads up that something involves violence or racism or whatever, sure, why not? It's not *censorship* to make people aware they should prepare (which ironically, means you could say that silly letter was a trigger warning letting students know about their future lack at the school—in which case, *very sneaky*, Chicago).

As for safe spaces, my own understanding is that it's also generally fine and courteous to give people space to despressurize and relax and be themselves, often without *me* around (or at least, if I am around, with me following rules others set). This is, I will be the first to admit, a *very* simplistic approach to what the concept of a safe space is. But it's the foundation on which I build out complexity regarding the subject.

Also, you know. I don't feel obliged to pretend "trigger warnings" are a liberal phenomenon; when they're basically conservative, they're usually called "ratings." Movie, TV and video game ratings, content advisory notes on music, etc—none of which in the US are currently dictated by the government, incidentally—they're pretty much so people don't get triggered (or get triggered by their children seeing something inconvenient for them as parents). I don't really have an opposition to ratings either. I mean, hell, back at the turn of the century I ran a video game site specifically calling out game elements ranging from violence to drug use to racism to nudity so people could decide whether or not to get a game, or get it for their kids, or be prepared for that content when it happened (here's one of the reviews https://web.archive.org/web/20000518044707/http://www.gamedad.com/framer.php3?nav=nav.php3&content=game_info.php3?gam_id%3d23). You know, kind of like trigger warnings. Conservative folks loved the site. *But that's different!* Well, no. It's really not.

Likewise I can think of several places online and off which qualify as "safe spaces" for non-liberals, where like-minded people go to rest and relax and not have to feel like they always have to be looking over their shoulder for the *politically correct thought police*, etc and so on, places that have rules that you have to follow, set by moderators or owners or whomever, and if you don't like it, there's the door. Whether they're called "safe spaces" or not is neither here nor there. Apply the duck test to it.

And that's fine too—with safe spaces and trigger warnings, however you choose to label them, everyone needs their gathering holes and has their sensitivities and desires companionship with others whose journey is similar to theirs. Sometimes you need a respite from the world, because very often the world is work. It's *courteous* to let others have them, and if necessary, to offer them. It would be lovely if people stopped pretending they don't exist all across the human experience, including across the political spectrum.

8. I don't believe the Chicago approach, or that silly letter, means fewer liberals (or conservatives! Or any other political orientation!) are going to come out of the school, a belief buttressed by looking at the rather wide cross-section of political positions and opinions that its alumni espouse. A school that counts both Saul Alinsky and Milton Friedman among its graduates can encompass a wide scope of thought; the alumni issuing forth from it since the heady days of the tenure of Alinsky and Friedman appear similarly varied in their politics. This is good for the school and it's good for the people who attend it today— they are going to meet up with people not like them, and argue with them, and hopefully come away with a better understanding of opposing positions, and their own. And who knows? Maybe they'll even become and remain friends with people who don't think in lockstep with them. It happens. It happened to me. And that is a definite positive of a Chicago education.

UTOPIAS

Ken Baker asks:

If you don't mind a question about another writer's work: The Culture in Iain M. Banks' series of novels is depicted as a Utopia. There is no need for money or laws, virtually any material thing anyone wants is available for the asking, everyone is beautiful and lives a long, happy life (except sometimes for people who are actively involved in other cultures and civilizations).

That all sounds nice. But, assuming the necessary technology eventually exists, human nature being what it is, is this a realistic future? And would a life free from all challenge be a satisfying life?

I'll answer with specific regard to Banks, and then assay the general concept of utopias and humans.

First, with regard to The Culture, I don't think it's a universe free from all challenges; there are plenty of challenges and adventures that people in The Culture may choose to take. Indeed, in *The Hydrogen Sonata*, our main character has spent her life—and modified her body—to attempt the performance of the musical piece that gives the book its title, and is notoriously difficult for anyone with fewer than four arms to attempt. Now, maybe you might argue that this isn't a *true* challenge, but I don't know; most people don't specifically radically change their physiognomy to do a specific thing if they don't consider it a central challenge to their life.

The difference between the challenges of The Culture and the challenges of, say, current life on this planet is that the ground level of the challenges of The Culture are elevated from basic needs. Here in the US, the ground level challenge is to achieve the economic means to stay alive and comfortable—get a job that gets you money so you can pay for food, shelter, education, medical needs, and so on. Failing this ground level challenge means going hungry and/or lacking a home and/or dying early from otherwise avoidable heath issues and/or being trapped in a cycle of poverty, along with your children, who inherit your ground level challenges.

The Culture gets rid of those particular ground level challenges, so the question now becomes: What are your challenges when you *don't* worry about, say, starving or dying early? It's not that there are *no* challenges. It's just that the challenges don't end with you dead in an alleyway because you can't afford to eat.

Indeed (and to now generalize) this is what utopias for humans essentially are: The removal of physical *want* and *need* to allow the multiplicity of operative *choice*. Choices can be challenges and many humans desire challenges—things which offer (or at the very least, appear to offer) meaning and achievement to one's life. So even in a utopia there should be challenges galore. Otherwise one may meaningfully argue that the society isn't a utopia at all. Utopias, in my opinion, minimize want, not choice and opportunity for achievement.

One may even argue that utopias should offer *more* opportunities for personally meaningful challenges because baseline needs are sorted, and that these additional challenges might seem frivolous to someone who is just surviving, but for the citizens of the utopia might have actual meaning. If you don't think that's possible, ask yourself why the Super Bowl and the Oscars draw in millions of viewers every single year, when the "achievement" those participating in it gain is based fundamentally on entertaining others. They both have meaning because of their context in a society that allows for enough wealth and leisure time to allow exceptional entertainment skills to *become* an achievement. Your ancestors on the savanna would would look at an Oscar as a useless shiny thing, and in their context, they'd be entirely correct. In our context, it's still shiny, but not useless. And in a utopia, maybe an award for, say, origami is one of the highest achievements one could aspire to, because why not? In a utopia, that sort of cleverness and dexterity could be (literally) prized.

(Before anyone notes it: There are already awards for origami. They just aren't widely known outside their specific community, he said, looking at his own shelf of community-specific awards.)

Here's an important thing to note about utopias, which I think is often overlooked (although not by Banks, as he wrote up The Culture): Utopias still have humans in them, which means that not everyone in them is going to be happy all the time. If you eliminate certain needs and wants, the part of the brain that focuses on achieving those needs and wants (or alternately desiring them) will focus on some other subject, and will be happy or unhappy about that. People will still have doubts and longing and desire and unhappiness to the same extent they do now. They just won't worry they'll, you know, *starve*.

How am I confident about this? Because some people *already* live in a utopia: In our world, they're called "rich people." Rich people (usually) have their baselines sorted and don't have to worry about food and shelter and health care and such things; they lead enviable lives with lots of opportunity for leisure. But in my experience they're not always happy, and their lives are not always problem-free. They have exchanged one set of problems for another, and while their problems are ones many people wish they had, they still weigh on the mind. In a utopia, where the baseline standard of living is the same as that of, say, a tech firm VP living in Irvine, California, people will still have problems. Maybe better problems. But still problems.

And I suspect that's why, when people actually live in a culture that seems utopian to us, here in the early 21st century, they won't recognize or appreciate it as utopian, any more than we recognize that the average life of a 21st century American citizen is utopian to, as an example, a European serf in the 11th century ("You can leave the estate? What? There *are* no estates? And you have all your teeth and don't have tumors on your face? And everyone can *read*? And what is this 'cell phone' thing you have? MY GOD MUSIC AND PICTURES

ARE COMING FROM IT IS IT POSSESSED"). For the people of a utopia, it will just be...life. And they will wonder what it will be like for the people who *finally* get to live in a utopia, centuries away from their own experience.

THE WAYS THE SCALZI WOMEN ARE BETTER THAN ME: AN INCOMPLETE LIST

<table>
<tr><td>Jul</td></tr>
<tr><td>6</td></tr>
<tr><td>2014</td></tr>
</table>

Last week, as part of my general "try to lose weight and get a little healthier because you're middle-aged now and you don't want to *die"* thing, I started going to the local YMCA to use its weight room and indoor track, with my daughter as my workout partner. She's been on the powerlifting team at her school for the last three years, so she's knowledgeable about the weights in a way I am not, and is thus a good person with whom to work out. At the end of our first session, I tweeted the following:

> *Let it be known that my daughter can lift more than I do. Because she's on her school's weightlifting team, and also because she's awesome.*

This naturally aroused the derision of the hooting pack of status-anxious dudebros who let me live rent-free in their brains, prompting a predictable slew of tweets and blog posts about how this is further proof of my girly-man status, hardly a man at all, dude do you even lift, and so on. I noted this to my daughter.

> **Me:** *Some dudes online are making fun of me because you lift more than I can.*

> **Daughter:** *That's because they're pathetic losers, dad.*
> *#point*

Should it be a surprise that my daughter, who has been on a powerlifting team for three years and has taken medals at competition, can lift more than I, who has not seen the inside of a weight room since high school? I don't think so; I think it would be mildly surprising if she couldn't. She has training and endurance that I don't. It's also equally possible that even if she had not had her previous training, if we had gone into that weight room, she still might have been able to lift more than me. I would have been fine with that. If I keep at it, over time it's possible I'll lift more than she can. It's also possible, however, that I won't.

And if I never lift more than my daughter? Well, and if that happens, so what? One, I'm not sure why I should feel threatened or belittled by my daughter's abilities of any sort. Call me *nutty*, but I *want* my daughter to be accomplished and capable, and even more accomplished and capable than me, whenever that's possible. It's a parent thing. Two, I'm not using the weight room to express my *manliness*, or as a zero-sum crucible to measure my personal worthiness against other human beings, because that seems, I don't know, kind of *stupid* to me. I'm using it because I want to be in better shape than I am now. I fail to see how collapsing into a testerical pile of insecurity over the fact my daughter can lift more than I can will help me with my actual goal of becoming more fit.

Of course, it helps that I'm not one of those quivering bro-puppets who lives in constant fear that a woman might actually outclass him in something, and that if she does, it means that his balls have shrunk three sizes that day. This is a good thing, because in point of fact the Scalzi women, Krissy and Athena, are better than and/or outclass me in several ways. For example:

1. I've already noted that Athena out-lifts me. Krissy, it should be noted, is stronger than either of us; she is in point of fact unusually (I like to say *freakishly*) strong. I will note that I am perfectly capable, strength-wise; childish dudebro taunting online aside, I do fine for myself in that department and always have. Krissy has always been substantially stronger than I. It was never even a point of contention.

2. Krissy also has more physical endurance than I do. I was just joking to her today about the fact that if she lived 10,000 years ago, she would run down gazelles on the savannah because, like the Terminator, she would *just keep coming*. Again, I do just fine in the stamina department (anyone who has seen me dance for three hours straight can vouch for this). Krissy outclasses me by a mile.

3. Both Athena and Krissy are better shots than I am, Athena with a bow and Krissy with guns and rifles. And I'm decent with a bow.

4. Krissy is the financial brains of the Scalzi outfit, since both by inclination and by training (she has a degree in business) she has an analytical mind for numbers. I do my part on the business end—my very first published book was on finance, and I was a consultant for financial services companies over the years—but the day-to-day administration and planning fall to her, with good reason.

5. Athena writes better at her age than I did at the same age. It's not even close. She will point out that she has the benefit of a parent who writes, with whom she can talk about both the craft and business of writing, and I cheerfully concede that point. Nevertheless, I've read her stuff, and I re-read the stuff I wrote at her age. My work at that age is pretty good. Hers is better.

6. Krissy is one of the best "straight-line" thinkers I've ever met; she can examine a situation, crystalize the issue and offer a solution quickly and dispassionately—and correctly. This is such a useful and critical skill that I actively spent years learning from her how to do it. I'm pretty good at it now. She's still better, enough so that whenever possible, I always confer with her to double-check my own thinking.

I could go on—I could go *on and on*—but I assume you get the point.

Now, no doubt the status-anxious dudebros will delight in my *shocking admissions* here, because they are silly little boys who apparently think that a man who can happily live with, and help raise, women who are better at various things than he is (including things they entirely erroneously suppose to be inherently *masculine*) must be therefore weak and inferior and *girly*. Two points here.

One, there's the obvious point that in the Scalzi household "girly" means *strong* and *smart* and *capable* and *better than decent with ranged weapons*. All of which I would happily be. So yes *sign me up for girly please.*

Two, and to repeat, these sad, frantic lumps of manflesh are proclaiming that a man who is pleased to share his life with women who are strong and smart and capable, and who has no problem acknowledging when their skills are superior to his, is somehow actually *lesser* for it. This should tell you all you need to know about the intelligence and sensibleness of such a world view.

I'm going to let them keep that silly, stunted world view. I'm going to keep mine. Because among other things, my world view has allowed me to share my life with, and share in the life of, the two best people I know: My wife, and my daughter. I am delighted in all the ways that they are the best, and also, better than me.

WEINSTEIN, RATNER, TOBACK, ETC

Another day and another dude in the entertainment industry accused of sexual assault and harassment: Today it's Brett Ratner, who six women accused of impropriety in a *Los Angeles Times* article, including actress Natasha Henstridge, who recounts an encounter two decades ago that basically amounts to rape, and Olivia Munn, toward whom Ratner has been pretty much a horny shit for more than a decade now. It's been a pattern that once a few substantive accusations are out there more come forward (see: Harvey Weinstein, James Toback, Bill Cosby), so I don't expect the next several days are going to be very happy ones for Ratner. Nor should they be.

I imagine it's likewise a very uncomfortable time for a lot of men in the entertainment industry right now, as they search their own pasts, recalling incidents that they are probably hoping to God are not dredged up toward the light of day by the women (or men! Or non-binary folk!) they've been horrible to, as the "whisper network" stops being whispery and starts talking out loud and unafraid. Ratner is the most recent powerful man in this particular barrel, but it's deeply doubtful he's going to be the last.

I don't doubt it's uncomfortable for everyone else in the industry, too, for all sorts of reasons. Let me explain it in personal terms: Currently I have several projects in various stages of development for television and film, mostly with people I've met with and liked but fundamentally know very little about except through the scope of their work. I am *praying* that none of them has been carrying on as a creepy, harassing piece of shit. Because, aside from all the very serious problems with *that*, there's the extra added concern of what it will mean for the aforementioned projects, which would then have a radioactive person attached to them who no one will want to do business with, if not for ethics then for optics. I have ethical and also *purely business-related* reasons for hoping my associates are not fucking creeps. Multiply my position by everyone in entertainment right now, and you see the problem.

(And to be fair, the problem is in both directions: The people I have my options with know me mostly through my work, too. They don't know what I'm doing in the rest of my personal and professional life, either, or whether or not I'm a creepy creep who creeps creeptastically, and my creepularity has simply just not been revealed to them—the "whisper network" doesn't reach to where they are. I've not been asked to attest that I'm *not* a harassing piece of shit. They're taking it on faith that I'm not.)

So basically everyone in entertainment right now, you could say, has the smallest inkling of what it's like to be a *woman* in the entertainment industry, and not to know whether the person you're meeting with will blow up *your* project or *your* career because of *their* behavior. Let's not overextend the simile—the chances I or lots of other dudes will face a "casting couch" situation to get a project made approaches zero, for example—but certainly the question of "who are you *really* and how will who you are hurt me and my goals?" is one lots of people are asking in a different way these last several weeks.

On a vaguely-related note, someone sent along a bit from a detractor of mine who was hoping that I would be outed as a harassing creep because wouldn't that be *perfect*, ha ha ha. Which will tell you two things: One, I don't need to seek out people saying awful things about me because people feel free to send those along, so I have a crowd-sourced clipping service of people being shitty to me; and two, my detractors are terrible people.

This fellow is going to be disappointed, I think. Consent is important to me, and historically speaking I've been able to take "no" for an answer. Likewise I make an effort not be a harassing shithead of a dude (spoiler: It's not *that* difficult to make that effort). I try to live my life so that people don't feel like I'm just waiting for the right moment to be a creepy fuck to them.

With that said: Are there times I might have made someone uncomfortable, or said or did something they found creepy? Yes, probably! I'm not perfect and as I've written about before, the decision as to what's creepy rests with the other person, not me (or you). So it's certainly possible something I've done or said rang some worry bells in someone else's head, and they prefer not to be near me or have anything to do with me. In which case **a)** totally fair, and **b)** I'm sorry.

Which is all easy to *say*, mind you. One of the things that the recent weeks has done is to cause me to go back and really look at how I have interacted with people, particularly women, over the years. I can think of times now where I've revised my opinion of my past actions downward (how I dealt with my long-term crush in high school is one example—I used to think it was puppy-dog swoonish and now I think it's a little sad and creepy), and others in more contemporary times where I feel like I can do better and will try to. I think at least some of my detractors are of the opinion that I hold myself up as a paragon of perfect behavior and thought, and, well. Let's just say I live in my own mind and know it better than they do. Trust me, I'm so *not* perfect. But I do try to be *decent* to people, and that's a constant process.

(I do have a useful rule of thumb, with my actions toward other people and with life in general, which is: *Is this something I'd tell Krissy about?* If this answer is anything other than "yes, of course, unreservedly," then there's a problem, which, incidentally, is a cue for me to talk to her about it *right then*. You would be surprised—or possibly you wouldn't—at how useful this rule has been over the years. You may also assume that there's *very little* my wife doesn't know about me.)

To go back to the entertainment industry, none of this is done yet: More people (mostly dudes) are going to be exposed for their harassing and assaulting actions, and even *more* people are going to have their lives and livelihoods thrown up in the air because of the fallout. It's necessary but it's going to be a mess. And it all could have been easily avoided. All it takes is *not* harassing, assaulting or treating other people like shit. Try doing *that*, entertainment dudes! You'll be (tragically) surprised how effective it is.

WHO'S COOL
AND WIIO'S NOT

May

9

2018

On Twitter, Washington Post columnist Alyssa Rosenberg and I were having a brief discussion of coolness, and I mentioned that the next time I saw her I would tell her my theory on what makes some people cool, and most people not. Whatever readers, sensing perhaps they would not be there for that private conversation, asked for me to explain it in public.

So, fine, here is my theory on "cool" and why some people will never be cool. And to explain it, let me use a couple of examples, namely, me and my wife Kristine.

I am, to put it bluntly, *not* cool. This does not mean that I am not (or at least could not be) a good person, or a nice person, or a person that people are interested in meeting, or someone who is creative or does interesting stuff, and so on. What it means is, when I meet people, I generally want them to like me. I like to be liked. This aspect of my personality means I expend time and effort and energy to find the ways and means to help people decide if they want to like me. It doesn't always work (and sometimes I decide *I* don't want to like someone), but generally it does; I'm mostly likeable, and by now I'm pretty good at reading people. But the point is, there's a flow of conversational and personality energy coming out from me, hoping to draw the other person in, to help create a space we can both be comfortable in, and maybe even be friends together.

Krissy also generally likes to be liked; who doesn't? But the thing about Krissy is that she's perfectly fine if you don't like her, either, and her particular personality means she doesn't worry about either condition. She is a lovely and wonderful and delightful person, and also, she's pretty much entirely self-contained. Your approbation or opprobation is neither here nor there to her. As a result, she doesn't send out a lot of energy when you meet her initially. Energy and effort goes *to* her, rather than *from* her, and then depending on what she decides, you get to be friends with her, or not. She's never less than polite and kind and correct with people; I've never known her to be cruel or standoffish, unless someone richly deserved it. But fundamentally she's a person people want to impress, rather than the person trying to impress people. In other words: she's cool.

Much shorter version: If you're the sort of person who wants people to like *you*, you're not cool. If you're the sort of person who people wished you liked *them*, you're cool. Likewise, *things* that are cool are things you have to do the work to approach; not-cool things come out to find you.

"That's just the difference between an introvert and an extrovert!" I hear some of you say. Well, no. As it happens, I'm the actual introvert in the family, and Krissy is the actual extrovert. I put out energy and effort despite eventually wanting to withdraw from people and recharge in my room; Krissy draws people in and then once they're in her circle of friends, she's ready to party. I think there may be some correlation between introversion and coolness (shyness can be confused with coolness, for example), and extroversion with not-coolness, but it's not one to one.

Indeed we can come up with lots of reasons why people are cool or not cool, but I'm not sure that any one of them is a constant. People who are beautiful seem to automatically go to the head of the line in terms of coolness, as an example, but I know lots of people who I think are gorgeous who are also deeply not-cool in their personalities, and vice-versa. Some creative people I know are cool; many are not. Some people would say "coolness is confidence" but anecdotally I don't think anyone would say of me that I'm *not* confident, and yet I don't consider myself cool at all. Most nerds are really not cool, and yet I can think of a few who totally are. And so on.

Also, and to be clear: Coolness, or lack thereof, is not a value judgment. Some awesome people and things are not in the least bit cool; some real trash is found under the "cool" umbrella. I do think at least some of the valorization of "coolness" comes from the simple fact that most people and things aren't in fact genuinely cool. Most people like to be liked; in situations where people feel comfortable, and on their own terms, they send out energy to others and hope to draw others in. Likewise, most creative things in the stream of commerce aren't meant to be difficult to approach; they're made, bluntly, to sell, to *someone*. At the end of the day, something that is "cool" or not is neither here nor there to its value (and its value to *you*), and cool people are still people and you can like them or not, depending.

Now, here's a couple of caveats to the "coolness" thing. The first is that "cool" is obviously very often shorthand for "a person or thing or action I like and/or admire," as in "I love that dude, he's so cool" or "That movie was really cool" or "That was a cool thing you did." If you're using "cool" that way—and pretty much everyone does—I'm not going to argue with you about it. The ridiculous fungibility of the English language means things can be "hot," "cool," "bad," "good," and "sick" simultaneously, and all meant positively, even when those words (again, obviously) have their own separate meanings in different contexts, and shades of difference in this one. When I'm talking about "cool" and "not cool" I'm scaling it down to a very specific context (and also, I should note I'm making a qualitative distinction between "not cool" and "uncool," the latter of which has specific negative connotations, and while I'm at it, between "not cool" and "warm," the latter of which has its own positive connotations. Wow, my philosophy of language training is getting a workout today).

The second caveat is that not-cool people and things can have situational coolness thrust upon them. I am by no stretch a cool person, but in events like readings and signings and appearances, I get to be a temporarily cool person, because lots of energy is being directed at me by people who have come to see me, and the dynamic of the event is that I can't really return the energy in kind.

The coolness generally dissipates the moment I'm off the clock, thank God, because I'm not *actually* famous and thus am not cursed to be recognized everywhere I go. That sort of coolness is performative and I can't imagine having to perform it all the time. It's difficult for not-cool people to be cool on a regular basis. It's like ill-fitting shoes. I imagine for cool people the opposite is true—being in a situation where they would have to send out energy all the time to other people would be exhausting.

I like that my wife is cool; from a sociological point of view it's been fascinating for me to watch people react to her over the last quarter century. I imagine that she feels the same way about me, watching me do my thing with people as I get to know them, and they me. I think as a couple we make a pretty good team because we are content to be who we are. I like my not-cool self. And I enjoy trying on a daily basis to get my super-cool wife to decide to like me. It's fun. And so far, so good.

Why The ACA
Matters to Me

Oct

2

2013

Over on her site, author Kameron Hurley tells the story of how she almost died because she didn't have enough money to manage her adult-onset Type 1 diabetes. It wasn't that she wasn't working—first she worked for a company through which she had (crappy) insurance, and later she was hustling as hard as she could as a freelance writer. It was because the way insurance has been handled in the US made it very difficult for her to get insured, *stay* insured and to afford to *be* insured—and the alternative to being insured here in the US is so much worse that it simply beggars description.

Thing is: Kameron's story? Not unusual for writers in the US. I don't have enough fingers and toes on my body to count off the writers in my own personal sphere who are hardworking, who are hustling as much as they can with their work, who had the medical boom dropped on them by life and were screwed because they didn't have health insurance, or couldn't get health insurance that was even remotely within their financial means. I can't tell you the number of writers I know personally who have gone begging online or to family and friends to cover a catastrophic medical issue. Not to mention musicians, artists, actors, and any other sort of creative people.

Or anyone else, for that matter, who doesn't live in the magical bubble of work that carries benefits. I was at the store the other week, listening to the woman in front of me in the checkout line cough like her lungs were trying to escape through her throat, and heard her friend admonish her for not going to the doctor. And the coughing lady gave her a look, and it was a look I knew really well from days of old, the one that said, *and just how am I going to afford* that, *do you think?*

In my professional life, I've been fortunate. I've always had good health insurance, either through my employer or through my wife's, and the one brief time I paid full freight for our health insurance, I was able to afford it (although I had to incorporate, hire my wife and then attach myself and our child as dependents on her policy, because it was massively cheaper that way—which also points out the stupidity of how health insurance is done in the US). I'm also aware how fortunate I have been for someone in my field; I am one of the few self-employed writers I know who *doesn't* have a health insurance tale of woe.

I'm also aware of how many people I know—not just writers but people in general, among friends and family—who have *no* margin of error when it comes to their health. If they get sick, their *most rational option* is take some Tylenol and hope it goes away. Because they can hardly afford to go to the doctor and even if they do, what is the doctor going to do? Give them a prescription for something they really can't afford, or send them along to a specialist they also can't afford, or tell them they have some problem or issue they can't afford to fix. Out comes the Tylenol. Out comes the look the woman in the checkout line gave her friend.

Now, here comes the Affordable Care Act, and its various marketplaces for insurance. God knows it's not the perfect system—it's really *not*—but for the first time in my adult memory it means that people can find an insurance plan with decent coverage, including the basic preventative care that can address so many problems early and much more cheaply than if people wait until they find themselves in an emergency room, for a price scaled to their income and their ability to pay. It means all the people whose previous rational options for health care consisted of being sick *because it was cheaper than getting well* have a better option, both for themselves and for the rest of us (you didn't think those ER visits came for free, do you? Oh, we *pay* for them, my friends).

And of course some people oppose it. They give all sorts of financial and economic reasons, which don't hold up to scrutiny, particularly over the long term, as the benefits of a healthier population and throttling of expanding costs come into play. In the end, a lot of the opposition stems from the fact that the United States still has a thick layer of angry Calvinism to it, the sort that suggests that if you are poor, or sick, that you did something to deserve it and that you should just have to deal with it because after all it is your *fault*. Well, I'm looking real hard to see how Kameron Hurley *deserved* to get adult-onset Type 1 diabetes. I'm coming up with a blank. They only thing she can be blamed for—and to be clear, *blame* is hardly the accurate word for it—is handling her illness in the way that the circumstances of her life dictated, first with her (bad) insurance and then later with none. Yes, sometimes people do foolish things, and get sick or hurt. But lots of people *don't* do foolish things, and get sick or hurt anyway. In the real world, this angry Calvinism is nonsense (and even people who do foolish things should have affordable health care).

I know too many people—too many people who work hard—for whom the ACA is a lifechanger, a way for them to finally be able to not have to choose between health care for themselves and their families and all the other bills they have to pay. When I see the Congresspeople who shut down the government as a way to stop the ACA, among all the other problems I have with them is the fact that I see a group of people who are, essentially, looking at people I know and care about and saying to them, *just fucking die, already*.

I'm not inclined to look kindly on the people wishing my friends and family dead. I'm going to remember the ones who did. I am also going to remember the ones who instead chose to help them.

Why I Didn't
Go To Bennington
College

Feb

15

2014

I read the *Esquire* profile of Peter Dinklage this morning, and it noted that Dinklage is a graduate of Bennington College, class of 1991. Which made me think, *huh, I could have been a classmate of Peter Dinklage's*, because I was also class of 1991...and I had also been accepted into Bennington. Indeed, when it came time to choose colleges, my final two choices were Bennington and the University of Chicago. There is an alternate timeline in which I zigged instead of zagged, went to Bennington and, possibly, hung about with Dinklage in the New England wildernesses of Vermont.

I've told people before that I almost went to Bennington, and when I tell them that—to the extent that they know about Bennington College at all—some of them wonder why I didn't go there. On paper at least, it seems like a better fit for my personality, at least when I was a teenager: It's an arty, freeform school that has spit out excellent writers and novelists with regularity, including Donna Tartt, Jonathan Lethem, Kiran Desai and Bret Easton Ellis (whose writing I'm not hugely in love with, but you can't say he's not successful in the gig), as well as scads of other creative folk.

So I would have spent four years with a bunch of kids very much like me in an atmosphere of unfettered creative ferment. Plus, at the time there was something like an 8 to 1 female/male ratio, which to a seventeen-year-old straight boy was a definite plus, in theory at least. I was all for it. And Bennington was all for me, it appeared—halfway through my interview for the school, the alumni stopped saying "if you go" and started saying "when you go," and Bennington itself offered me flat-out the best amount of scholarship money of any school I was accepted to.

So why didn't I go? Because as attractive as Bennington was, and it really was attractive, at the end of the day I knew myself. I was creative and artistic and full of big ideas, but I was also madly, deeply, *truly* unstructured. Bennington was similarly unstructured, by intention. Which was attractive but also not really what I needed. Left to my own devices, I would devolve into a puddle of inertia. The University of Chicago is many things, some positive and some negative, but the one thing it is not is unstructured. It could provide a pedagogical spine I could slop my unstructured, creative self around.

There were other ancillary reasons as well (Bennington has only 600 students, and coming from a high school with 360 people, I wanted something a bit less intimate, for one; U of C had a worldwide reputation and deep resources; Chicago is a hell of a town), but at the end of the day, it came down to structure. I didn't have it, so I needed a school that did. I picked U of C and have never had cause to regret it.

(I am, I would note, still largely unstructured; that I have achieved as much in my life as I have is in no small part due to having a wife who aside from every other amazing quality she has is super organized and gets things done, including for me.)

Still, my choice of Chicago over Bennington should not be read as a criticism of Bennington; it was a tough choice and for good reason. Every once in a while I think about how my life would have been different if I had taken the leap and gone Bennington. It's impossible to say, but I suspect among the several differences might have been that I would have become a novelist sooner, probably wouldn't be writing science fiction (I see myself becoming more of a Sam Lipsyte or Gary Shteyngart sort of writer—or at least wanting to be a writer *like* them), and I suspect would be doing the Park Slope thing or something very close to it. I would hope I would have had the sense to marry someone like Krissy, as I don't suspect I would have met her in this particular timeline.

And, hey, I probably would have partied with Peter Dinklage a time or two. There would be worse things to have in one's memory banks.

WHY I DON'T DRINK OR USE DRUGS

Mar

24

2016

'm fairly open about my teetotaler status, which led Thomas Hewlett to ask:

You've mentioned several times that you don't drink alcohol. I do a lot of work with addiction/recovery and I'm wondering about your relationship to alcohol and drugs and what led to your decision to not drink. Or is this simply a case of "that stuff doesn't taste good"?

It's true: I don't drink alcohol except in very rare circumstances (like, half a glass of champagne at my wedding), I've never smoked cigarettes, I've never taken an illegal drug, and outside of Novocain at the dentist's office, I'm generally reluctant to take legal drugs either; my wife always expresses surprise if I go to the medicine cabinet for ibuprofen, for example. So what's the story there?

Well, to begin, and initially the reason I avoided the stuff, my family has *really bad* addiction issues. I'm a child of alcoholics and drug users, and I've seen first hand what the stuff can do to people whose brains are wired to leap out of their seats when drugs are around, not only in family members but in the people who were around my family. Many of the people I knew growing up were either struggling with addiction, or trying to get clean, or dealing with the shitshow of a life that is crawling out of the hole that addiction puts you in. All of which reinforced the idea for me early on that this was not what I wanted for my life, or in my life.

This did mean when I was younger I could be pretty humorless about alcohol and drugs. When I was a little kid I was convinced a single beer or puff from a joint would put you on the fast track to being (in the words of *South Park*) homeless on the streets giving handjobs for crack, and I would sometimes freak out about it. I got better about this as I got older and learned that not everyone had the same addiction problems as I saw in the people around me (this is where I note that for a large part of my childhood my mother was active in the Alcoholics Anonymous community, so I really *was* surrounded by addicts, albeit ones trying to get and stay clean). But, yeah, as a kid I was definitely not cool with a beer and a joint. I figured it meant you were doomed. *Dooooooooomed.*

On a personal level, the residual effect of that childhood paranoia manifests itself with a continued personal lack of interest in alcohol or drugs. I'm no longer paranoid that a single shot of hard liquor or a toke would turn me into an uncontrollable gibbering addict, but on the other hand given my family's inarguable problems with the stuff I don't feel the need to play the odds, either. I'm not foolish enough to think I *don't* have all the features of an addictive personality, nor am I foolish enough to believe that age and understanding will have much compensatory effect against my body's physical desire for addictive stuff. All in all, best to leave the stuff alone. There are other things to keep me occupied.

When I was younger, there were some people who were amazed that I didn't drink or do drugs. "Aren't you curious?" was a question I got a lot (answer: No, because I'd seen enough of it in my life, thanks), sometimes followed by the person, almost always a dude, who would be all "Dude, I'm *totally* getting you drunk tonight!" because he thought he was doing me a favor by making me relax through alcohol. It didn't work since someone trying to get me drunk made me rather more tense (this sort of thing was almost always about alcohol, I'd note. People smoking pot would offer you the joint, but if you didn't want it, they were always "cool, whatever" and off it would go to the next person).

Occasionally when I was younger someone would get offended that I didn't drink, because they thought I was judging them for drinking. Well, when I was a kid, sure, I'd do that. By the time I was drinking age, I didn't care what other people were doing with their bodies, unless it was directly affecting me. Which is the way I feel today. I don't drink; I'm fine if you do.

Nowadays, at age 46, no one is in the least offended that, or usually even curious about why, I don't drink or do drugs. At this age, everyone knows people who *stopped* drinking or doing drugs, because they are in recovery. No one blames them for it, because everyone knows someone whose life got righteously screwed up because of substance abuse issues. If not drinking or doing drugs is what it takes for you *not* to have a messed-up life, good on ya. I do assume at this point that most people who notice that I don't drink or do drugs assume I have some substance abuse history. Well, it's true, I do; just not *mine*. I also don't mind if people assume I'm in recovery. It's not correct, but it's not an insult, and if someone is judgey about people in recovery, then they're the asshole.

(This is the point where I will note that I know a lot of contemporaries in recovery from drugs and alcohol, and they have nothing but my respect and admiration. Recovery is *hard*, man. Admitting you have a problem is hard. Quitting a thing your body is crying for is hard. Making amends to the people you hurt is hard. Staying on the recovery path each day, every day, is hard. Part of the reason I never started drugs or alcohol is that I saw close up at an early age how *fucking* hard recovery is. I'm not entirely sure I could do it. Given what the alternative to recovery is, that's not good. So, yes: People in recovery? You rock, I salute you. Keep on keeping on.)

At this age there are other reasons I don't drink or do drugs. In the subject of alcohol, first off, I'm cheap, and alcohol is expensive and I don't understand how people just throw their money down that particular hole (to be fair, I feel this way about Starbucks, too). Second, alcohol has calories and as a middle-aged dude who already weighs more than he likes, I don't see why I should add to my woes in this regard. Third, given what I know about myself in terms of where I make conscious efforts to inhibit my behavior, I'm pretty sure I'd be a raging asshole when I'm drunk. You know that thing I wrote once, about how the failure mode of clever is asshole? It's not just a pithy statement. It's a reminder to me of my own failings. I expect that were I drunk, I'd try to be clever *all the time*, and would fail.

With drugs, well. I've never been a fan of the recreational use of pot, since that shit stinks like wet dogfarts and causes jam bands, neither of which fill me with joy. Pretty much all the other recreational drugs that exist out there just seem like a fast track to either being an asshole and/or losing a bunch of your teeth in one terrible fashion or another. The exception here seems to be psychedelics, which I worry that if I took would cause me to freak out more than I would like, which means that such a freakout would likely be a self-fulfilling prophecy.

Finally with both drugs and alcohol, at the end of the day I like being in control of my own self, as much as I can be, because I'm responsible for my actions and my self. Given what I know of myself and my likely addiction issues, drugs and alcohol would make it harder for me to be in control of myself. This would make me very unhappy, and that in itself would have a number of unpleasant knock-on effects.

All told: Drugs and alcohol are not for me, thanks.

But if they're for you—and you're not swimming in addiction issues (in which case please seek help), and you're not bothering anyone else with your fun (and if you are, stop being an asshole)—then that's great, and enjoy yourself. Anyone who's seen me at a convention knows my natural habitat there is in the bar, hanging out and laughing with people. I wouldn't be there if I was spending my time pursing my lips in disapproval at people loosening up through judicious use of booze. I am a lifetime designated driver, and I'm cool with that, too; I like making sure people get home safe.

I'm not a pot enthusiast, but generally speaking I'm for its legalization, and while I'm less sure about blanket legalization for other currently not legal drugs, the more I look at the mess that is the US response to drugs, the more I lean toward the general libertarian idea of "legalize it all, tax the shit out of it," with a substantial chunk of that tax earmarked for treatment of addiction (rather than, say, incarceration, which is what we have now and which isn't working particularly well as far as I can see). My personal prohibition against any of this stuff should not imply one for everyone else.

But yeah, for me, prohibition it is. The good news is, so far, my life has done okay without drugs and alcohol. They're not things I feel a lack of.

Why My Wife
is Amazing,
Part 73,592

Conversation between me and Krissy yesterday:

Me: With all this bullshit around health care, and the possibility of pre-existing conditions and insurance caps coming back, we should probably look into supplemental insurance.

Krissy: I got us supplemental insurance years ago.

Me: You did?

Krissy: Yes. I even have policies for very specific things.

Me: Like what?

Krissy: I have an insurance policy on your hands.

Me: My hands?

Krissy: You're a writer. You use your hands. If something happens to your hands, it's a problem. We'll need to pay for someone for you to dictate to.

Me: You've insured my *hands*.

Krissy: Yes.

Me: I'm not going to lie. That's literally the sexiest thing you've said to me this whole damn month.

WILL HUMANS SURVIVE?

Mar

21

2016

We're getting cosmic for this question, from Greg, who asks:

Earthlings have 4 billion years to figure out space colonization before the sun goes red dwarf and consumes the earth Galactus style. They also have 4 billion years before the Andromeda galaxy collides with the Milky Way galaxy, which will likely require massive technology to survive. Can we pull it off? Can we even survive that long?

Well, before we begin, let me make a few corrections here.

<nerd>

Actually, the sun will *not* turn into a red dwarf, it will turn into a red giant, which has a very real chance of expanding out to the size of Earth's orbit, swallowing it up in the process. That's likely to happen closer to five billion years from now, not four billion years from now. Not that it will matter because a mere billion years from now the sun is going to be brighter and hotter than it is now, which will likely turn Earth into something like Venus is today, i.e., a hellish world where greenhouse gases have run amok, so that's probably the deadline we're working within.

Also, the Andromeda Galaxy colliding with the Milky Way Galaxy? While it is likely to happen in 4 billion years or so, it's unlikely any of the stars in either galaxy will collide with each other—the distances between stars is just too great. It's possible (although unlikely) the solar system might be ejected into deep space because of the gravitational effects of two galaxies merging, but the solar system itself should be fine. Mind you, by that time the Earth would be uninhabitable *anyway* because of the sun heating up, but the galactic smash-up will be neither here nor there to that.

</nerd>

So: The now amended question is: Will humans figure out space colonization before the Earth is rendered uninhabitable by the sun, which barring anything else will almost certainly happen a billion or so years from now, and will we survive that long in any event?

The answers: Maybe, and probably not.

Last part first: Humans, which is to say the species *Homo sapiens*, is about two hundred thousand years old, which is actually not that old as species go. We evolved out of previous species of the genus *Homo*; probably *Homo heidelbergensis*, which went extinct around the time we showed up (probably coincidence, I'm sure). Before *heidelbergensis* was *Homo erectus*, from which it was likely descended, and which has also gone extinct. And so on and so forth.

Here's the thing about species: Generally, they don't last very long (geologically speaking). Over time, most species are likely to do two things: Evolve into another species, and/or go extinct. To be clear, sooner or later, every species goes extinct (see the ticking time-bomb of the sun, above); only some evolve into something else. But it is very rare, generally speaking, for a species to last more than a few million years.

Why? Because the Earth is an unstable place, given enough time—temperatures go up, then they go down. The amount of gases in the atmosphere fluctuates significantly. Ice ages happen. Global warming occurs. Every now and again an asteroid drops in to really screw everything up. Die offs of the majority of all the extant species on the planet have happened several times (and some folks are warning that we're in the early stages of a new one, thanks to human activity messing with the planet). When the ecologies change, the niches that species developed to take advantage of change too. This is rarely a good thing for the species in question.

Current humans have existed for a mere 200,000 years, in a genus (*Homo*) whose oldest member existed only 2.5 million years ago—barely even yesterday in geologic time. It would be optimistic in the extreme to suggest that *Homo sapiens*, as it exists today, will still be with us a billion years from now—400 times as far into the future as our entire genus extends into the past. Given the assiduousness with which we're currently reworking the ecology of the planet (unintentionally or otherwise), we're probably making it more difficult for the species to last another 10,000 years, much less a billion.

But we're smart! I hear you say. Sure, that's true, but does it then follow that **a)** we're smart enough not to basically kill ourselves by wrecking the planet, **b)** that our intelligence means that evolution is done with us. The answers here, if you ask me (and you did) are: We'll see, and probably not. In the latter case, there's an argument to be made that our intelligence will *increase* speciation, as humans intentionally do to our species what natural selection did unintentionally before, and do it on a much shorter timescale, in order to adapt to the world that is currently rapidly changing under our feet, in no small part because of our own activities.

So, no. Human beings, meaning *Homo sapiens*, will almost certainly not be here a billion years from now. We're probably not even going to be here 100 million years from now, or 10 million years from now, or, hell, even a million years from now. The question is whether our evolutionary descendants will be around, a new branch (or branches) of the genus *Homo*. My guess is: A million years from now, yes, and we may even recognize them as human. Ten million years from now, maybe, but we could probably only vaguely see them as being descended from us. A hundred million years from now, if our descendants are still around, there would be no family resemblance at all. A billion years from now, well. Remember that your direct ancestors from a billion years back were single-celled eukaryotes who had just figured out this great new thing called "sex." That's how far back in time we'll be from any of our descendants then.

Now, as to the other question, will we have figured out space colonization by a billion years from now, sure. Look, if we *really* decided that space colonization was something we wanted, we could have a couple million people in space in the next hundred years, easy. The issue to my mind isn't really *technology*—I suspect we have the tech to make roughly serviceable colonies in space (and on the moon and on Mars) right now, and we could scale up from there in the next hundred years, no problem. The issue is whether we want to make the *effort*, and swallow the frankly ridiculous set up and maintenance costs, of permanent space colonization. Barring a *Seveneves*-like catastrophic event, we probably won't, because why would we? We've got a nice planet down here, even if we're currently mucking it up a bit, with lots of raw materials and space to work with. It's easier to try to work with what we have down here, at the bottom of a gravity well, than send people up there and try to make *that* work.

I mean, yes, sure, *eventually* the sun will eat the planet, and it will swaddle it with greenhouse gases long before then. But again, the operative phrase here is "geologic time." These events are going to happen so far out in the future that the human mind—the *Homo sapiens* mind—literally cannot process how far out in the future it will be. I mean, shit. We think waiting two days for something to arrive to our house via Amazon Prime shipping is *forever*. To make a mind constructed like that consider the unfathomable expanse of a billion years is folly.

Rather than worry too much about a billion years from now, or five billion years from now, I'd rather have us think about the next hundred years, and what we're going to do with them. Make no mistake, when we talk about the fact we're "wrecking the Earth" what we mean is that we're wrecking it *for us.* As soon as we're gone, there's no other species taxing the planet to the same extent we are. What life remains—and life *will* remain—will speciate out to take advantage of how the planet is then, and will fill the niches, and over time the planet will change again, and speciation will happen to take advantages of those changes, too. The Earth doesn't need us, and it won't miss us when we're gone. It'll just…go on. It will do that if we die off, or if we take to the stars. But honestly, the first of these is far more likely than the second.

I'd like for humans to be here in a hundred years, and in a thousand. After that, we can worry about the next million years, and then the next ten million, and so on, until we get to the billion year mark and a much hotter sun. We've got a lot of time between now and then, however. First things first.

WOMEN
AND GEEKDOM

| Apr |
| **13** |
| **2013** |

n e-mail, Brian asks:

Women in Geekdom. Why is this all exploding now? Where is it going?

I am assuming Brian means women in geek-related fields taking a stand against the both latent and overt sexism in those fields and having to deal with outsized, histrionic freakouts some geek dudes are having about it in response.

What's happening? To explain, let me go to one of my favorite little bits in the film *The American President,* which I think these days is best known as writer Aaron Sorkin's rough draft of *The West Wing.* The scene has President Andrew Shepherd navigating his way through a Christmas party at the White House and coming across a florid, very concerned man in a green jacket:

INT. RESIDENCE - NIGHT

An informal Christmas party is underway with maybe 20 GUESTS, some of them familiar faces.

SHEPHERD and a GREEN-BLAZERED MAN

> GREEN BLAZERED MAN (GILL)
> Mr. President, militant women are out to destroy college football in this country.

> SHEPHERD
>
> Is that a fact?
>
> GREEN BLAZERED MAN (GILL)
>
> Have you been following this situation down in Atlanta? These women want parity for girls' softball, field hockey, volleyball...
>
> SHEPHERD
>
> If I'm not mistaken, Gill, I think the courts ruled on Title 9 about 20 years ago.
>
> GREEN BLAZERED MAN (GILL)
>
> Yes sir, but now I'm saying these women want that law enforced.
>
> SHEPHERD
>
> Well, it's a world gone mad, Gill.

Right now geekdom is positively *stacked* with Green Blazered Men, who are shocked and concerned that women in geekdom are suddenly not just satisfied with the *idea* that they have equal standing, opportunity and engagement in the geek world—they are actually *pushing* for it to happen, and pushing *back* against the men who are resisting that, whether that resistance is passive, aggressive or passive-aggressive. Or to put it another way, more and more women in the geek world seem to be *done* with the idea they need to just put up with this shit anymore, and it's making the men who have been dishing out the shit—whether they knew they were dishing it out or not—a little defensive. And when Green Blazered Men feel defensive, they sometimes also get sort of angry.

Which doesn't precisely answer the question of *why now?* Well, the best answer for this I can come up with is that it's the *second decade of the twenty-first century*, isn't it? If I were a woman geek being asked to put up with a whole bunch of sexist bullshit in my community, and pretend it wasn't happening and that this is what actual equality in my community looked like, I would *hope* that my response would be to say, loudly and publicly, "you've got to be *fucking* kidding me." So that there *are* women who are actually saying this, loudly and publicly, doesn't surprise me and is also something I support.

And of course those women are catching hell for it. Many male geeks (it seems to me) are unaware of their casual sexism and/or have uncritically bought in to how things have always been in the culture, because why wouldn't they? It's a nice set-up for them (and by them I should note I mean *us*, because, hi, I'm a male geek). I think people are inherently conservative about social structures that favor them, because **a)** *duh*, and **b)** most people assume their own life experience is similar to other people's even when they're told otherwise and are given specific examples. When they're confronted with this ignorance, they feel defensive and feel like the *real* problem is the person who is complaining, because they themselves are *not bad people*, therefore the person making them feel bad *must* be.

Add this to the fact that a lot of male geeks are also emotionally immature and/or seeking status with other male geeks—male geekdom is *extraordinarily* status sensitive, which is a subject worthy of its own separate discussion—and it's not surprising that an immediate reaction by so many male geeks to women pushing back is HULK SMASH. The Internet obviously facilitates this sort of thing by allowing for anonymity and gatherings of like-minded folks who offer a comforting bubble of "my thinking is how everyone thinks." So it's easy for hordes of anonymous male geeks to strike out at women—who often do not have the same sort of anonymity when they complain publicly about the sexism of the geek world, and who indeed have a target painted on them as soon as they open their mouths.

This is not to paint every male geek with the same brush. There are plenty of male geeks who are also fed up with the sexism of geekdom; there are others who show their ass with a bout of public sexism—intentional or otherwise—who then actually pay attention to what women and others are telling them about that sexism and try to do better (there's often a difficult "but I'm not a sexist!" protest phase to this, followed by a 101-level discussion of sexism, which is its own issue. Lots of smart, clever people don't like to think *they* need entry-level enlightenment.).

Also, sexism in the male geek world does exist on a sliding scale, from jackassed geek bros who loathe and fear women and everything about them that they cannot penetrate at the top, to the dude who for no particularly good reason suspects women aren't good at FPS games but is otherwise fine with women geeks at the bottom. Some of these dudes will find it easier to let go of their sexism than others.

And with that said, the final reason I think this is all exploding now is because I think the acceptance of overt and covert sexism in geekdom *is* on its way out—not as a feature (it will always be there, because some people are just fucking sexist assholes, and also, geeks) but as a dominant aspect of the field. A useful example of this I can offer is what happened in the first decade of the twenty-first century, when a ton of US states suddenly passed laws and state constitutional amendments banning recognition of same-sex marriage. It happened because a bunch of people who were abjectly terrified that gays and lesbians would have equal access to the rights and privileges of marriage were able to leverage the latent and often unexamined homophobia of a bunch of other people into terrible, bigoted, hateful laws.

Why then? Because Massachusetts allowed same sex marriage, and because gays and lesbians as a class had begun saying "enough of *this* shit," when it came to being denied the right to marry, and it just plain freaked out a bunch of people who didn't understand why gays and lesbians couldn't be happy knowing they *could* get married, just as long as it was to someone of the opposite sex (no, really. This was an argument for a while). And then the more organized members of the freaked-out brigade looked at the demographics of gay acceptance and realized the clock was ticking.

They were right. Here in 2013 a more than bare majority of Americans approve of same sex marriage, marriage equality is the law in several states, and the percentages are going up in both cases. There will be places and people who will need to be dragged into the world of marriage equality kicking and screaming, but it's a question of when, not if, at this point. Too many people, gay and straight, have decided this is a thing that will be.

And so with the geek world. Women geeks are largely done with letting this sexist shit go uncommented upon, a growing number of men geeks are siding with them, and that number is going to continue to grow. Women geeks certainly aren't going to shut up now—too many of them are all in on this. Good for them.

But, yeah, sexism in geekdom is a thing, is *still* a thing, and will *continue* to be a thing for a while. Not every male geek is going to just willingly unload his sexism. Whether they want to admit it or not—whether they consciously *know* it or not—they see it as having value; something that offers status and an exclusive identity. They like their green blazer.

WONDER WOMAN: A SMASH, POSSIBLY IN DIFFERENT WAYS THAN YOU THINK

Aug

3

2017

This next weekend *Wonder Woman* is very likely to crack the $400 million mark at the domestic box office, which in itself is a significant feat (only 26 other films in the history of cinema have managed it) but is particular good news for the Warner Bros studio and its DC universe of films, after the critical failures of the two most recent DC films, *Batman v. Superman* and *Suicide Squad*, both of which *Wonder Woman* has now outgrossed...

...Well, sort of. *Wonder Woman* is the undisputed champ of the three films in the domestic box office arena, but in the global arena, right now (and, given the late date of *Wonder Woman*'s theatrical run at this point, probably ultimately), *Wonder Woman*'s overall box office performance is right in line with *BvS* and *Suicide Squad*, and both of those films have outperformed *WW*'s box office in key areas. *BvS* has a larger global gross ($873 million to $790 million), and *Suicide Squad* has a larger foreign box office ($420 million to $393 million). At this point, two months since release, it's possible but unlikely *WW* might catch up with those numbers (it'll be easier for the film to pass *Suicide*'s foreign BO than *BvS*' global). But when all the theatrical grosses are tallied, again, *Wonder Woman*'s box office performance is likely to be right in line with its DC siblings' performance.

Given that *Wonder Woman*'s box office overall is not substantially different than that of *BvS* or *Suicide Squad*, why is it being hailed as the savior of the DC universe film franchise? There are a few reasons. One, both *BvS* and *Suicide* were critical (if not financial) flops, dark and gritty and depressing slogs that no one really seemed to like all that much, even if the films did in fact pack people into theaters—$330 million and $325 million in domestic grosses are excellent returns. *Wonder Woman*, on the other hand, was a critical success—which was useful for itself but also deemed important for the future of the DC franchise as a whole. Three critical flops would (presumably) have made it difficult to sell the Avengers-like *Justice League* film that's next on the slate.

Two, despite global box office being the primary engine for Hollywood these days, domestic (i.e., US and Canada) box office is still hugely influential in terms of perception. As an example, this summer's *The Mummy* is widely considered to be a flop despite the fact that worldwide it's grossed $400 million to date. Had *The Mummy* done $200 million domestically and $200 million foreign, it wouldn't be seen as a flop; if it had done $300 million domestically and $100 million in foreign sales, it'd be one of the summer's winners. *Wonder Woman* outgrossed its DC siblings here at home, and "here at home" optics still matter.

Three, the financials of *Wonder Woman* are probably more advantageous to Warner Bros than *BvS* or *Suicide*. First, it was a cheaper film to produce: $125 million, where *BvS* was twice that, and *Suicide* was $150 million. Second, Warner (generally) gets to keep more of the money a film grosses domestically than internationally, where the grosses have to be shared with distributing partners and are otherwise divvied up in less advantageous ways.

Finally, because *Wonder Woman* is a woman-centered superhero film with a woman director, and the common wisdom was that the film outperformed financial expectations. Why this bias persists is a long discussion for another time (it's worth noting that only one other film has outgrossed *Wonder Woman* domestically so far this year, and that's *Beauty and the Beast*, another woman-focused film, and the one film remaining on the theatrical schedule this year that will outgross it will be *The Last Jedi*, which also has a woman as the protagonist), but it's there.

It's worth pointing out that of the four reasons I've given here, three of them are explicitly *perceptual*, rather than about the financial bottom line, and the one that's about the financial bottom line is probably the one least publicly discussed out of all of them. The perceptual issues *aren't* fake issues (I'll explain why further down) but I think it's worth pointing out that, perception aside, Warner Bros' DC universe films from *BvS* onward are doing just fine financially, with an average box office of $802 million globally between them, and an average domestic gross of $350 million. Which, incidentally, is higher than the average domestic *and* worldwide gross of the (to date) 16 Marvel cinematic universe movies, which are $306 million and $776 million, respectively.

Which leads me to think a couple of things. The first is that generally film quality doesn't mean all that much for a superhero film's box office as long as it has **a)** brand name recognition and **b)** some really excellent marketing behind it. Two-thirds of the DC films get knocked for being crap, but those two films also outgrossed ten of the sixteen Marvel films both domestically and worldwide, all of which have better critical reputations than *BvS* or *Suicide*.

Next up, even if *Wonder Woman* had been a critical flop, I think it's an open question as to whether that would have had a major *negative* impact on the financial performance of *Justice League,* the next DC film in the release barrel. To be clear, I think *Wonder Woman*'s critical and perceptual superiority to *BvS* and *Suicide* is *beneficial*—it now means *JL* is likely to get to or even surpass $1 billion in worldwide grosses (and get more than $400 million domestically). But I suspect that had *Wonder Woman* not been a perceptual and critical smash, *JL* would still end up in the same $750 million-to-$850 million range the other DC films have managed to this point. These are essentially fool-proof movies, which all things considered, has been a very good thing for Warners, indeed.

This means I also suspect that even if *Wonder Woman* had not been a critical success, it still would have done reasonably well at the box office: In the $250 million-to-$300 million range domestically and double that globally. And again that's down to familiarity and marketing and the long pent-up desire to have a woman superhero head up a movie, and especially Wonder Woman, the best-known woman superhero. The critical/perceptual box office premium here is significant—roughly 25% of the box office gross—and nothing to discount. But recent box office successes in the form of *Beauty and the Beast, The Force Awakens* and *Rogue One* shows us that established franchises (Star Wars and Disney live action remakes, respectively) don't automatically take a financial penalty for having women in the lead role (I'm not even bringing up *Twilight* or *Hunger Games* here, which established themselves in the lit world before jumping over to film). *Wonder Woman*, I think, would have been perfectly *financially* successful even if it had been critically received only marginally better than *BvS* or *Suicide Squad*.

The real issue here, to my mind, is how there's still *any* hesitancy to front women characters in franchises, superhero or otherwise. There's pretty clearly no significant financial penalty for doing so *if* your franchise is already up and running and your marketing is focused; honestly, at this point there's only *upside*, if you manage to make the film *better* than its male-focused franchise siblings. That upside is perceptual in the short run, as it largely was here with *Wonder Woman*. But in the long run it's likely going to add to your franchise financial bottom line. In this case, *Justice League* will almost benefit from *Wonder Woman*'s perceptual halo.

And further out than that—well. It will be interesting to see which film will have the bigger opening weekend: The next Batman, or the next Wonder Woman. I do know which one I am more interested in seeing right now.

It's All Beautiful and Nothing Lasts

Oct

20

2014

"It's all beautiful and nothing lasts." It's a phrase that showed up in a dream of mine last night, as something I said to my wife as we were crossing a street in a big city. The street was where her father's family's farm used to be, in the dream—something that had some resonance in the real world, as her father's family's farm is now part of the Dayton International Airport. The dream me made the comment not about the farm in particular, but about life in general, prompted by the farm turned city street.

And it's a true statement. All of it is beautiful, and it doesn't last. I'm old enough now to be at the point where I see the movement of life, and me through it, to see people I like and love pass away and to see people I like and love grow up and become who they are. People move, stay and move again; houses become homes, and homes become vacant houses once more. Strangers become friends and sometimes become strangers again. Life happens and it's a gorgeous thing—all of it, even the annoying parts—and it doesn't last. It's all temporary and doesn't stay.

Before you ask: I'm fine. Everyone around me is fine. Even my pets are fine. Indeed, generally speaking, life is very good. If I had to peg a predicate cause for any of this, it would be going to a memorial service of a distant relative yesterday, who I knew only from family reunions, and coming across a comment in a discussion thread from my friend Jay Lake, which because it was part of a back and forth with several other people, momentarily gave the illusion that he was still with us, alive and engaged. But I think it's just simply more that I'm now aware that life moves, and I do too.

One thing I think is worth noting is how my brain phrased the statement: "It's all beautiful and nothing lasts." This is a qualitatively different statement than it would have been if the dream version of me had said "it's beautiful but nothing lasts." That to me feels defeatist—what's the point of acknowledging the beauty of life if it just goes away. That fact that it *doesn't* last is why you should acknowledge it: it *won't* stay, it will be gone and you will be gone, too. But while you live, that beauty exists and it is there for you to love and cherish, and to be a part of and to add to if you can.

It won't last. Nothing lasts. But it's here, and you should be here for it, and in it.

Thank you for being part of it, in this moment. I appreciate it, and the moment we're sharing. I hope you do too.

ACKNOWLEDGMENTS

Once again I'm delighted that Subterranean Press allows me to publish collections like this with them. My thanks to everyone there, and particularly to Bill Schafer, Yanni Kuznia and Geralyn Lance.

Nate Taylor did the artwork for this. He's awesome.

Gail Cross did the design. Likewise awesome.

Shannon Page did the proofreading. She is awesome, too.

A quick thanks to Wordpress, which has hosted Whatever on its VIP service for ten years now, and to 1and1.com, which hosts the rest of Scalzi.com. I literally couldn't have done it without you.

And of course thank you to Kristine and Athena Scalzi, who live with me and keep me sane and make me happy. Every book I write is about the two of you, whether that's obvious or not.